W9-DBC-974

LONDON'S NEWCOMERS

The West Indian Migrants

CENTRE FOR URBAN STUDIES

The Centre was established at University College London in January 1958. It is its object to contribute to the systematic knowledge of towns, and in particular of British towns; to study urban development, structure and society; and to link academic social research with social policy.

The Centre undertakes and assists a variety of relevant studies in this country; it also keeps in touch with comparable research in other countries. In its work, the Centre attempts to bring together the interests of the social sciences and those of allied fields, such as public health and town planning.

The members of the Committee which governs the Centre for Urban Studies are listed below.

Chairman: R. G. D. ALLEN, Professor of Statistics, University of London, at the London School of Economics and Political Science.

Vice-Chairmen: SIR WILLIAM HOLFORD, Professor of Town Planning, University of London, at University College London.
J. M. MACKINTOSH, Emeritus Professor of Public Health, University of London.

Director of Research: RUTH GLASS, Honorary Research Associate, University College London.

S. T. BINDOFF, Professor of History, University of London, at Queen Mary College.

ASA BRIGGS, Professor of History, University of Leeds.

W. GORDON EAST, Professor of Geography, University of London, at Birkbeck College.

T. FERGUSON, Professor of Public Health and Social Medicine, University of Glasgow.

C. DARYLL FORDE, Professor of Anthropology, University of London, at University College London.

D. V. GLASS, Professor of Sociology, University of London, at the London School of Economics and Political Science.

C. A. MOSER, Reader in Social Statistics, University of London, at the London School of Economics and Political Science.

L. DUDLEY STAMP, Emeritus Professor of Social Geography, University of London.

MAIN AREAS OF WEST INDIAN SETTLEMENT IN LONDON

Map 1

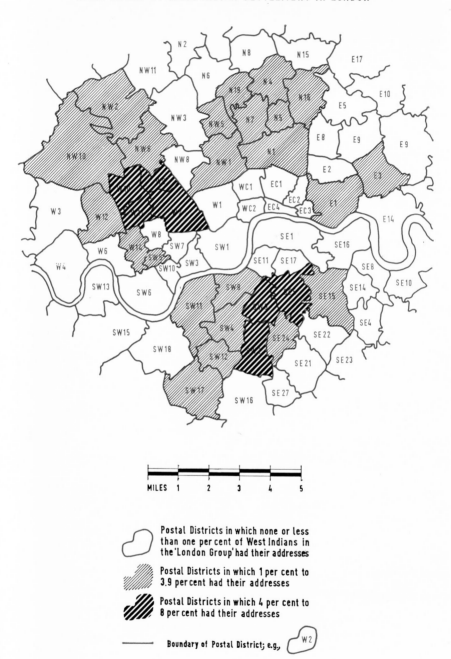

Frontispiece

Centre for Urban Studies
University College London
Report No. 1

LONDON'S NEWCOMERS

The West Indian Migrants

RUTH GLASS
assisted by
Harold Pollins

HARVARD UNIVERSITY PRESS
Cambridge, Massachusetts
1961

FIRST PUBLISHED IN GREAT BRITAIN IN 1960
by
Centre for Urban Studies, University College London
and George Allen & Unwin Ltd
under the title:

Newcomers
The West Indians in London

© Centre for Urban Studies, 1960

DA
125
W4
G7

42909 THIS BOOK IS SET IN 10 ON 11 PT TIMES ROMAN (SERIES 327)

PRINTED IN ENGLAND BY
HAZELL WATSON AND VINEY LTD
AYLESBURY AND SLOUGH

TO DAVID

Contents

APPENDICES

MAPS

Acknowledgments

FIRST, I want to thank the staff and associates of the Centre for Urban Studies for their help. Mr. Harold Pollins, the main research assistant for this enquiry from October 1958 to February 1960, collected a good deal of the material and wrote the original draft, referred to in the Preface, before it was decided to expand the report. I have drawn from parts of his draft and from his additional notes, especially in Chapter I, but also in some passages of Chapters III, IV and V. The responsibility for the final text and interpretation is, however, mine.

Several of my colleagues have contributed greatly, both during the earlier stages of the enquiry and during the most difficult final stage of revision since the beginning of this year. Mr. Wolf Scott was closely associated with the arrangement and analysis of the data for the London Group and Sample of West Indians, presented in Chapter II. Appendices A and B are largely the result of his work. Mr. John Westergaard has done so much to help me by his criticisms, by filling in gaps, checking sources, and doing the tedious job of proof reading, that I have been unable to keep count of my debts to him. But I know that it would have been impossible to get the book to press without him. Mr. Stephen Hatch, too, assisted in various ways; and he compiled the index. I am grateful to Miss Bridget Dalison for her follow-up of discriminatory housing advertisements; to Miss E. U. Chesterton for drawing the maps; to Mr. I. C. Cannon for giving advice on typographical and similar matters; and to Mrs. Joyce Forbes for her skill in typing successive versions of the manuscript.

We have obtained indispensable material from the Migrant Services Division of the Commission in the United Kingdom for the West Indies, British Guiana and British Honduras. I am indebted to Mr. Garnet H. Gordon, C.B.E., Q.C., the Commissioner in the United Kingdom for the West Indies, British Guiana and British Honduras, and to Mr. Ivo S. de Souza, the Secretary of the

Migrant Services Division, for their permission to extract data from the records of the Division. In addition, Mr. de Souza and several other members of his staff have been most patient and thorough in answering our many enquiries on a variety of subjects.

I should further like to thank the following people and organisations. Mr. A. H. Pickwoad, the Liaison Officer of the Barbadian Immigrants' Liaison Service, has supplied essential information; Mr. Frank Fenton Jeremiah has done the same repeatedly; Mr. Barry Carman and the British Broadcasting Corporation have given us permission to include Mr. Carman's interview as Appendix C and also to quote extracts from his other interviews; Dr. Henry Durant, the Director of the British Gallup Poll, has made data collected by his organisation available to us for further analysis; the Willesden International Friendship Council have allowed us to quote an extract from their so far unpublished survey.

Among the many others who have been helpful in giving us leads, information and in discussing relevant questions have been the London County Council; the Race Relations Committee of the Society of Friends; Professor L. C. B. Gower; the Rev. C. S. Hill; the Rev. Marcus James; Miss Claudia Jones, the Editor of the *West Indian Gazette*; Mrs. Joan Maizels; Mrs. Sheila Patterson and Mr. Frank Pilgrim.

The reader will see that I have also good reasons for being grateful to the authors of various studies, novels and articles referred to, or quoted, in the text, as well as to many anonymous people.

My private debts—to David, Helen and Robert Glass—are in a separate category. They will have to be acknowledged elsewhere.

Preface

IT would not occur to anyone who writes a book on criminology to state in the preface that he is opposed to murder. Nor would it occur to any reader to complain that an author who makes such a statement is not objective. Unhappily, however, the elementary principles of ethics on matters of prejudice and discrimination are not as yet equally axiomatic. A book on the relations between white and coloured people in Britain has to begin before the beginning.

It is thus necessary to say at the outset that I am not dispassionate on this subject. I share "the very definite opinion" expressed in a single phrase not long ago by Lord Winster: "... discrimination because of race, colour or religion is an intolerable insult to the human dignity of an individual."[1] And I have to add that I regard such discrimination also as an intolerable insult to the dignity of the society in which it is practised. This is my premise—or my bias, if the reader should wish to call it that.

Of course, this premise is by no means incompatible with optimism on the status of the new minority in Britain. In the early stages of our enquiry I started from the assumption that optimism was justified. Indeed, so long as one looks at the situation of coloured people in Britain from 'outside'—judging from casual observations in a few places and from a cursory review of public opinion—it is possible to maintain the idea that there are no grave actual or potential 'white-colour problems'. The picture looks far gloomier when we watch it closely. Even then, it is still much brighter than in some other parts of the world. In terms of the standards of this country, however, there is cause for serious and urgent concern. The reasons for arriving at a view less sanguine than the initial one are summarised in the last chapter, which has had to be an inconclusive conclusion.

This inevitable revision of assumptions also determined a change in the scope of our enquiry. As a part of its research programme, adopted in 1957, the Centre for Urban Studies had planned a series

[1] *Parliamentary Debates*, H.o.L., 19th November 1958, col. 660.

of small-scale investigations into the growth and conditions of several minority groups in London. It was, and is still, intended to include reports on these investigations—covering the Irish, the Jews, the Poles and the West Indians—in a symposium on *London People and Places*. The West Indians were chosen because they are the largest coloured minority group in this country, and also the only one about whose characteristics and distribution in London reliable data could be obtained. Preparatory work for the survey of West Indians was begun during the summer of 1958—before the disturbances in Nottingham and Notting Dale had drawn public attention to the 'colour question'. A draft of a chapter on the West Indians for the London symposium was completed in May 1959.

At that stage, it became evident that a brief survey of the subject was quite inadequate. It could, in fact, easily be misleading—just as misleading as so many of the popular ideas both about colour and the conditions of the coloured in Britain. Moreover, as public opinion on such matters was in flux and public memories of relevant events were surprisingly short, it was appropriate to follow the development of opinion and to record such events.

The range of our enquiry had, therefore, to be widened in some directions, though narrowed in others. Methods of fact-finding had to be adapted accordingly. In general, the paucity of knowledge about the coloured minority—and even more the lack of self-awareness in the reactions of the white majority towards them—is both a symptom and a contributory cause of negative features in the situation of the newcomers. In some respects, however, the difficulties of collecting information were a by-product of comparatively positive, though perhaps only transitory, circumstances. Originally, we had assumed, for example, that it would be feasible to follow up the statistical data for the 'London Group' of West Indians, presented in Chapter II, by a household sample enquiry in one or two districts of London where the coloured migrants were believed to be concentrated. But the data for the London Group showed that there are as yet no substantial 'coloured quarters' in London, though there is a danger that such quarters may develop. So far, many of the migrants are still dispersed over a rather wide area of the London region. Thus at present a truly representative group of coloured Londoners could only be reached by a census, or by a survey covering a large sample of all Londoners. As we ourselves could not undertake so ambitious a project, the account of the migrants' problems of settlement and adjustment had to be derived from a variety of other, less satisfactory sources.

So the book grew, though not as systematically, comprehensively and concisely as the topic deserves. It can be regarded as no more, and was intended to be no more, than an essay in contemporary history. As such, it had to draw from diverse evidence—direct observation and enquiry; statistical records and documentary material, published and unpublished. As such, the book also suffers from all the limitations imposed in commenting on current rather than on past history.

There are other disadvantages. The record had to stop at an arbitrary date line—June 15, 1960. And the subject has no definite boundaries, socially or geographically. In writing about the West Indians in London, the focus of attention has often to be shifted— from the West Indians to London society and institutions. Nor is it permissible to ignore conditions and events outside London. The sub-title of the book is, therefore, inevitably imprecise.

More embarrassing still are the terminological difficulties. Many of the words which have to be used because no others are available are highly ambiguous, emotionally loaded or simply wrong. They tend to have a dichotomous, 'we' and 'they' connotation. The word 'colour' is an obvious example. The term 'British' has to be used when we mean the 'local' people, though of course the West Indians are British, too. 'Migrant' is a defective substitute for the even less suitable word 'immigrant'. The terms 'race', 'racial' or 'race relations' are worst of all: 'race' is not a scientifically valid category; 'race relations' are not discrete phenomena, but the term implies that they could thus be considered. Although I have avoided such words as much as possible, I must apologise for not having been able to do so altogether.

'Prejudice' and 'discrimination' hardly require definition any more. (Prejudice can be described as a negative, suspicious, hostile or contemptuous attitude towards a group as a group—an attitude which is usually associated with the assumption of that group's inferiority. Discrimination can be defined as the denial of oppor-tunities and rights to members of a group because they belong to that group, irrespective of their individual capacities and behaviour.) Perhaps I should stress that I regard the concept of tolerance not in a passive but in an active sense, in keeping with the traditions of European thought and politics.

RUTH GLASS

London,
June 1960

1

Introduction

The New Minority Group

"BLACKS invade Britain" shouts the *Black and White News*, the news sheet of the White Defence League. "Send the coloured immigrants home" says Mosley's Union Movement.[1] "Britain's Coloured Guests" was the title of a neutral and factual article in the *Radio Times*.[2] All the terms—aggressive and friendly—which are used to refer to the newcomers underline, deliberately or inadvertently, the uncertainty in the status of the new minority group.

The term 'our coloured guests' (or 'visitors') indicates one of several, not necessarily consistent, attitudes of liberal-minded people in Britain towards the migrants from the West Indies, from Africa, from India and from Pakistan. A guest is welcomed; he is treated with courtesy and with respect. But a guest stays for a limited period. And indeed many of the coloured people in Britain, too, think and speak of their stay here as temporary.

But while some go back to their countries of birth, it has to be taken for granted that a coloured minority now exists in this country and will continue to exist here. It is a rather small minority, about 210,000 people altogether (including West Indians, Africans, Indians and Pakistanis) according to an official estimate in December 1958[3]; and since then this number has not greatly increased. It is thus less than one-half of one per cent of the total population of Great Britain. Though the coloured minority group is small, it presents a new situation: it has come into being mainly during the last ten years.

There is thought to have been a noticeable Negro population in London in the eighteenth century, but in the subsequent century it

[1] The statements of the White Defence League and of the Union Movement which are quoted are constantly repeated in the verbal and published pronouncements of these groups. (See Chapter V, Part 2.) The West Indians resent the term 'immigrant'; as they are British citizens, they refer to themselves not as 'immigrants', but as 'migrants'; and this is the term which we have, therefore, used generally in this essay.

[2] An article in the *Radio Times* of 12th December 1958, which introduced a wireless programme broadcast in the following week.

[3] *Parliamentary Debates, H.o.C.*, 5th December 1958, cols. 1580–1.

disappeared, and from 1900 until 1948, there was only a trickle of coloured migrants into Britain. Usually they settled in dock areas in the provinces and in London. Some coloured people lived also in Soho, and a few students and professional men in other scattered parts of London. But until the last decade it was possible to walk through many London districts without ever seeing a coloured person, except perhaps an itinerant Sikh pedlar, carrying a large suitcase of ties and braces, or the traditional 'black doctor' (usually an Indian) who, in working class districts, was often a subject of superstitious reverence.[4]

Nowadays, the number of coloured people in Britain is higher than ever before; they are far more visible: despite some concentrations, they are more dispersed throughout the country. They also participate to a greater extent than before in general economic life, and their legal status in this country, as citizens of the Commonwealth, is now definite. Previously, coloured seamen in Britain were often treated as 'coloured aliens', even if they came from a country within the Empire. This is no longer the case. In this new situation, the attitudes of white British people to coloured British people, who come to live here, are changing too.[5]

Attitudes have to change, moreover, not only because there are many new features in the distribution and conditions of the coloured migrants in this country. It is not its size, nor its novelty as such, which makes the present coloured minority in Britain so important. Because of the growing significance of coloured peoples in world affairs, their status in 'advanced' countries has begun to be regarded as a yardstick against which a nation's civilisation is measured. What happens to Negroes in the South of the United States, in South Africa, and in Britain is of far more than local interest. And as Britain is now looked upon as the centre of a multi-racial Commonwealth, the treatment of coloured people in this country, especially, commands world-wide attention and concern.

Interest and concern are growing in Britain, too. The Nottingham and Notting Dale disturbances in the autumn of 1958, and the

---

[4] There was also, of course, the temporary phenomenon of American Negro soldiers in Britain during the war. For Soho, see: 'Soho in Sepia', in Stanley Jackson, *An Indiscreet Guide to Soho* (London, 1945). For a short account of the early history of coloured people in Britain, see: K. L. Little, *Negroes in Britain*, London, 1948.

[5] As a result, the existing studies of coloured groups in this country give now only a partial picture. This is true also of the very rapid survey made by Clarence Senior and Douglas Manley in 1955: *A Report on Jamaican Migration to Great Britain*, Kingston, 1955. (An abridged version of this report was published in the *Fabian Research Series*, No. 179, 1956.)

murder of a West Indian in May 1959, evoked reactions and activities of many kinds. Since September 1958, news of discrimination in dance halls, hotels and in industry has been under constant observation; it is reported in newspapers, and is frequently the subject of questions in Parliament. Coloured characters appear in novels, in plays and films.[6] The 'colour problem' is featured on radio and television.

No other recently arrived minority group has aroused emotions and controversies of the same intensity and scale. There has been far less interest, for example, in the migration of Poles to Britain during and after World War II than in the migration of West Indians, although the number of Poles settled here is very similar to that of West Indians. The Poles, moreover, are in certain respects, of which language is only one, more alien than West Indians. But the West Indians in Britain are more noticeable than the Poles, irrespective of class differences between immigrants and natives, and between different groups of immigrants. And while it may be true that, as some people argue, the difficulties of all newcomers to Britain are alike, it is also true that coloured people meet these difficulties in an accentuated form. They are not simply migrants: they are coloured migrants. A white newcomer can hide, or eventually lose, the obvious signs of his foreignness; a dark skinned man cannot wash off his colour.

His distinctiveness often causes antagonism; but it also frequently evokes ardent sympathy. Whatever the reasons for these contradictory responses, there is no doubt at all that the colour question does produce vehement reactions, negative and positive. As yet, there appear to be comparatively few people in Britain to whom colour is invisible.

West Indian Migration

This survey deals with those coloured migrants who have come from the British West Indies—that is, those from the various territories which belong to the West Indies Federation, and also those from British Guiana and British Honduras. They have been chosen for separate consideration not only because they are the largest coloured group in Britain, but also because their traditions have linked them closely to this country for a long time. The majority of West Indians, unlike other coloured migrants, have English as their main language. Their main religion is Christian. West Indian

---

[6] There has been one important feature film, *Sapphire*, dealing, *inter alia*, with many of the problems revolving around coloured people in London.

education has been focussed on Britain, and the overt patriotic feeling shown by West Indians towards Britain is often greater than that shown by 'native' British people. Of course, the West Indians do not form a homogeneous group, and they have links with other nations, apart from Britain. Those of East Indian origin have much in common with some Indian communities. Their experiences in the United Kingdom are often similar to those of Africans. Nevertheless, the considerable number and the specific characteristics of West Indian migrants in Britain permit a separate discussion of their conditions in this country.

All figures of the number of coloured people in Britain are estimates or guesses. Statistics collected by the Government are hardly more exact than those produced by unofficial bodies. However, two sources, in particular, are useful. The first is the Population Census. While the Census in Great Britain does not distinguish people according to colour of skin, it does give country of birth. The second are the statistics kept by the Migrant Services Division of the Commission in the United Kingdom for the West Indies, British Guiana and British Honduras. The Division arranges to meet all parties of West Indian migrants to Britain; its records provide, therefore, fairly reliable indications of the course of West Indian immigration.

On the basis of both these sources it appears that there were towards the end of 1959 about 126,000 coloured West Indian migrants in Britain.[7] This total excludes the number of coloured children who were born in this country and who have remained here. That number is unknown.

The general trend of recent migration to Britain can be traced from the statistics which have been published, although these are slightly inconsistent and not precise. There are annual figures of all West Indian arrivals in Britain, and also separate figures for Jamaicans only. The number of migrants was small until 1953; it then increased suddenly and reached a peak in 1956. In 1958, and during the first half of 1959, there was a sharp decline in the number of new arrivals, but in the second part of 1959 the number had again increased.

The pattern of migration, however, has changed in recent years.

[7] In 1951, according to the Population Census, there were in England and Wales some 15,000 people whose 'birthplace or nationality' was given as the West Indies. (*General Report*, Table 49.) Since then until the end of 1959, according to the Migrant Services Division, about 125,000 West Indians have come to Britain, giving a maximum number of 140,000. From this figure we must deduct perhaps one or two thousand white West Indians, who were included in the Census figures, and also those coloured migrants who have returned home, at least 11,600, as estimated by the Migrant Services Division.

(A) Annual Migration

Year	All Migrants	Jamaicans only
1948	—	547
1949	—	307
1950	—	357
1951	1,000	898
1952	2,000	1,293
1953	2,000	1,270
1954	10,000	8,000
1955	24,473	18,561
1956	26,441	17,302
1957	22,473	12,354
1958	16,511	9,992
1959	20,397	12,573

(B) West Indian Arrivals in Britain

Year	Men	Women	Children	Unclassified	Total
1956	13,921	9,380	652	2,488	26,441
1957	11,412	9,385	874	802	22,473
1958	7,662	7,768	1,081	—	16,511
1959	10,057	8,219	2,121	—	20,397

(C) Number of West Indian Arrivals in, and Minimum Number of Departures from, Britain

Year	Arrivals	Departures
1956 and 1957	48,914	4,800
1958	16,511	2,300
1959	20,397	4,500
TOTAL	85,822	11,600

[8] It should be noted that all the figures quoted and shown in the following tables are very approximate, and that they are also of uneven accuracy for different years. Only round figures for annual arrivals are available for the years before 1955; no separate statistics for West Indian women and children who arrived in Britain were kept before 1956; and it was only in that year that the figures of the departures of West Indians from Britain began to be compiled. These latter figures represent the minimum number of departures. The statistics here quoted are derived from the West Indies Commission, and from various Jamaican sources, such as the *Report on Jamaica, 1956*, H.M.S.O., 1957 and the *1957 Economic Survey, Jamaica, Government of Jamaica*. G. W. Roberts and D. O. Mills, *Study of External Migration Affecting Jamaica; 1953–55*, University College of the West Indies, Jamaica, 1958 (originally published as a Supplement to *Social and Economic Studies*, Vol. 7, No. 2, 1958), also give figures of Jamaican migrants for the three years of their study (see p. 45). Although their figures differ slightly from those quoted here, they show the same general trend.

Before 1957, the majority of migrants from the West Indies were adult males. But since then, the number of West Indian women and children who came to Britain has increased steadily: in 1957, it was estimated to be equal to that of male migrants; in 1958 and 1959, more women and children arrived than men.

Thus there are signs that West Indians are becoming more settled in Britain. But there are also indications to the contrary, for the number who are known to have returned to their home territories since 1956 (the first year for which figures of departures are available) has steadily increased. It is estimated that about 86,000 West Indians have arrived in Britain from the beginning of 1956 to the end of 1959; at least 11,600 have gone back during that period, though it is not known whether they have done so permanently. The ratio of departures to arrivals was considerably higher in 1958 and 1959 than in the previous two years: it was roughly one in ten in 1956 and 1957; but one in seven in 1958; and one in five in 1959.

West Indians are used to travelling in search of work, but the desire to go to Britain has only recently become strong. Already in the 1880's there was a large-scale movement from Jamaica to work on the Panama Canal, which remained the main reception area for Jamaican emigrants for some thirty years, followed in importance by the United States and Cuba. With the completion of the Canal in 1914, the United States became the main receiving area until 1924, when immigration was restricted by American legislation. Generally speaking, for the next 20 years the net movement was inward, and the Caribbean territories did not become exporters of population again until after World War II.[9]

The main causes of migration in the recent post-war period are fairly evident. First, there is the pressure of population. G. W. Roberts's study of the population of Jamaica, the largest of the West Indian islands, shows clearly that the rate of growth of population, already high before the Second World War, has increased since then. "Indeed since 1950 the island has consistently shown rates of natural increase in excess of 2 per cent which, despite some emigration, results in a rate of growth nearly twice that prevailing in the middle of

[9] See: George W. Roberts, *The Population of Jamaica* (Cambridge, 1957); George W. Roberts, 'Emigration from the Island of Barbados', *Social and Economic Studies*, Vol. 4, No. 3 (1955), pp. 245–88; W. F. Maunder, 'The New Jamaican Emigration', *Social and Economic Studies*, Vol. 4, No. 1 (1955), pp. 38–63; C. F. Cumper, 'Population Movements in Jamaica, 1830–1950', *Social and Economic Studies*, Vol. 5, No. 3 (1956), pp. 261–80; C. G. Hill, 'The Migration of Jamaican Workers to England', *Report on Jamaica, 1956*, H.M.S.O., 1957, pp. 34–8.

the nineteenth century."[10] The details of growth vary from territory to territory: Trinidad and British Guiana have experienced greater natural increases than other islands because of their large populations of East Indian origin. Aggravating this pressure on resources there have been natural disasters—floods and hurricanes—which have caused unemployment and poverty.

The second main cause of recent migration, linked with the first, is the high level of unemployment and under-employment in the West Indian territories. The general low level of wages and the lack of opportunity have caused West Indians to look outside their islands for economic improvement.

Thirdly, doors to other countries have been closed. The 1952 McCarran-Walter Act reduced the flow of West Indians to the United States of America to a mere trickle, and entries to other countries on the American continent, previously open to West Indian migrants, have also been made more difficult.

West Indians thus began to turn to Britain, and it is not surprising that they should be inclined to do so. By upbringing they are British, and they have the legal right to enter the United Kingdom freely. Their image of this country was a promising one. They heard of Britain's post-war economic development. The ease with which jobs could apparently be found in Britain contrasted sharply with the lack of employment opportunities in the West Indian territories. The stories of some 8,000 West Indians who served in the Royal Air Force in Britain during the Second World War also became well known at home. A number of these people reached commissioned rank; and all those who served were greatly impressed not only by the absence of discrimination in the armed services, but also by their introduction to an advanced industrialised economy. Some of them remained in Britain after the war.

Altogether, the general background of recent West Indian migration to Britain is similar to certain aspects of the post-war migration of the inhabitants of another Caribbean island, Puerto Rico, to the United States of America. The Puerto Ricans, too, have suffered from poverty and over-population on their island; they are drawn to the prosperity of the United States; and as they have American citizenship, they can enter the U.S.A. without any legal bar.

Just over ten years ago, West Indian migration to Britain began in a small and unorganised way. There were not many regular steamship services between the Caribbean and Britain, but services soon expanded in response to the growing demand. Similarly, in the West

[10] George W. Roberts, *The Population of Jamaica, op. cit.,* p. 307.

Indies, the arrangement of passages to Britain developed into a sizeable business. Roberts and Mills write of Jamaica:

> "Numerous travel agencies have sprung up and many, though maintaining their headquarters in Kingston, have extended their operations throughout the island by means of sub-agencies.
>
> The advertising campaigns promoted by competing agencies in urban and rural areas have apprised many Jamaicans of the possibility of emigrating to the United Kingdom. Some agencies have been paying specified sums to individuals who 'sign up' customers. The facilities offered to their clients have also helped to promote emigration. The provision of passages on easy payment plans, or on the furnishing of securities and other credit facilities have greatly extended the range of persons able to emigrate."[11]

Most of the West Indian governments have merely permitted migration to go on, but one of them, that of Barbados, has actually given assistance to migrants. The island is the most densely populated territory of the West Indies Federation, with heavy unemployment, and it has a long history of emigration. The Barbados Government has granted loans to migrants, and has helped to secure employment and accommodation in the receiving areas. But the number thus aided is small. On the whole, migrants from the Caribbean make their own arrangements to reach Britain, neither hindered nor helped by their governments. There are few restrictions. Some West Indian authorities have warned intending migrants of the housing and employment difficulties in Britain; but they have not put any obstacles in the way of those wishing to migrate.

When people in the West Indian Federation apply for passports, they are liable to special procedures on two grounds: age and criminal record. Applicants who are under 18 and over 50, as well as those who have criminal records, are separately examined, and may have their applications refused. But these screening procedures are not applied with the same thoroughness in all the different territories, and there is the further complication that passports which are issued for travel between the various islands can be used also for travel to Britain.

While a migrant makes his own decision about his move to Britain, he is not ignored by the authorities on his arrival here. In 1953, a Jamaican Civil Servant was seconded for duty in Britain as a Welfare Liaison Officer. He and his staff were attached to, though not financed by, the Colonial Office. His duties were taken over by the British Caribbean Welfare Service which was established in 1956, and which also assumed additional functions. In December 1958, this organisa-

[11] Roberts and Mills, *Study of External Migration affecting Jamaica, 1953–55*, p. 5.

tion was given a more definite official status, and accordingly re-named the 'Migrant Services Division of the Commission in the United Kingdom for The West Indies, British Guiana and British Honduras'.[12] It has been, and still is, one of the functions of these various bodies to supervise the arrival of migrants in Britain. Opportunities for doing so have improved over time, so that the Division now knows, from information supplied by the West Indian governments, when to expect parties of migrants.

Many of the ships which carry West Indians are French, Spanish and Italian. Thus the migrants often land first on the Continent, and continue their journey to Britain by train and cross-Channel steamer. Here they are met first by officials and later also by friends. The arrival of a typical party of migrants, in November 1958, might serve as an example of their reception in this country.

In this group of 82 West Indians, there were 44 women and 12 children—a higher proportion than in the earlier years of migration. They had travelled on an Italian boat to Genoa, and from there to Folkestone, accompanied by a French courier, who was employed by the shipping company. His party also included some 50 German and Dutch people. At Folkestone, two officials were waiting for the West Indian group—one from the British Caribbean Welfare Service, the other from the British Council. These two cooperate in the reception of migrants; the latter is especially concerned with students, including student nurses. The arrangements for meeting such parties are well organised: the Caribbean Welfare Service in London (now the Migrant Services Division) has advance information of migrant parties and of their routes; the immigration authorities at the British port know the exact number to be expected from information cabled to them by the immigration officers on the cross-Channel steamer. The couriers, too, have lists of the West Indian passengers and pass these on to the Caribbean Welfare officer at the dockside.

The West Indian passengers came ashore last, many of them still in summer clothes, with some improvised extra covering to meet the harsh November day. They went quickly through passport control while the two London officials stood by, in case there were any special questions. Two coaches on the boat-train had been reserved for the West Indian party so that the two officials could go around and ask everyone whether they had a place to go to. The actual addresses, in many different parts of London, were not listed. The

[12] The organisational change in 1956 was due to an expansion of activities: other governments of the West Indies, in addition to that of Jamaica, began to contribute finance for welfare work in the U.K. In 1958, the organisation became a part of the West Indies Commission in the U.K.

officials simply wanted to find out whether the migrants knew their destination or not. Everybody had an address to give. The officer from the British Council wrote down the names of students and young girls. If nobody came to meet them at Victoria, the British Council would look after them.

But at Victoria the platform was crowded. There was a mass of dark people; about a hundred friends and relatives were waiting to greet the newcomers. Soon they were all dispersed. No official body has a record of where they have gone to; and no official body knows for certain where they are now.

II

Characteristics and Distribution of West Indians in London

1. THE DATA

THE only comprehensive source of information about West Indians in London is the Migrant Services Division of the West Indies Commission. The Division performs many functions, in addition to meeting parties of migrants, and keeping statistics of arrivals. In general, it provides a link between West Indian newcomers and the institutions of British society. While the Division itself has no funds for welfare purposes, it guides migrants to the social services and, if necessary, to welfare agencies which exist here. Its staff are prepared to give advice on all sorts of questions—on matters of employment, education, housing, health, and on personal problems as well. They deal with people wishing to be repatriated; they also supervise the travel arrangements for the considerable number of children, born in Britain, who are sent home to the West Indies. (It is usually expected that at the age of five they will return to their relatives in this country to attend school.) The Division has an Industrial Relations Section, concerned with all aspects of employment, and its officers help a great deal in putting migrants into touch with employers. The Division, moreover, tries to co-ordinate the activities of the various West Indian voluntary associations, and it runs courses for them on methods of organisation.

There are, therefore, few West Indians, especially in London, who have not come into contact with the Division, or with its predecessor, the British Caribbean Welfare Service, at some time or other, and who are unaware of its activities. The Division's offices in London are visited by many West Indians who want advice on a variety of questions, or who make use of its other services. Such visits have been made since 1953, when a Welfare Liaison Officer was first appointed, and they have continued through the various changes in organisation. Since early in 1954, records have been kept of all personal interviews; as far as possible, each visitor's circumstances (origin, age, address and occupation, for example) have been entered on a standard record card. These files were later taken over and continued by the British Caribbean Welfare Service, and subsequently by the re-named agency—the Migrant Services Division.

Although the Division, like its predecessors, is concerned with West Indians in the whole of the United Kingdom, nearly all the personal callers live in the London area, at least at the time of their interviews, and this was true also of those who came for advice to the offices of the previous agencies. The record cards of these visits, of which there were about 5,000 altogether at the end of 1958, thus provide useful data on the distribution and characteristics of West Indians in London. Indeed, no other equally extensive and reliable data are at present available.

We were able to extract the relevant information, and this was done in two ways. First, the addresses on all the cards were copied and mapped. Though some were incomplete, there was still a total of 4,691 usable addresses, to which we shall refer in this chapter as the 'London Group'. Second, a random sample of over one in four (actually two-ninths) of all the London Group cards (which had been sorted by sex of applicant and year of interview) was taken. For each of the cases in the Sample the details from the original records were copied and then tabulated. There were 1,070 individuals—782 men and 288 women—in this 'London Sample', as it is here called.

Are the London Group, and consequently the London Sample, representative of West Indians in London? As there is no information comparable in scale and detail to that provided by these sources, it is not possible to answer the question with complete certainty. Some tests can, however, be made, and their results are positive.

To begin with, certain external data are available—on the number of West Indian men and women who have come to this country in recent years, by origin and year of arrival, and also on the previous occupations of migrants. The detailed comparison of these data with the sample results, as given in Appendix A, has led to the conclusion that the London Sample can be regarded with confidence, in particular so far as male migrants are concerned. The Sample is consistent with the kuown characteristics of West Indians who arrived in the United Kingdom from the beginning of 1951 to the end of 1957. (Both the earlier and the latest arrivals are slightly underrepresented.) There are some minor discrepancies: the London Sample contains proportionately fewer women, fewer Jamaicans and possibly more non-manual workers than are included in the external data, which relate to migrants in the country as a whole. The first discrepancy, in the proportion of women, though slight, might be of some importance. But the others are too small to throw serious doubts on the validity of the London Sample of West Indian men; they might, moreover, be due to differences in the coverage and accuracy of the various sources of information, and to selective migration to London.

In conjunction with the rather scanty external data, it is also necessary to consider the inherent plausibility of the London Sample. The Migrant Services Division—as its predecessor, the British Caribbean Welfare Service, which dealt with the majority of cases in the Sample—is undoubtedly an important agency for West Indians in London and well known among them all. It can thus be assumed that those who came to its offices with their questions are a representative, and not a highly selected, group—especially in view of the fact that the migrants, however varied their backgrounds and conditions, still face common problems on which they need advice from the official agency. This assumption was confirmed by the composition of the London Sample: it includes people of diverse origins, ages and occupations. While it might have been expected that black-coated workers would have fewer problems, and would, therefore, be less likely to visit the official agency than West Indian manual workers, this was not the case. Thus the London Sample can be regarded as a reliable one for the vast majority of post-war male West Indian migrants in London—for those who arrived during the seven-year period from 1951 to 1957. For West Indian women, however, the Sample appears to be less trustworthy. As they do not make use of the official agency to the same extent as men, and as housewives, in particular, would have fewer reasons to make such visits than others, it is also probable that those who do go are not representative of all the age and social groups of West Indian women in London.[1]

It must be emphasised, moreover, that not all the information which the London Sample provides—about both men and women—is of equal value. The details were originally noted for a specific administrative purpose—that of assisting the official agency in carrying out its advisory functions. The records were not designed as a basis for a social survey of West Indians in London. Thus not all the particulars for which space was allotted on the standard record card were systematically entered for everyone. Information is complete or

---

[1] As the Sample for women might well be less representative than that for men, the results are given separately in the subsequent parts of this chapter—except with reference to those aspects which are not, as the analysis showed, likely to be affected by any bias in the selection of women who visit the official agency. The pattern of geographical distribution in London, for example, was the same for men and women.

almost complete for the whole London Sample on sex, age, territory of origin, year of arrival in this country, date of first interview with the official agency, on their London addresses at that time, and on the kind of problem on which advice was sought. The details on the migrants' last occupations in the West Indies are also fairly well known. But those on their occupations in London are more meagre—largely because many migrants come to the official agency in search of jobs, and are in fact unemployed at that stage.

As, of course, only adults visit the official agency, the West Indian child population is omitted from its records, and the cards contain no information on certain important aspects—on marital status, family size and composition, on moves in London and to other parts of the United Kingdom. Nor is it known how many of the migrants in the London Sample have since returned home. It is not possible to derive from the Sample an estimate of the total number of West Indians in London at the end of 1958.

Despite these limitations, it is, however, well worth while to consider the London Sample in some detail. It gives an accurate picture of the geographical pattern of West Indian settlement in London. It also indicates some of the main demographic and social features of the new minority group. So far, a good deal of the information which has been circulated about the migrants has been based on vague hearsay. The new concrete data, though still sparse, dispel some current misconceptions.

2. ORIGIN, SEX AND AGE

West Indian newcomers to London have the typical characteristics of long distance migrants. They do not represent a cross-section of the population of the Caribbean territories. They are a select group. They are predominantly young; more men than women migrate, and also more people of the higher than of the lower occupational grades.

Origin

Some territories, moreover, have contributed more than their proportionate share to the total migration to this country. This is true especially of Jamaica, the largest of the Caribbean islands. In 1958, the population of Jamaica was about 45 per cent of the total estimated population of the West Indies territories. But almost 60 per

cent of all West Indian men in the London Sample came from Jamaica
and 70 per cent of the women; and these proportions are very similar
to those of official estimates and statistics for West Indian migrants
in the country as a whole.

TABLE 1

London Sample   TERRITORY OF ORIGIN OF MIGRANTS

Territory of Origin	Men	Women
	%	%
Jamaica . . .	57	70
Trinidad and Tobago .	9	6
Barbados . . .	7	6
British Guiana . .	8	5
Other Territories . .	19	13
TOTAL		
Per cent . . .	100	100
Number . . .	782	288

NOTE: The 'other territories' are the Leeward and Windward islands (Antigua,
Montserrat, St. Kitts-Nevis, Dominica, Grenada, St. Lucia, St. Vincent) and British
Honduras.

However, the proportion of Jamaicans among new arrivals has
not been a constant one. Since 1953 it has steadily decreased: almost
80 per cent of the men in the London Sample who arrived here in
that year or before were Jamaicans, but only 45 per cent of those
who came in 1957 and 1958. On the other hand, the proportion of
migrants from Trinidad and from the smaller territories has increased from year to year. (These trends are also repeated in the
external data for all West Indian migrants to the United Kingdom.)

Female Migrants

The migration pattern of women, in terms of their origin, repeats
that of the men, but after some delay. Presumably this is the case because women tend to follow their husbands or male relatives when
these have already been settled here for some time. Thus the decline
in the proportion of women from Jamaica, and the increase in the
proportions of those from other islands, during the 1953 to 1958
period, have been similar to the respective changes among male
migrants, but not quite so great.

TABLE 2

London Sample

YEAR OF ARRIVAL IN THE U.K. OF ADULT MIGRANTS BY TERRITORY OF ORIGIN

Territory of Origin	Year of Arrival of Migrants in the U.K.												TOTAL	
	1953 or Earlier		1954		1955		1956		1957 and 1958					
	Men Only	All Migrants	Men Only	All Migrants	Men Only	All Migrants	Men Only	All Migrants	Men Only	All Migrants			Men Only	All Migrants
	%	%	%	%	%	%	%	%	%	%			%	%
Jamaica	77	81	72	75	64	67	47	50	45	53			57	60
Trinidad and Tobago	8	7	3	3	4	4	12	11	14	11			9	8
Barbados	4	3	3	3	9	9	9	9	7	5			7	7
British Guiana	4	3	8	7	3	3	12	10	7	8			8	7
Others	7	6	14	12	20	17	20	20	27	23			19	18
TOTAL														
Per cent	100	100	100	100	100	100	100	100	100	100			100	100
Number	75	90	107	137	189	247	243	344	168	252			782	1,070

The growing proportion of women and of children among recent arrivals indicates that husbands have been asking their families to join them. At the 1951 census, 41 per cent of all the adults born in the West Indies and living in England and Wales were women. The figures of Jamaican migrants to this country from 1953 to 1955, in the study by Roberts and Mills, show similar percentages for those three years. According to the Migrant Services Division, the proportion of women among annual arrivals has been increasing since 1956: in 1958, every second adult migrant from the West Indies was a woman.[2]

There are fewer women in the London Sample than among all West Indian migrants who have arrived in the United Kingdom since 1951, as shown by the estimates and statistics of the Migrant Services Division. The latter proportion for the country as a whole is just over 40 per cent; that in the London Sample is 27 per cent. (The two percentages would have been very similar if the London Sample had included wives who, after an interval, followed migrants who arrived here before 1955.) The London Sample does, however, show the same steady proportionate increase in female migration as is seen in the general figures for the country as a whole.

Year of Arrival

The London Sample also reflects the general curve of annual arrivals from the West Indies to the United Kingdom: the increase in number year by year from 1951 to 1956, and the decline which occurred in 1957 and 1958.

The table of annual arrivals indicates that the term 'newcomer' is by now rather a misnomer for quite a number of West Indians in London. By the end of 1958, one in ten of the men in the Sample had lived here for five or more years; well over two-thirds for two to four years; and about one in five had come more recently.[3] About one in

[2] G. W. Roberts and D. O. Mills, *op. cit.*, p. 37. See also Appendix A. During the past few years, the Migrant Services Division has counted children separately among annual arrivals of West Indians in the United Kingdom. The proportion of children has increased from about 3 per cent of all West Indian migrants to the U.K. arriving in 1956 to 10 per cent of those arriving in 1959. (See Chapter I, p. 5.)

[3] It is possible, of course, that a few of the migrants who arrived in the early fifties have since returned home or gone to other parts of the country. But their number is probably offset by that of West Indians who have been established here for a considerable time, and who tend to be under-represented in the Sample. It can thus be assumed that Table 3 gives a realistic account of the length of stay of West Indian men in London.

TABLE 3   Year of Arrival in the United Kingdom and Ratio of
London Sample   Female Migrants

Year of Arrival	Percentage Arriving Each Year		Women as % of Total Arrivals in Each Year
	Total	Men Only	
1953 and before .	8	10	17
1954 . . .	13	14	22
1955 . . .	23	24	24
1956 . . .	32	31	29
1957 . . .	17	16	31
1958 . . .	7	5	40
TOTAL			
Per cent . .	100	100	27
Number . .	1,070	782	288

TABLE 4
London Sample   Age of Migrants on Arrival

Age Group	Men	Women
	%	%
15–19 . . .	6	9
20–24 . . .	27	24
25–29 . . .	24	23
Sub-Total .	57	56
30–34 . . .	13	14
35–39 . . .	13	10
Sub-Total .	26	24
40–44 . . .	7	8
45–49 . . .	6	7
50–54 . . .	2	3
55 and over . .	2	2
Sub-Total .	17	20
GRAND TOTAL .	100	100
Total Number .	738	276
Age Unknown .	44	12
Total Sample . .	782	288

TABLE 5

London Sample

AGE OF MIGRANTS ON ARRIVAL IN THE U.K. IN SUCCESSIVE YEARS

| Age Group | Arrivals in Different Years | | | | | | | | | |
| | Men | | | | | Women | | | | |
	1954 and Before	1955	1956	1957 and '58	Total	1954 and Before	1955	1956	1957 and '58	Total
	%	%	%	%	%	%	%	%	%	%
Under 30 . . .	62	57	54	56	57	48	49	60	62	57
30–39 . . .	24	29	28	25	26	21	20	26	18	24
40 and over .	14	14	18	19	17	31	31	14	20	19
TOTAL .	100	100	100	100	100	100	100	100	100	100

two—those who arrived before 1956—can be expected to have made their initial adjustment.

Age

As so many of the migrants are young people, they are likely to have the capacity to adapt themselves to their new environment rather quickly. When they arrive here, the largest single age group, both among men and women, is that of people who are between 20 to 30 years old. Over 50 per cent of the men and 47 per cent of the women were of that age when they came to England. And few of them were over 44 years old—only 10 per cent of the men and 12 per cent of the women.

The age distribution of West Indians in the London Sample is essentially alike for men and women, and also for migrants from the different Caribbean territories. There have, however, been some changes in the age structure of successive annual 'cohorts' of migrants. In recent years, the percentage of men who are over 40 when they arrive here has increased—slightly but steadily. Among women, there has been the opposite tendency: proportionately more young women, under 30 years, have come here than before.

It is relevant to note the natural shifts in age distribution which have occurred among the adult migrants in the London Sample since their arrival in this country.[4] Although they are still a young group, the definition of 'youth' has, of course, changed. The majority are now over 30 years old: they are at a stage when they would be expected to support families, and to look for settled employment.

TABLE 6

London Sample   AGE OF MIGRANTS

Age Group	Men		Women	
	On Arrival	In 1959	On Arrival	In 1959
	%	%	%	%
Under 30 .	57	41	56	44
30–39 .	26	33	24	30
40–49 .	13	19	15	17
50 and over	4	7	5	9
TOTAL .	100	100	100	100

[4] As children are not included in the records of the official Caribbean agency, it is not possible to derive from our data a picture of the present age structure of all West Indians in London.

3. OCCUPATIONS IN THE WEST INDIES AND IN LONDON

Occupations at Home

Although the migrants are asked to state their previous occupation in the West Indies when they visit the official agency, not all of them in fact do so. Some have been too young to have had any, or regular, employment before they came to this country; others may have been unemployed for some time. Thus quite a number of the replies to this question—especially from women, many of whom have presumably not worked before—are incomplete or too vague for the present purpose.

Nevertheless, there is sufficient information to provide a useful indication of the previous occupational characteristics of the migrants, in particular as this information is consistent with that derived from other sources. (See Appendix A.)

Before they left for England, the employment status of the men and women in the London Sample was as follows:

Employment Status in the West Indies:	*Men*	*Women*
	%	%
In full-time employment		
(*a*) Details known . . .	78	27
(*b*) Details vague . . .	7	4
	—	—
	85	31
Definitely never worked before; or in part-time employment, or in full-time education . . .	2	7
Employment status unknown . .	13	62
TOTAL		
Per cent	100	100
Number	782	288

Adequate details were, therefore, available for four-fifths of the men, and for just over a third of the women—including in both groups those who had definitely never been in paid employment before they arrived in England. For people who were known to have had an occupation (78 per cent of the men; 27 per cent of the women) their last one in the West Indies was recorded.[5]

While the range of previous occupations of the migrants in the London Sample is a wide one, there are also definite indications of selection. One in four of the men, and one in two of the women, had been non-manual workers. Indeed, only just over one in five of both the men and women had been in a rather low occupational grade, and had been employed in the West Indies as a semi-skilled or un-skilled worker, or as a farm labourer. Thus the migrants are not drawn equally from the various occupational groups in their home territories. The proportions of black-coated and of skilled workers among them are greater, and that of agricultural workers is smaller, than the corresponding proportions in the employment structure of the West Indies as a whole.[6] Such selective migration, in terms of occupation and age alike, might well have potential adverse effects on the economy of the West Indies.

Of course, selective migration—of the young and the skilled—also implies that the West Indies' loss might well be Britain's gain, or, in this case, London's gain. This is not to say that the migrants neces-sarily have the particular capacity for the jobs which are open in the areas to which they go. Nor are West Indian and London occupa-tions with the same name and apparent rank, in fact, always com-parable. In some respects, the hierarchy of occupations might well be different. In Kingston as in London, moreover, some descriptions, like that of a shopkeeper, carry ambiguous meanings; they give no precise indication of status and training. But even if all the possible qualifications are kept in mind, the occupational background of the migrants is still an encouraging one. In a period of normal economic activity, they could surely be absorbed in the vast London labour market, with its great range of opportunities. They have brought with them a sufficient diversity of experience, a sufficient share of skill, and certainly a considerable share of youth and vigour. Peo-ple who write to the newspapers to complain that England has be-

[5] A comparison, in terms of age, origin and year of arrival, of the men whose previous employment status or occupation were unknown with the others, for whom these details were known, has shown that the former and the latter are alike in their main characteristics. The omission of the 'unknowns' from the count is thus not likely to have disturbed the picture of the previous occupational structure of the migrants in the London Sample.

[6] For a detailed discussion of the effects of selective migration on the labour force in Jamaica from 1953 to 1955, see G. W. Roberts and D. O. Mills, *op. cit.*, pp. 68 ff.

come the "dumping-ground for the world's riff-raff"[7] will find no support in the table below.

TABLE 7

London Sample PREVIOUS OCCUPATIONS OF MIGRANTS IN THE WEST INDIES

Occupation	Men	Women
	%	%
Professional Workers	1	—
Quasi-professional Workers	6	16
Shopkeepers and Assistants, Salesmen . .	5	16
Clerks, Typists	12	18
Total Non-manual Workers . . .	*24*	*50*
Manual Workers: Skilled	46	27
Semi-skilled . . .	5	18
Unskilled	13	5
Total Manual Workers	*64*	*50*
Farmers	9	—
Farm Labourers and Fishermen . . .	3	—
Total Agricultural Workers . . .	*12*	—
GRAND TOTAL (all with known occupations):		
Per cent	*100*	*100*
Number	608	77

NOTE: Our classification of occupations is in accordance with that of the Registrar General. The group of cooks, waiters and others in personal service (just under 2 per cent of the males and 4 per cent of the females) has, however, been included in the category of semi-skilled workers and not in that of non-manual workers.

The various previous occupations of migrants are not evenly represented in the different age groups. As might be expected, there is some relation between status and age. Professional and quasi-professional workers tend to be older than the others: a higher proportion of them than of the clerical and manual workers are men over 40.

[7] *North London Press*, 8th May, 1959. Similar statements are frequently made, even by people in the well-informed sections of British society. Thus it was said, for example, not so long ago in the House of Lords (by the Earl of Swinton): "Of course, the great majority of people who come into this country, certainly from the West Indies, are unskilled men." (*Parliamentary Debates*, H.o.L., 19th November 1958, col. 646.) In fact, however, the "great majority" of West Indian migrants are black-coated or skilled workers.

TABLE 8 PREVIOUS OCCUPATIONS IN THE WEST INDIES BY TERRITORY OF ORIGIN

London Sample

(Male Migrants)

Occupation	Territory of Origin					
	Jamaica	Trinidad and Tobago	Barbados	British Guiana	Other Territories	Total
	%	%	%	%	%	%
Professional Workers .	3	22	5	22	7	7
Other Black-Coated Workers .	13	32	7	22	19	17
Total Non-manual Workers	*16*	*54*	*12*	*44*	*26*	*24*
Manual Workers: Skilled .	47	42	58	33	45	46
Semi-skilled .	5	4	9	4	5	5
Unskilled .	13	—	21	13	18	13
Total Manual Workers .	*65*	*46*	*88*	*50*	*68*	*64*
Farmers .	14	—	—	6	4	9
Farm Labourers and Fishermen .	5	—	—	—	2	3
Total Agricultural Workers .	*19*	—	—	*6*	*6*	*12*
GRAND TOTAL *Per cent* . .	*100*	*100*	*100*	*100*	*100*	*100*
Number . .	345	55	43	46	119	608
Per cent . . .	57	9	7	7	20	100

Far more noticeable than the variations by age, however, are the distinctions in the occupational distribution of migrants from the different territories. Jamaica, Barbados and the smaller territories (including British Honduras) send a smaller proportion of black-coated workers to Britain than Trinidad and British Guiana. The majority of men from Barbados had previously been skilled manual workers. Almost all the farmers and farm labourers in the London Sample come from Jamaica; just under one in five of the Jamaicans has had an agricultural occupation.

Occupational selection has been increasingly noticeable among the migrants who have come to England in successive years. The proportion of black-coated workers has been higher among the recent than among the earlier arrivals: it has grown steadily year by year, both among men and women. Fewer men in the middle ranges of the occupational hierarchy migrated in the last few years than before; the proportion of unskilled manual workers, too, has increased —though only among men, not among women.[8]

More significant than the actual shift in the occupational structure of migrants is its consistency. For the same shift has steadily occurred among both men and women, in all age groups, and also among migrants from different Caribbean areas. Jamaica, too, like the other territories, has recently sent proportionately more black-coated workers to London than before, and also a higher percentage of unskilled manual workers.

[8] It might be thought that the steady increase in the proportion of black-coated workers among recent arrivals can be attributed to the simultaneous changes in the age composition and origin of migrants which have already been referred to. Recent male migrants tend to be older than the earlier ones (while the trend among women is in the opposite direction); and there is some 'bunching' of male non-manual workers in the older age groups. Moreover, there were proportionately fewer Jamaicans among the migrants from 1956 to 1958 than among those in the years before then. And as there is a lower percentage of black-coated workers among Jamaican migrants than among those from other territories, a decline in the Jamaican contribution to West Indian emigration could have the effect of raising correspondingly the proportion of non-manual workers among the total arrivals from the Caribbean territories.

However, neither explanation is sufficient, as a more detailed analysis showed. The change in age composition—relevant only in the case of men—has barely contributed to the shift in the occupational structure of recent 'batches' of migrants. The decline in the proportion of Jamaicans has had a slightly greater effect, though still only a marginal one. But quite apart from the combination of these two factors, there must have been other independent reasons for the increasing proportion of black-coated workers among recent arrivals. These reasons will presumably be found not in London, but in the economic conditions of the West Indies.

TABLE 9

London Sample   PREVIOUS OCCUPATIONS OF MALE MIGRANTS BY PERIOD OF ARRIVAL IN THE U.K. AND BY TERRITORY OF ORIGIN

Previous Occupation in the West Indies	Migrants from Jamaica		Migrants from All Other Territories		All Male Migrants	
	Arrival in the U.K.		Arrival in the U.K.		Arrival in the U.K.	
	1950–55	1956–58	1950–55	1956–58	1950–55	1956–58
	%	%	%	%	%	%
Non-manual Workers . .	13	20	28	35	18	28
Manual Workers: Skilled .	51	41	52	40	52	41
Semi-skilled	10	10	5	7	8	8
Unskilled	9	18	12	15	9	17
Farmers . . .	17	11	3	3	13	6
TOTAL						
Per cent . .	100	100	100	100	100	100
Number . .	187	158	85	178	272	336
Arrivals in each period as % of total arrivals in each group .	54%	46%	32%	68%	45%	55%

NOTE: A few migrants who arrived before 1950 have been included in the group of those who arrived up to 1955. In this table, farm labourers and fishermen have been included in the group of semi-skilled manual workers.

Occupations in London

The migrants' aspirations for jobs in London are largely determined by their previous occupations in the West Indies. There is a considerable, and indeed a growing, proportion of West Indian men and women who hope for a job with middle class status; there is also an increasing proportion of men who are apparently used to unskilled manual work. But the largest single group of men—even among those who have arrived here since 1956—is still that of skilled manual workers. Have the migrants with varied occupational backgrounds been successful in finding the jobs for which they were looking here?

It seems that many of them have been disappointed, at least in the early period of their stay in London, and that quite a number are likely to remain disappointed unless they forget their previous aspirations.

Although the London Sample does not provide a full record of the migrants' employment experiences, it does give some indications. Indeed, the records on London occupations are incomplete just because a large number of West Indian men and women visit the official agency in order to get advice on how to get a job. And many of the men, especially, go to their official 'advice bureau' soon after their arrival here, when they have not yet been employed in London. The women tend to go at a later stage, when they have already lived here for some time. For that reason, the Sample contains information on London occupations for a higher proportion of women than of men—for 52 per cent of the women, and for 42 per cent of the men.

But while the occupations of only a minority of men have been recorded, it is this minority which has had, in fact, experience of the London labour market. They are mainly people who had already lived here for some time when they visited the British Caribbean Welfare Service (or the comparable earlier or later agency).[9] Therefore, they have had at least one job in this country already, usually in London. (For those who have had several jobs, the last one was recorded.) With increasing length of stay their chances of having been employed here have clearly increased, and those who have lived here for some years also have slightly better jobs (in terms of occupational status) than the more recent arrivals.

Everyone who walks around London knows that West Indians are employed in public transport, in the post office, and in the service of local authorities. They are seen working on building sites, in

[9] This is illustrated by the following table. (Footnote continued on p. 28.)

factories, in restaurants and cafés; West Indian nurses have become familiar to patients in London hospitals. It looks as though the new-comers have varied manual and non-manual occupations; in this respect their situation appears to be better than that of the smaller number of coloured people in Britain before the war who had serious employment difficulties.

Although everyday observation is to some extent confirmed by the Sample records on the London occupations of migrants, these records also show that the new minority group is by no means free from employment problems.

Both the men and women in the Sample had a variety of jobs in London. The men who had obtained skilled manual work were in fifty different kinds of occupation: among them were mechanics, fitters, painters, moulders, drivers, tailors, compositors, radio and electrical engineers; the largest individual group in this category was that of carpenters. The list of occupations of the semi-skilled

EMPLOYMENT STATUS OF MIGRANTS IN LONDON
(London Sample)

Employment Status in London	Length of Stay in the U.K. at the Time the Record was Taken				Women
	Men				
	Arrival in U.K. Within Same Year	Arrival in U.K. In Previous Year	Arrival in U.K. Two or More Years Before	Total	Total
	%	%	%	%	%
Employed:					
Occupation known	18	64	83	42	52
Details vague .	6	9	8	7	15
Sub-Total .	24	73	91	49	67
Others: (Mainly those who were not yet employed) .	76	27	9	51	33
TOTAL					
Per cent .	100	100	100	100	100
Number .	437	170	175	782	288
Total Per cent .	56	22	22	100	

NOTE: Among the 'others', whose occupations in this country are not known, are also a few in full-time education, and—among the earlier arrivals—some people who sought advice on prob-lems unrelated to employment, and therefore did not mention their London occupations. But most of the 'others' had not lived in this country long enough, at the time of their visit to the official agency, to have held a job. On the other hand, 77 per cent of those whose occupations in this country have been recorded, had arrived in the previous calendar year, or in earlier years.
Information on the London occupations of women is more extensive—covering a larger number of cases—than that on their occupations in the West Indies, presumably because many women had not been employed there. For men, the position is reversed.

and unskilled men, too, is a fairly long one. Among the former were machinists, stokers, packers, bus conductors and relayers, employed on the railways. Many of the unskilled men (about one in two of them) simply described themselves as labourers or factory hands. Others were working as porters and cleaners, as garage or lift attendants, as dishwashers and bottlewashers, as messengers and roadsweepers.

Proportionately more women than men had office jobs as clerks and typists, and there was also a number of nurses. Among the women who had manual work, two kinds of employment were predominant. One group were working as domestic and kitchen assistants in restaurants, hotels, hospitals and canteens. The others were employed as machinists and finishers in the clothing industry.

While West Indians in London have thus undoubtedly entered many different occupations and industries,[10] their jobs are within a fairly narrow range of status, and indeed mostly of rather low status. In London, 60 per cent of the men and 66 per cent of the women had semi-skilled and unskilled manual jobs. In the West Indies, in their previous occupations, only 21 per cent of the men and 23 per cent of the women in the Sample had been in these rather low categories. There seems to have been a downgrading, and it is especially noticeable in the case of black-coated workers. Before they left the West Indies, 24 per cent of the men and 50 per cent of the women in the London Sample had been in non-manual occupations. But in London, only 6 per cent of the men and 23 per cent of the women had obtained comparable jobs.

Changes in Occupational Status

The distribution of the migrants' occupations in London differs greatly from that of their previous jobs in the West Indies. But the comparison between these two distributions does not show the employment experience of individual West Indian men and women. A considerable number of men had not yet found work in London when they visited the official agency. Some other men and many women had not been previously employed in the West Indies—or had not stated their previous occupation—but had obtained jobs in London. It is, therefore, necessary to consider in more detail the experience of

[10] For West Indian men, transport appears to be the most important individual industry group (as distinct from occupational group). But a fair range of industries, including building, engineering, catering and distribution, are represented. The industries which women enter most frequently are professional services (e.g., hospitals) catering and clothing.

TABLE 10

London Sample   OCCUPATIONS OF MIGRANTS IN LONDON

Occupation	Men	Women
	%	%
Quasi-professional Workers	2	14
Clerks, Typists	4	9
Total Non-manual Workers . . .	*6*	*23*
Manual Workers: Skilled	34	11
Semi-skilled . . .	17	49
Unskilled	43	17
Total Manual Workers	*94*	*77*
GRAND TOTAL (all with known occupations)		
Per cent	*100*	*100*
Number	330	150

NOTE: While in the West Indies some of the migrants had been in professional occupations, and others had been in the group of shopkeepers and salesmen (5 per cent of the men and 16 per cent of the women had been in the latter category), in London none of the migrants in the Sample had obtained jobs in either of these categories. The group of women in quasi-professional occupations in London (14 per cent of the total) consists of nurses who are able to continue their training and their original occupation here. As there is this group of nurses, the range of status is wider, and the percentage of the non-manual category is greater, for West Indian women than for the men in the Sample, so far as their London occupations are concerned.

TABLE 11   OCCUPATIONS IN THE WEST INDIES AND IN LONDON

London Sample   Men Whose Occupations Both in the West Indies and in London are Known

Occupation	Proportion in Each Occupational Group	
	In the West Indies	*In London*
	%	%
Non-manual Workers. . .	27	5
Manual Workers: Skilled . .	52	33
Semi-skilled .	7	18
Unskilled .	14	44
TOTAL		
Per cent . . .	100	100
Number . . .	236	236

NOTE: Those who had been farmers in the West Indies have been included in the non-manual category.

a smaller group of migrants whose occupations both in the West Indies and in London are known.

It is useful to make this comparison, especially as the smaller group, for whom all the relevant particulars are available, is representative, in terms of various characteristics, of all the West Indian men in the London Sample. (The smaller group has essentially the same distributions of occupations in the West Indies and in London as were found for the whole sample of male migrants.) Thus the indications derived from the general record of occupations are confirmed. Downgrading, in terms of occupational status, has indeed been frequent. Just over half of the West Indian men in this group, whose jobs both before and after migration were recorded, have in this country an occupation with a lower rank than they had previously.

Occupational Status in London Compared with
Status in the West Indies

In London:	Male Migrants
	%
Same status as previously . .	41
Higher status than previously .	5
Lower status than previously .	54

TOTAL	
Per cent . . .	100
Number . . .	236

NOTE: In this comparison, quasi-professional and clerical jobs have been regarded as being of the same status grade. When men who were farmers in the West Indies are excluded from this group, the proportions with the same, higher and lower status in London respectively are still very similar to those shown above. The same is the case also when only the experience of those men is considered who had been in London for at least one year at the time when their jobs here were recorded. Proportionately more West Indian women than men appear to maintain their previous occupational status in London. However, the number of women in the Sample whose jobs both in the West Indies and in London are known is rather small.

It is the managerial and black-coated workers who have found it especially difficult to continue their previous occupations in London. Most of them (86 per cent) were employed as manual workers here, and over half as unskilled labourers. But apparently the change of status has also been a drastic one for many of the men who had done skilled manual work in the West Indies.[11] Almost 40 per cent were in

[11] It is sometimes argued that this downgrading is not in fact very drastic, because the claim to skill made by many West Indians is false, at least by English standards. In support of this view, it is said that a considerable proportion of

unskilled jobs in London, and 7 per cent in semi-skilled jobs. On the other hand, some of the migrants, who had previously been in jobs which require no particular skills, have been able to improve their status and to enter skilled grades in London.

Of course, occupational status is not the sole criterion by which the economic success of the migrants can be judged. A lowering of status, as a result of migration, does not necessarily imply a decrease of income. Some unskilled labourers in London might earn more than some professional men in the West Indies; and in this country, too, manual work, even of fairly low skill, is sometimes better paid than non-manual work. Nevertheless, it is not easy for a professional or black-coated worker to accept the role of a factory hand or road-sweeper. Moreover, occupational status and job security tend to be correlated. And status matters a great deal to any new minority group, and especially, in present circumstances, to the members of a coloured minority group. The indications that there are problems of this kind cannot, therefore, be shrugged away.

4. GEOGRAPHICAL DISTRIBUTION IN LONDON

It is not known how many West Indians live in London, or in any individual borough, in 1960. The last enumeration of people born in the West Indies, in the Census of 1951, can no longer give any guide. During the disturbances in the autumn of 1958, one figure was widely quoted—that of about 40,000 West Indians in the London area. But it was based on a rash guess and became accepted by virtue of mere repetition.

A little more has become known recently about the geographical distribution of West Indians in London, but in this respect, too, the information so far available was bound to be impressionistic and

---

West Indian migrants, including those who call themselves 'skilled workers', are illiterate. This is, however, not the case. Figures of illiteracy among male migrants from Jamaica during 1954 and 1955 are given by Roberts and Mills, *op. cit.*, p. 53. (The test of illiteracy used was the migrants' ability to sign their names.) Of a total of 16,089 male migrants, 288 (less than 2 per cent) were found to be illiterate. In this group of migrants, there were 9,714 who claimed to be skilled workers; 84 of these (well under 1 per cent) were illiterate. These proportions of illiterate people among West Indian migrants (as distinct from the West Indian population in the home territories) are not unduly high, in comparison with illiteracy ratios in the adult populations of advanced Western countries.

vague. As coloured people are particularly noticeable when they live close to one another, and have thus been visible in some districts—in Brixton, North Kensington and Kilburn, for example—it has been thought that they are all highly concentrated in a few parts of London. In fact, however, the impressions derived from general observations have been misleading. The addresses of about 4,700 West Indian migrants in the 'London Group' show a more complex pattern of distribution than has so far been thought to exist.[12]

Stable Pattern of Distribution

There is every reason to assume that the geographical distribution of the London Group is representative of that of West Indians who have arrived in London since 1951, in general.[13]

The districts in which a considerable number of migrants are known to live (though nobody knows how many) are shown up clearly on our map of West Indian addresses in London. The main features in the pattern on this map have, moreover, been fairly stable for some time. They are essentially the same for migrants who gave their addresses a few years ago as for those who gave them recently, for those who arrived in successive periods as for the whole group of West Indians. While individual migrants may move from a particular

[12] In this section, we are referring to the 'London Group'—the 4,691 West Indian men and women whose addresses were recorded and mapped—whenever the geographical distribution of the migrants, in general, is considered. For the distinctions in this distribution—in terms of the origin and occupations of migrants, for example—we are using the data from the London Sample of 1,070 cases. As the Sample was drawn from the London Group, the proportionate geographical distributions of the former and of the latter are alike. The London Group, with the larger number of cases, provides a more detailed picture of the geographical distribution as such.

[13] Thus it is possible to obtain a realistic picture of the pattern of settlement, although we are not able to derive from our data an estimate of the proportionate distribution of the total West Indian community, including all women and children, in the different areas of London. We have also compared our information with indications derived from several other sources. West Indian officials and individuals have drawn our attention to particular streets in which migrants live. The officers of local authorities could not give figures of the actual numbers of West Indians in their boroughs, but were able to point to the streets in their areas where migrants tend to cluster. We visited the various districts several times so as to make our own observations. We also noted the addresses of all West Indians mentioned in eleven local London newspapers for a period of three months. Mrs. Sheila Patterson gave us a list of addresses of West Indians in South London which she had collected during her study in Brixton. The existence of several areas of fairly concentrated West Indian settlement, which had been indicated by these and other sources, was later confirmed, and also shown with more precision, by the data for the London Group.

42909

house—and it cannot be assumed that all those in the London Group can still be found at the addresses which were recorded—it seems that their rooms or flats are taken by other West Indians. In general, therefore, West Indians are still found in the streets, and in scattered houses, in which migrants have lived at any one time in recent years.

As more migrants have come to London, some extension of West Indian settlements has, of course, occurred; in several districts of London, the proportion of West Indians in the population has also grown. But apparently the geographical expansion of the migrants has not been commensurate with the increase in their number. As the absolute increase has not been great, in relation to the total population of London, and as there has been also since 1956 an uneven decline in the annual number of new arrivals, the latter have been absorbed in the London area without a significant change in the pattern of West Indian addresses.[14] Apparently, the newcomers have moved into houses, dispersed in many different parts of London, which had already been occupied by some West Indians, and also into those districts where migrants were living fairly close to one another. And it seems that there has been more doubling-up, and presumably more crowding, in the rooms and flats of West Indian tenants.

Dispersal of Migrants Throughout London

Even before the influx of new migrants during the past three years, the geographical distribution of West Indians in London had been a rather scattered one, and this is yet another reason why its pattern has hardly changed. Irrespective of their length of stay in this country, and at various points of time since the early fifties, the migrants in the London Group have had addresses in many different parts of the conurbation. By the end of 1958, there were West Indians in all but two of the metropolitan boroughs in the County of London, and in twenty-two other local authority areas in the adjacent counties of Middlesex, Surrey, Kent and Essex. (There were no migrants in the metropolitan boroughs of St. Marylebone and Bermondsey; and there were also none in the City of London where only some 5,000 people live nowadays.)

But while West Indians are dispersed throughout the London region, they are not evenly distributed within it. The vast majority— well over four-fifths of all those in the London Group—live in the County of London, although the County contains only two-fifths of the total population of the London region. Comparatively few

[14] See Table 13, and also the further comments on the continuity in the geographical distribution of West Indians in London.

REINALD LIBRARY
ROGER JUNIOR COLLEGE
EVERDOUGH WASHINGTON

TABLE 12   GEOGRAPHICAL DISTRIBUTION OF WEST INDIANS
London Group   Addresses of Migrants in Greater London by Boroughs

Address	Per cent Living in Each Area
Islington	9·3
Kensington	12·1
Paddington	9·9
Hammersmith	3·2
Fulham	2·2
Sub-Total in these northern and western metropolitan boroughs	36·7
Lambeth	18·4
Wandsworth	6·5
Camberwell	4·8
Battersea	3·6
Sub-Total in these southern metropolitan boroughs	33·3
Hackney	2·8
Stepney	2·6
Sub-Total in these eastern metropolitan boroughs	5·4
Fifteen other metropolitan boroughs . .	11·0
TOTAL COUNTY OF LONDON . . .	86·4
Willesden (Middlesex)	6·5
In 21 other areas of Middlesex, Surrey, Kent and Essex	7·1
GRAND TOTAL	
Per cent	100·0
Number	4,691

N.—4

migrants live in the outer suburbs—old or new, middle class or working class.[15]

Thus the map shows some concentrations of West Indian addresses in the northern, north-western and western sectors of the County of London (stretching out into Willesden in Middlesex) and also on the other side of the river, mainly in the south-west, including the edge of the south-eastern districts. Apart from two small clusters of West Indians in the East End, however, there are very few migrants in the whole eastern sector of London, north and south of the Thames— both in the areas which have lost population and also in those which have grown, relatively or absolutely, during the last three or four decades. (See Map 1.)

While there are several clusters of West Indian settlements, these are in different parts of London; and there is also a scatter of individual addresses over a wide area. The highest proportion of West Indians in any one borough is in Lambeth, where just over 18 per cent live; Kensington and Paddington, with 12 per cent and 10 per cent respectively, are next. And there are only three other boroughs— Islington and Wandsworth in London County and Willesden across the border—where more than 5 per cent of all the West Indians in the whole London Group have settled. Just over a third of the group live in those northern and western metropolitan boroughs, and an almost equal proportion in those southern parts of the County, where some concentrations of West Indians occur.

Areas of Concentration

The actual areas of concentration can be identified when the map of London is sub-divided in more detail, and when the distribution of West Indian addresses throughout the 118 postal districts in London is considered.[16] A minority—just over one in five—of the migrants are scattered over 71 postal districts; and there are only fourteen districts in which there are no West Indians from the London Group at all. However, while almost 80 per cent of the migrants live in 30

[15] Four metropolitan boroughs in particular—Lambeth, Kensington, Paddington and Islington—have a considerably greater proportion of migrants than of the population of London County as a whole. Almost 50 per cent of all the West Indians in the whole London Group are in these boroughs (or 58 per cent of those who live in London County); but only 23 per cent of the population of the County as a whole were resident in these four boroughs on Census day in 1951. The latter percentage has not changed since that time.

[16] As borough boundaries frequently run across postal districts, the aggregates of West Indian addresses by postal districts are similar to, but not identical with, those in particular boroughs or groups of boroughs. The total London Postal Area is, moreover, larger than the County of London.

postal districts, the clusters in most of these are rather small. There are only seven postal districts—five of them north of the river on the west side, and the others in the south—in each of which 4 per cent or more of all the West Indians in the London Group have settled.

Postal District		Per cent of the London Group West Indians Living in Each District
S.W.9	Stockwell . .	8
S.W.2.	Brixton . . .	4
S.E.5.	Camberwell . .	4
	Sub-Total . .	*16*
W.9.	Maida Hill . .	6
W.11	Notting Hill . .	5
W.2.	Paddington . .	4
W.10	North Kensington .	4
	Sub-Total . .	*19*
	TOTAL . .	*35*

Of course, the clusters of West Indian settlement are not in fact divided by the boundaries of postal districts, and thus the pattern of distribution is seen more clearly in the following table which is a statistical summary of Map 1. (In this table, the postal districts which contain, individually, more than one per cent of all the addresses of migrants in the London Group, and which are adjacent to one another, have been grouped together.) The table also illustrates the stability in the pattern of West Indian addresses in London in successive periods.

Among the six areas in London in which some concentrations of West Indians have existed for some time, there are two which have continued to be of particular importance. Each contains well over one fifth of all the West Indians in the London Group. The first is the rather extensive West area, which stretches from Paddington, through North Kensington and Notting Hill, to Shepherd's Bush and Hammersmith. The second is the South-West area where the focus of the migrants' settlement is Brixton, Stockwell and South Lambeth. It seems that there have been some slight shifts in the respective importance of these two areas since 1955. Apparently, in recent years, proportionately fewer West Indians have moved to the West area,

TABLE 13   ADDRESSES OF WEST INDIANS—MEN AND WOMEN—IN SUCCESSIVE PERIODS

London Sample

Address at Year of Interview with Official Agency

(i) Areas of West Indian Settlement	(ii) 1954–55	(iii) 1956	(iv) 1957–58	(v) Total London Sample	(vi) Per Cent Increase in Each Area from 1955 to the End of 1958
	%	%	%	%	%
A. Main Areas					
West	32	24	22	24	370
North-West	11	7	8	8	370
North	12	15	14	14	580
East	4	3	3	3	370
Sub-Total: Northern Areas	59	49	47	49	410
South-West	17	23	23	22	620
South-East	4	9	8	7	790
Sub-Total: Southern Areas	21	32	31	29	660
B. Other Districts	20	19	22	22	515
GRAND TOTAL *Per cent*	100	100	100	100	485
Number	221	255	594	1,070	

NOTE: As the geographical distributions of West Indian men and women are alike, the figures for the total London Sample are shown. The distributions of the London Sample and of the London Group are identical. There are seven districts in the West area, and the same number in the South-West area; three each in the North-West and South-East areas, eight in the North, and two in the East area. The main areas of West Indian settlement consist altogether of 30 postal districts. The composition of the main areas is shown on Map 1.

and more to the South-West area, than have settled in the London Region as a whole.[17] And these respective trends have also occurred fairly consistently within each of these two areas, in their various constituent postal districts. From 1956 to the end of 1958 the influx of migrants into Notting Hill, in the West area, for example, appears to have been proportionately smaller, and that into Brixton, in the South-West area, proportionately greater than the total West Indian immigration into Greater London during this three-year period. Thus the popular assumption that Notting Hill is the main reception area for coloured migrants is not correct.

On the whole, however, the small shifts in the pattern of distribution are far less noticeable than its continuity. Like other minority groups, the West Indians have followed the routes of previous migrants from their countries; they have moved into areas, and also into particular streets within these areas, where people from their territories had settled already before 1956. Indeed, the outlines of the six main areas of West Indian settlement have hardly changed during the last three years: the migrants are concentrated in the same postal districts in which smaller groups of West Indians had been located before.[18] The percentage of migrants who live outside the areas of

[17] These indications are derived from the London Sample, as shown on Table 13, col. vi. By the end of 1958, the total number of migrants who had been interviewed by the official agency was almost five times larger (485 per cent) than it had been three years earlier. But the increase in the West area during that period was considerably smaller (370 per cent) and that in the South-West area considerably larger (620 per cent). Of course, these figures are only illustrations of a trend; for various reasons (which have been discussed above, page 14) they cannot provide a precise assessment of shifts in geographical distribution. They are, however, consistent not only with general observations, but also with other analyses of the results of the London Sample. As the majority of migrants visit the official agency soon after their arrival in this country, the geographical distribution of West Indians in London, as seen in Table 13, is confirmed if the actual year of arrival of migrants in the U.K., and their length of stay here at the time at which their London addresses were recorded, are taken into account. The same continuity in the pattern of addresses, and the same slight shifts in the pattern, are visible if the more detailed aspects of the distribution are considered.

[18] This point should be noted. The clusters have grown absolutely, but—apart from some minor modifications—not proportionately, in relation to the increasing number of West Indians in London. In other words, if a map of West Indian addresses in London had been drawn three years earlier, it would have shown the same districts as places of relative concentration which are shown as such here, and thus the same main areas of settlement, although the number of migrants was then much smaller. There seems to have been no significant 'overspill' of West Indians into adjacent postal districts. This is presumably partly explained by the fact that many of the recent migrants are relatives or friends of those who came earlier; the newcomers share rooms which were already occupied by West Indians, or they find rooms nearby.

concentration has also remained constant. Just over one fifth of all the West Indians in the London Group live outside these areas and have addresses which are scattered all over the County of London and its fringes.

Geographical Distribution of Different Groups

There are some slight differences in the geographical distribution of West Indians who belong to different occupational groups, and also more marked differences in that of migrants from different territories in the Caribbean. As might be expected, the addresses of West Indian men and women who have non-manual occupations in London are more often scattered than those of manual workers: 28 per cent of the black-coated workers in the London Sample live outside the six main areas of West Indian settlement, as compared with 17 per cent of the manual workers. It is presumably easier for the salary earners than for the wage earners in the new minority group to disperse throughout London, and indeed they often want to find accommodation in districts into which other migrants have not yet moved. A recent advertisement by a coloured professional man—"Room wanted, but not in Notting Hill"—expressed a fairly typical preference of middle class migrants.

But while social distance between West Indian wage and salary earners is often reflected in geographical distance between them, migrants who come from the same territory in the Caribbean tend to live fairly near to one another in London. This is true especially of people from Barbados, from British Guiana and from Trinidad, the majority of whom are concentrated in the main areas of West Indian settlement north of the river.[19] Considerable proportions of each of these groups in the London Sample are clustered, moreover, in a particular district in the northern sector of London. Over 40 per cent of the migrants from Barbados, and about a third of those from British Guiana, live in the West area, and 28 per cent of those from Trinidad in the North area. The Jamaicans are in general more widely distributed than the migrants from other territories; but there is one cluster of them in South London, in the South-West area.

[19] More than half (55 per cent) of the migrants from Barbados in the London Sample, 58 per cent of those from British Guiana, and 62 per cent of those from Trinidad live in the main northern areas of West Indian settlement, as compared with 42 per cent of the Jamaicans and 49 per cent of all the West Indians in the London Sample. There are similar differences in the distribution of migrants from various territories in the individual parts of the main areas of settlement.

'Coloured Quarters'

When the addresses of migrants in the London Group are pin-pointed in detail, the dual features of their distribution—concentration and dispersal—are even more clearly visible. And it is then also apparent that the general pattern of the location of West Indians throughout London is repeated on a small scale within each of the main areas of West Indian settlement, and in particular in the western and southern sectors. (See Maps 2 and 3.)

The West area, for example, contains here and there some streets in which several, or quite a number of, migrants live, often in adjacent houses; but there are many other streets in which only one or two West Indian addresses can be found. In fact, there are very few dense geographical clusters of West Indians in London, and they exist only in a few districts, mainly in and around Brixton and North Kensington, with occasional patches further north. Less than one in five of all the migrants in the London Group had their addresses in the streets in which these fairly dense clusters occurred.[20] And over 40 per cent were in streets in which there were as yet no indications of multiple West Indian tenancy. (See Table 14.)

While there are several fairly dense concentrations of West Indians in London, these clusters are certainly not 'ghettoes', as the maps of West Indian addresses and their summary on the next table show. The images of Notting Hill and Brixton as the 'Harlems' of London are still far from reality. Only a small proportion of West Indians in London live in these particular places, and in most parts of these districts it is not the coloured people but the white people who are predominant.

In the whole of London, there are only two streets—in Brixton—which are almost entirely occupied by coloured migrants. There are also a few other streets—in that area and in the western sector—where the majority of people, or almost a majority, are coloured. But usually more white people than coloured people are seen at the windows, on the doorsteps and in the streets—even in the districts

[20] As shown by Table 14 in outline, and by Maps 2 and 3 in detail, even in the areas of comparatively concentrated West Indian settlement, only a minority of the migrants lived in rather dense geographical clusters—23 per cent of all those in the northern and southern areas. And outside these main areas of West Indian settlement, the migrants' addresses were still more widely scattered. Outside the main areas, there were only nine postal districts (in which 6 per cent of the total London Group had their addresses) where some indications of clustering could be seen. These nine districts are at the edges of the main areas of settlement; most of them are adjacent to the South-East area.

in which West Indians are concentrated and live near to one another. And there are no schools anywhere in London in which coloured children are more than a small minority. As yet London has no 'coloured quarters' of the kind found in American cities.

Map 2

WEST AREA
THE MAIN CLUSTERS OF WEST INDIAN SETTLEMENT

Number of West Indian addresses per house

- ○ One per house
- ◉ Two or three
- ◒ Four or five
- ● Six or more

NOTE: These are addresses of individual West
Indians or their households. For example,
when there are three West Indian addresses
per house, these would refer either to three
separate individuals or to three separate
households.

Map 3

SOUTH-WEST AND SOUTH-EAST AREAS
THE MAIN CLUSTERS OF WEST INDIAN SETTLEMENT

Number of West Indian addresses per house

- ○ One per house
- ◉ Two or three
- ◑ Four or five
- ● Six to ten

NOTE: These are addresses of individual West
Indians or their households. For example,
when there are three West Indian addresses
per house, these would refer either to three
separate individuals or to three separate
households.

TABLE 14
London Group

GEOGRAPHICAL CLUSTERS OF WEST INDIANS IN LONDON*

Areas of West Indian Settlement	Migrants Living in Streets where they are:—					Per cent in Each Area
	Dispersed	Hardly Clustered	In Minor Clusters	In Denser Clusters	Total	
	%	%	%	%	%	%
A. Main Areas						
West	19	19	24	38	100	24
North-West . .	39	23	35	3	100	8
North . . .	44	26	19	11	100	14
East . . .	44	26	30	—	100	3
Sub-Total: Northern Areas	31	22	25	22	100	49
South-West . .	24	19	31	26	100	22
South-East . .	27	34	14	25	100	7
Sub-Total: Southern Areas .	25	23	26	26	100	29
B. Other Districts . .	92	6	2	—	100	22
GRAND TOTAL						
Per cent . . .	43	19	20	18	100	100
Number . . .	2,018	885	939	849	4,691	4,691

* The definitions of the degrees of concentration are based on the number of addresses of individual West Indians (or households) in a particular street. (They do not refer to the total number of West Indians in a street, but to the number of addresses given separately by the migrants who visited their official agency.)
    Dispersal: one or two addresses of West Indians (individuals or households) in a street.
    Hardly clustered: three or four addresses in the same street.
    Minor clusters: five to nine addresses in the same street.
    Denser clusters: ten or more addresses in the same street.
Of course, as the length of streets and their building density differ, these definitions give only an indication of the degrees of concentration. Nevertheless, Table 14 gives an accurate outline of the pattern of distribution which is visible in our detailed maps of all the addresses of the 'London Group' West Indians in the main areas of settlement. Two of these maps are reproduced here. (See Maps 2 and 3.) They show the location of West Indians in those postal districts—in the West, South-West and South-East—in which the concentration of migrants is most marked.

III

Problems of Settlement and Adjustment

1. HOUSING

THE outline of the characteristics and distribution of West Indians in London points to the two main problems which they as a group are facing in their settlement here: employment and housing. It is these two problems, above all others, which are mentioned at once by all those who are familiar with the situation of the migrants. Both are often the chief difficulties of any new minority group in a large metropolitan area. And of course, there are also problems of a personal kind, as well as the more subtle trials of adjustment which all migrants, irrespective of their origin, social class and colour, meet when they arrive in a new country. But in the case of the West Indians, all difficulties—general or personal, major or minor—are complicated by the inescapable question of colour prejudice. It is bound to enter any discussion of their experiences in finding work and homes in London.

When the West Indian newcomers visit their official agency, they ask most frequently for advice on questions of employment; housing (as the table below shows) is low down on the list. But this is not a reflection of the comparative importance of the various difficulties. Housing is at least as serious a problem as employment; indeed, in general it appears to be the harsher and the more stubborn one. The list is indicative of the kinds of advice which the official agency can offer. The staff of the Migrant Services Division (as that of its predecessors) are in touch with employers and employment exchanges; they are, therefore, often able to aid West Indians in their search for jobs or better jobs. But they can rarely assist the migrants in finding lodgings, or better lodgings than they have already. In that respect, the West Indians in London have usually no other help than that which they can give to one another.

TABLE 15   TYPES OF PROBLEM ON WHICH WEST INDIAN
London Sample   MIGRANTS SOUGHT ADVICE FROM THEIR
                  OFFICIAL AGENCY FROM 1954 TO 1958

Problem	Men	Women
	%	%
Employment . . .	75	62
Travel	8	12
Education . . .	6	4
Family and Personal .	6	12
Legal, Tax and Insurance .	4	3
Housing	1	7
TOTAL		
Per cent . .	100	100
Number . .	782	288

The First Bases

When newly-arrived West Indians are asked on the boat-train to
London if they have an address to go to, they usually produce an
air-mail letter from a relative or friend. The address on the letter will
be their first in London. This has been the experience throughout the
recent period of migration, while in the early fifties there were also
some migrants who arrived hopefully without any address. Temporary accommodation had to be found for them—occasionally in
Salvation Army hostels and similar institutions—by the welfare
officers (from the Colonial Office, the London County Council and
the Red Cross) who met them. Similar provisions have also been
made for nurses and student nurses, and for the Barbadians who
come to Britain under their Government's scheme. It is one of the
tasks of the West Indian welfare officer who is employed by the
London Transport Executive to find lodgings for the people who
have been recruited by the Executive. But only a minority of migrants
have been helped in that way. The majority have obtained accommodation through their own personal contacts and efforts. While there
is no proof that they always go to the addresses which they give
initially, there is no doubt that most of them, like other migrants
here and elsewhere in the world, are in fact housed at the beginning
of their stay by the relatives or friends who preceded them.

It is not only the more recent migrants, since World War II, but also the small group of long-established coloured people in London, who have helped to provide temporary accommodation. Their houses became, virtually, hostels for newcomers from the West Indies. There was an unofficial 'reception centre' of this kind in North Kensington; there were several in Camberwell and Brixton; one in Islington, and one in Hampstead. A few of these temporary bases were outside London; two in particular became well known to welfare workers when migrants arrived asking to be directed to 'Sloobucks' (Slough, Buckinghamshire) and to 'Baldockerts' (Baldock, Hertfordshire).

As all these places are scattered (though most of them are within a radius of six miles from Charing Cross) the creation of a single 'coloured quarter', or even of several large areas of concentration, has so far been avoided. At the same time, of course, the original 'reception centres'—the rooms of some migrants; the houses of others who were already settled here—were also the nuclei for most of those patches on the London map where there are now clusters of West Indians. The migrants have tried to obtain more permanent accommodation in the immediate neighbourhood of their first temporary bases.

In a few cases, however, the location of these first bases was determined not only by the presence of earlier hospitable migrants in a particular district. It is partly a matter of chance, for example, which explains the recent settlement of West Indians in Brixton. When the first large party of migrants arrived in 1948 on the *Empire Windrush*, 242 were temporarily housed in Clapham Common Underground station, which had been a war-time air-raid shelter. A writer has described the episode as follows:

> "The Colonial Office was by now seriously concerned about the *Windrush* men. Mr. Creech Jones wrote to Councillor Jack Simpson, Mayor of Lambeth, whose borough was close to Clapham Common, and asked if some welcome could be arranged. Councillor Simpson took a look at the mayoral purse which allowed £600 for the whole year, and said he could entertain forty Jamaicans. So, on the afternoon of Wednesday, June 23rd, in a room over the Astoria Cinema, Brixton, a representative group of the Jamaicans took tea with the Mayor.
>
> Local officials and two M.P.'s were there. Colonel Marcus Lipton, Labour Member for Brixton, told the men that they should regard Britain as their second home. The Mayor added to his own good wishes the comment: 'When I heard of your coming here, I was moved. A journey like yours does not take place without good reason.' Afterwards, there was a free cinema show.
>
> Back at the shelter that evening, the forty men described the reception to their friends. They spoke with enthusiasm, joyous that a few people had taken the trouble to make them feel welcome. The

limited sum of money spent was not important: tea and cakes had been as effective as champagne. In the unknown and perplexing vastness of England, the Jamaicans now felt they could be sure of one place. Brixton was friendly. In Brixton they would make their homes."[1]

Most of these men were placed in local jobs which gave them an additional incentive to remain in the district.

Areas of Migrant Settlement

Although the areas in which West Indians tend to cluster—in North and West London and in the South—are by no means all alike, they have several features in common. Because of their history and location, and because of the physical structure of their dwellings, they can offer some sort of accommodation—however shabby or even dismal—to a considerable number of migrants from a low income group. Indeed, they are the only large-scale districts of the County of London and its fringes where such openings exist at present. Only a few people can nowadays be squeezed into the areas which were the traditional reception centres for newly-arrived minority groups—for the Huguenots, for the Irish, and for the Jews. By and large, West Indians cannot find lodgings in the solid working class districts of the East End and the southern river-side boroughs, which have a reduced but a rooted population and stable tenancies, and in whose cottages and latter-day 'model' tenements there is no space for further sub-division. Nor are the newcomers in current circumstances eligible for the new municipal flats or houses built by the London County Council and the metropolitan boroughs. The solid middle class and upper class districts—of Hampstead, Chelsea, Westminster, South Kensington and similar parts—are equally closed to all but a small minority of more prosperous West Indians. Even before World War II the people in these areas had already come to terms with current social conditions: the big houses had been converted for multiple use; rows of artisans' and coachmen's cottages had become fashionable residences; luxury flats had been built. And as since World War II there has been an acceleration of this trend—a growing aspiration of some sections of the middle and upper classes to 'return to town' rather than to cope with the disadvantages of suburbia—there has been an increasing competition for central London sites and for the previous tradesmen's and servants' residences, and consequently a sharp increase in their price. The process of middle class rejuvenation, which had occurred in old

[1] Joyce Egginton, *They Seek a Living*, London, 1957, pp. 65, 66. (Mr. Creech Jones was Secretary of State for the Colonies at the time.)

Hampstead at an earlier period, can now be seen in many different parts of central London—and especially in Notting Hill, Bayswater, Paddington and Islington. Where the chimney sweep and the tailor have lived before, the company director and the solicitor live now. No more aspidistras, but some new picture windows. With their fresh coats of paint (in Festival of Britain colours) the little old houses—two rooms up and two down—have become elegant town residences. These kinds of places are certainly far beyond the reach of migrants.

Many of the old 'mean streets' and squares have become so expensive, not only because the large Victorian houses are no longer suitable for the contemporary middle class way of life, but also because in general the residential capacity of Central London has been, and is still being, decreased. In part, this is the natural result of twentieth century conditions—of the increased demand for space for road traffic, for private homes, and for public and commercial services. As the physical pattern of the townscape changes, many residential buildings become obsolete. And as real estate values rise with the increasing competition for sites in Central London, the place of private houses is frequently taken by office blocks, by stores and hotels. Thus the scarcity of residential space is cumulative, and it is not effectively counteracted by the official policy for the planning of London. It has been the objective of the plan to reduce the resident population of the County of London and of its periphery. The planners want to 'export', not to 'import', population; patterns of development have been designed accordingly. It is not a policy which is hospitable to a considerable group of newcomers.

The choice of location for West Indian migrants is thus very narrow. In fact, they have hardly any choice. They have to stay fairly near to the central London labour market: to the majority, the outlying parts of the London Region—the territory of one-family houses, owner-occupiers and new municipal estates—are inaccessible. They cannot go to those central London districts—working class, middle class or upper class—whose patterns of occupation have been stabilised, nor to those which are in the stage of physical reconstruction, planned functional change or social upgrading. Therefore, the migrants have to go to patches of inner London which have been neglected, and which have been already for some time in the process of decline and social downgrading.

West Indians find rooms in streets where the tall houses, covered with grime and peeling plaster, display their decay. The streets have been by-passed because their location—near a railway, a noisy market, on a main traffic route, in areas of mixed land-use—has become an unfavourable one. And the four- and five-storey houses, usually with dark basements, which were built mainly in the late nineteenth century for the large households of the middle-middle classes, have been left to deteriorate also because they are so clumsy and ugly. It seemed hardly worth while to convert them properly into self-contained flats or maisonettes. (Indeed, some of them, near the Portobello Road and Paddington station, are so forbidding that they were a mistaken speculation from the start; they were never, or only briefly, occupied by the fairly prosperous families for whom they had been intended.)

Gradually, these houses have been sub-divided, though not adapted to multiple occupation. The kitchen, the bathroom, the toilet, which were once used by a single household, now have to be shared by several, and also by transient lodgers. Occasionally, some additional make-shift cooking facilities have been installed. Each of the rooms, once scrubbed by servants, is now often occupied by a separate group of people—by a family; the remnants of a family; by one lodger, or by several who pay their rent jointly.

Zones of Transition

The West Indians have not initiated the process of sub-division and decay: they are the latest group who have to look for lodgings in the streets which have the typical physical and social characteristics of 'zones of transition'. Since the thirties, these streets have become more sordid and also more cosmopolitan. They have been the reception areas for immigrants from other parts of Britain and from the Continent; for casual visitors to London; and for 'outsiders' at the fringes of society. But nowadays crowding and blight in such streets are becoming worse because the type of accommodation which they can offer is becoming more scarce. The arrival of the new migrant group has occurred at a period when the zones of transition are hemmed in on all sides—by the continued expansion of London's commercial centre; by the consolidation of socially homogeneous districts; by physical reconstruction; by the middle class invasion of the little streets which are adaptable to contemporary residential use; and also by the hopeless slums, which have apparently long been forgotten. It is by no means unusual to see decay and rejuvenation, both at various stages, in close juxtaposition. And the contrasts are accentuated because renewal is patchy: deterioration is unchecked in one street, while another, still good-looking, gets a fresh cosmetic treatment. And so density is increasing in the zones of transition: the new and the re-modelled houses nearby are not for those who move into the already tightly packed streets, which are the rejected remnants of middle class prosperity.

In and around North Kensington, in particular, such contrasts, and the warnings which they imply, are plain. The faces of the buildings tell whether they are the ones in which the migrants are concentrated. If you look at the condition of the streets, and their surroundings, you see an important aspect of the so-called 'colour problem'.

Much of the southernmost part of the district is still, or once again, largely middle class and upper middle class; it has clear affinities with South Kensington. Many of the generously built houses have been sub-divided into expensive flats; many of the little ones have been newly adorned and sold at high prices. The few coloured people who live here are mainly students from various parts of the world.

Further north, the picture changes. At the turn of the century, Charles Booth, in his massive survey of *Life and Labour of the People in London*, found that the streets in this part of the district, too, were occupied by "well-to-do" and "fairly comfortable" households. And groups of similar social status, together with some skilled workers, were still living here at the time of the *New Survey of London Life and Labour* in the late twenties.[2] Since then, there has been rapid deterioration. The tall houses, structurally similar to those of the south, are badly in need of repair: the woodwork is unpainted; window frames are rotten; plaster has fallen away from the outside walls, showing patches of bare brick. Occasionally, there is a gap in a long parade of terrace houses: the missing house seems to have fallen down. These are the streets of transition where a considerable number of West Indians have found rooms.[3]

[2] Charles Booth, ed. *Life and Labour of the People in London*. 3rd series: *Religious influences*, Vol. 3, *The City of London and the West End*, London, 1902. (See maps.) H. L. Smith, ed. *The New Survey of London Life and Labour*, London, 1930–35, Vol. 7, *The Western Area*, maps.

[3] Most of the streets in which West Indians are concentrated in North Kensington (as shown by the addresses of the 'London Group') had middle-class occupants both at the time of the Booth survey, and at that of the New London Survey. In fact, in the 40 years' interval between these surveys, there had been very little social downgrading in these streets. Their decline started after 1930. Only one in four of the migrants who live in the main areas of West Indian settlement in North Kensington (in those where clusters of West Indians are found) are in streets which were near the "poverty line" either in the late 19th century or in the early thirties—that is, in streets which were then classified as having a mixture of "poverty and comfort" or being of "moderate poverty". (And only 8 per cent are in streets which contained some elements of "degraded and semi-criminal classes" at the time of the New London Survey.) The area of concentrated West Indian settlement in Brixton was entirely occupied by middle-class people and skilled workers at the periods of both surveys.

The streets are often wide, and they are also lively. Especially in the summer months, the people congregate outdoors; they come out of their overcrowded lodgings as much as possible. There is a great deal of movement, and of visual diversity. On one corner of a dingy square, which still has patches of green and a few trees, there is a new block of flats on a site which had been bombed. Towards the south, the zone of transition is joined to the prosperous parts: there is no definite physical demarcation. Nor is there one northward and westward where the territory of the tall, increasingly decrepit terrace houses merges into meaner streets, with smaller houses, in which decay and poverty are firmly entrenched. Here at the fringes of the present zone of transition are Notting Dale and Kensal New Town— areas which were in transition in the late nineteenth century, and which have since become the rotten parts of the Royal Borough.

When Charles Booth wrote about these parts at the turn of the century, they were in a process similar to that—or at least regarded as similar to that—which is now taking place in the adjacent streets to the south. Talking of Notting Dale (which used to be known as "The Potteries") he said:

> "It has been, and is, a temporary halting place. Some of its denizens might stay only a night, some a week, others months or even years, but as a general rule, sooner or later, they were accustomed to move on. . . . The stream still flows, but of late the inward current has been met here by a stronger outward tide of a different character, consisting of the very dregs of more central London stirred up and dispersed by improvements or alterations involving the destruction of old rookeries, and the result is a perhaps unexampled concourse of the disreputable classes. As to this all authorities are agreed.
>
> These people are poor, in many cases distressfully so. . . . They form the most serious mass of the kind with which we have to deal; greater, probably, than any now remaining in any one spot in the central parts of London; and while the numbers elsewhere are decreasing, here they are increasing. Some years ago whole streets of houses built for classes who declined to occupy them were untenanted and in ruin, without even a pane of glass in their windows; now they are filled with people of this low class, and the bad element is spreading.
>
> It is not all the same in character. The district might be compared to a vessel through which a foul stream is flowing, leaving continually a deposit; to which is added this further uncomfortable feature, that as the flow and the deposit increase, so the capacity of the vessel increases also. But the deposit is less criminal and less disorderly than the stream, acquiring more the character of an industrial community. It settles down to, and comes to share in, the life and habits of the older inhabitants who have become suited to their environment."[4]

Since that time, Notting Dale and Kensal New Town (which was old already in the 19th century) have stagnated in blight. There have

---

[4] Charles Booth, *op. cit.*, *Religious Influences*, Vol. 3, pp. 152, 153.

been hardly any improvements for well over fifty years. The few
exceptions stand out: one large group of flats nearby has trans-
formed a street which used to be notorious for the 'rat-runs' under
the old, now demolished houses. A man trying to evade the police
could enter any house and disappear in the tunnel connecting the
cellars. But on the whole, except for the fact that the blare of wireless
from open windows has been added to the street noises, Charles
Booth's description of these districts and of their needs is still valid
today.

> "Notting Dale is an outlying portion of Kensington, and its condi-
> tion has been long felt to be a disgrace. Many schemes have been
> suggested and great efforts made to cope with it, and much disappoint-
> ment has been felt at the result; culminating at length in an almost
> despairing petition to the London County Council to take over and
> deal with the whole area, and though this has been refused, pre-
> sumably on the ground that so wealthy a locality should be able to
> manage its own affairs, it would really seem that nothing short of
> wholesale and drastic action would suffice."[5]

But there has been no wholesale and drastic action, although these
districts became notorious for their poverty, overcrowding and crime.
In 1924, Kensal New Town presented a picture which was no better
than that which Charles Booth had seen at the beginning of the
century.

> "Mr. Charles Booth describes this as one of the worst districts in
> London, and social workers recognise that Southam Street (with its
> 140 nine-roomed houses in which 2,500 people were living in 1923, an
> average of two persons to every room in the street), and the equally
> crowded rooms in the immediate vicinity, for bad housing accommoda-
> tion surpass even the Special Area of Notting Dale. It is the base-
> ments which are so appalling, those 'slum basements, where rheuma-
> tism and consumption and drink scribble their names on the dirty
> wallpaper'. . . . Naturally this part of North Kensington figures week
> by week in the police news."[6]

In 1951, this was the district with the highest rate of overcrowding
in London—five times greater than the average for London County
as a whole.[7] Still, Notting Dale and Kensal New Town remained

---

[5] Charles Booth, *ibid.*, pp. 156, 157.
[6] F. M. Gladstone, *Notting Hill in Bygone Days*, London, 1924, p. 202.
[7] In Golborne Ward (which includes the district known as Kensal New Town)
12·7 per cent of the population were living at a density of more than two persons
per room at the 1951 Census date. The comparable percentage of overcrowding
for the whole of North Kensington (consisting of four wards) was then 6·8 per
cent; that for the Borough of Kensington (including the northern and southern
parts) 4·6 per cent; that for the County of London was 2·5 per cent.

forgotten until they were suddenly in the news. It was in Notting Dale that the disturbances between white and coloured people occurred in September 1958. It was in Kensal New Town, in Southam Street by the railway bridge, that a West Indian was murdered in May 1959.

Since then, these districts have been much visited—by journalists, by welfare workers, and also by agitators. There have been numerous accounts of the physical conditions of their streets in the Press. But it is hardly realised that these are not the districts in which a considerable number of West Indians live. The houses here have either been neglected and overcrowded for far too long, or the remnants of their respectability have been guarded far too closely, to admit many newcomers.[8] Only here and there have coloured people found rooms in Notting Dale and Kensal New Town. Far more are concentrated in the adjacent streets—in the wedge between reconstruction in the south and stagnation in the north. And more migrants might still have to crowd into these intermediate streets if the present trends in inner London continue, and no alternatives are offered. If that happens, the zone of transition could become a coloured quarter. Competition for the limited accommodation which this zone can provide will certainly increase even more—though it is at its border, in the streets in which physical and social blight have long been settled, that tension between white and coloured people is already latent, and occasionally acute.

The physical condition of other places in London where West Indians cluster are similar to those of the North Kensington zone of transition. Brixton, in the borough of Lambeth, is less socially mixed than North Kensington, but there, too, good and bad housing are in juxtaposition. Two long streets had been deteriorating before the migrants came. All the fairly tall yellow-brick houses with basements look run down; the basement railings have been removed; the impression of congestion and decay is accentuated because the roads are used as car parks. These parallel streets have become almost a coloured ghetto: there is hardly a house in them which is not occupied by West Indians. The two streets are isolated. On one side, they

[8] The same is true also of the other dilapidated mean streets at the fringes of the zones of transition—of the streets in and around Paddington, for example, which were already very poor and had a migratory population in Booth's days. He said: "Many of the houses (in these streets) are let out in furnished rooms from day to day, and among the residents thieves and prostitutes abound ... the rooms are even sometimes tenanted by day and night, Box and Cox fashion." (Charles Booth, *op. cit.*, *Religious Influences*, Vol. 3, p. 122.) Such streets, as those in Notting Dale and Kensal New Town, have hardly been improved and have thus retained many of their late 19th century characteristics.

are cut off by a railway; on another by a main road; on the third by a new block of flats. On the fourth side, there is a street of quite different character: the small two-storey houses are well maintained; the front gardens are neat; there is solid working class respectability; and apparently there is not a single newcomer living here. Apart from the coloured children from the adjacent streets who go to the school in this road, there are no obvious signs of changes in the neighbourhood.

Housing Conditions

As the zones of transition become more dense, their housing conditions deteriorate, their rents go up, and thus density increases even more. Most West Indians live in poor lodgings and pay high rents—both in relation to the kind of accommodation which they have, and also in relation to their incomes. Most of them can afford such rents only when they crowd together. The typical situation is that a family, or several single migrants, share one room—often a small room—in which they sleep, cook and eat, and spend their free time when they cannot go outdoors. The 'furniture' of the furnished room is frequently very meagre. Sanitary and washing facilities are usually shared with other tenants. It would be hard for anyone to find a *modus vivendi* in such cramped lodgings; it is hard especially for people from a milder climate, with different social habits, who have been used to being a great deal in the open air.

The standard rent which the migrants pay for such a room is £2.10.0 or £3.0.0 per week. (A character in one of the stories of the West Indian writer, Samuel Selvon, speaks of "a two and ten room".) This figure is often quoted, but there are wide variations—upwards rather than downwards. There are also cases where the rent—£1 per head—is paid per person and not per room. If five single men share a room, the landlord obtains twice the 'standard' rent. Even higher rents are by no means unknown, especially in North Kensington.

In that district, too, there have been threats of violence against coloured tenants to prevent them from going to a Rent Tribunal to ask for a reduction in their rent.[9] Some 'shark' landlords have

---

[9] The tenant himself need not lodge an appeal with the Rent Tribunal; the borough councils have powers to do so. Some London boroughs have used their powers; Kensington, however, had not yet brought any cases to the tribunals by May 1959, when these matters were under discussion in the Press. In a report on the situation in Kensington at that time, *The Times* (May 21, 1959) also said: "The extortionate rents which are regularly charged for poor housing could be lowered by appeal to the Rent Tribunal. It is extremely difficult to persuade West

become notorious. Descriptions of the worst type of lodgings have appeared in novels and in newspapers; accounts of exploitation and intimidation were given in the Press, especially when the murder of a West Indian in that district in May 1959 had drawn public attention to it once again.

Of course, it would be wrong to generalise from such accounts. Not all West Indians live in sordid lodgings, pay extortionate rents and are afraid of their landlords. In some parts (particularly in several streets in North Kensington) they have indeed been plagued. In other districts of London, they have had few complaints; and they have also appeared freely before Rent Tribunals to put their case. And although most of the houses in which West Indians live are overcrowded, they themselves often see to it that their rooms, however shabby, are well-kept and do not look like slums.

But while individual efforts are made, and West Indians have diverse experiences in London, their common difficulties should not be underestimated. In general, they have been pushed into an unsatisfactory environment; and as matters stand now, this is not likely to be merely a transitory phase. Their poor housing conditions are not only the result of the general shortage of the kind of accommodation in inner London to which newcomers with limited, insecure means could get access, and which they could afford. The level of rents paid by the migrants is generally so high—relatively and often absolutely, too—that their range of choice should be wider than it is in fact. There is no doubt that prejudice and discrimination—subtly and overtly—limit their opportunities even more than can be explained by the present residential pattern of London. The West Indians themselves say so; all observers of their situation agree with them. And there is the well-known vicious circle. While high rents, overcrowding and sharing are in part caused, and certainly accentuated, by colour prejudice, such conditions, in turn, create prejudice. There is thus further deterioration, and more of the same.

It is, unfortunately, a classic situation. As the West Indians are wedged in and have to compete for scarce space and amenities with white tenants, many of whom have long been badly housed

---

Indian tenants to take this action themselves. Indeed the same is true of many other tenants in the area who are paying absurdly high rents, Irish labourers, for example, and old-age pensioners. In the first place many tenants have no idea of their rights, or even of the existence of the tribunal. But there is a more sinister reason for acquiescence. Cases have been known of appeals being withdrawn after intimidation by a landlord. Strong arm men are sent to beat up those who make objections; in other instances large sums have been offered for a tenant's silence."

themselves, tensions and frictions develop. And it is the newcomer who is made the scapegoat for physical and social claustrophobia—especially if he is coloured, and if his mode of living is not yet adapted to dense quarters in a cold climate. (If a few West Indians sing or talk loudly in the street late at night, or have extended parties in their rooms, they are all thought to be inconsiderate. If some are ignorant or disreputable, they are all classified accordingly.) An image is built up of the coloured man as the intruder who is to be blamed for frustration and deferment of hopes for improvements.[10] But it seems that this image is stronger and more persistent in the old slums at the edges of the zones of transition, or in adjacent streets which are in the early stages of transition, than among the West Indians' next-door neighbours, who cannot help seeing coloured people as individuals, not just as representatives of a fictitious stereotype.[11]

Still, it is difficult to avoid quarrels when several families share a cooker on a landing and an antiquated W.C. A crowded room is bound to be noisy; the time-table in one of them is not necessarily

[10] The Chief Housing Officer for Kensington is reported to have said: "Immigration into densely crowded areas made people on the (housing) waiting list suspicious and sensitive to the colour problem." (*Manchester Guardian*, July 3, 1959.) A few weeks earlier, *The Times* (May 20, 1959) reported: "It is often said that working class white people resent an influx of coloured neighbours because they 'lower' the district with their crowded houses, ignorant behaviour, and rowdy habits. This is emphatically not a satisfactory explanation of the interracial resentment in North Kensington at the present. The great majority of the coloured inhabitants are semi-skilled West Indian workers, with respectable habits, a strong ambition to do well for themselves, and at least as much education as their white neighbours. There are a few West Indians in the area who are either prostitutes or who live off the earnings of prostitutes; but they are an insignificant minority. Certainly the proportion of criminal or immoral elements in the coloured people in this area is smaller than among its white population."

[11] Thus in one district of Paddington, where white and coloured people have lived close together for some time, a joint Tenants' Association, the St. Stephen's Gardens Tenants' Association, has become well established. Another joint Association—the Powis and Colville Residents' Association—was formed towards the end of 1959 in a 'mixed' district in North Kensington. The Committee as well as the membership of this Association consist of both white and coloured people. Most members are tenants, but landlords, too, can join. The Association was established as a result of the wide publicity which was given, in the summer of 1959, to the intense dissatisfaction with bad housing conditions and high rents in North Kensington. Its formation was assisted also by several individuals and groups who are concerned with the improvement of race relations in the area. Within a short time, the Association had acquired about 160 members (a number which represents one-fifth of the estimated potential membership); and there were signs that it was growing rapidly. The Association is campaigning for the improvement of housing conditions and fair rents; for better garbage collection, street cleansing and street lighting; and it is also interested in the provision of social clubs and the upkeep of squares in the district.

synchronised with that in others. Irritations are infectious; hardships are cumulative.[12]

There are disputes not only between white and coloured tenants,
and between white landlords and coloured tenants, but also between
coloured landlords and white tenants. In some districts of London,
it is virtually impossible for the newcomers to obtain lodgings in
houses owned by white people. Whenever possible the migrants
themselves have, therefore, acquired property, freehold or leasehold
—usually dilapidated property which was not in demand, and for
which, so they tell, they have to pay an inflated price. When the
house is bought, it is not necessarily vacant: one part might still be
occupied by white tenants. Stories of strained relations between the
new coloured owner and the white tenants are told: it is alleged that
he tries to turn them out, or has actually done so. And no doubt
there have been cases of this kind.

The money for such a house is often raised by a co-operative
enterprise. Several West Indians pool their savings to pay the initial
deposit jointly. Soon the house is densely occupied; the individual
rooms are let to a queue of relatives and friends—to new arrivals
and to 'refugees' from other lodgings. Sometimes the accumulated
rent receipts are sufficient to buy another house, and yet another
one; a chain of ownership is formed. And this is still another
factor in the increasing density of West Indians in certain districts.[13]

Though coloured landlords, too, have faults, the migrants tend to
prefer them for many reasons. Elsewhere, they say, their rents are
often higher than those of white people; they have to pay a 'colour
tax'. And there are white people, especially again in North Kensington, who tell one another that their rents have gone up because
of the West Indian influx. It has been reported that some white

[12] "Some coloured men pay as much as £7 a week for a flat, furnished with
junk and lacking not only a bathroom but in some cases even a gas supply. High
rents lead to overcrowding. . . . The result is in many cases perfectly justified
resentment on the part of older white residents. It is annoying if you have to go
to work in the morning to be kept awake by loud conversation and blaring
music. And it is also natural to resent those who have pushed up your own rent
to an unreasonable figure by their arrival. Moreover, overcrowding also contri-
butes to the restless life of the young people who could not spend their evenings
at home, even if they wanted to, and have to find their amusement in the street."
The Times, May 20, 1959.

[13] This system of house-buying by coloured migrants exists also outside London. The *Manchester Guardian* (September 15, 1958) gave an account of such
co-operative purchases in one of the districts of West Indian settlement in Manchester, where they occur apparently for similar reasons as in London, and with
similar effects.

landlords have bought property in the zones of transition ". . . for the specific purpose of rack-renting coloured tenants who have few alternatives." "Cases are even known of landlords bringing in West Indian tenants and encouraging them to behave in an anti-social way in order to get rid of sitting tenants so that higher rents can be charged."[14] When West Indians see advertisements of vacant rooms which say "coloured welcome" or "coloured only", they tend to be rather apprehensive. They suspect that they might be welcomed because they would have to pay inflated rents.

However, they do not often see such advertisements. The 'anti-coloured' ones are more frequent, as anyone knows who looks systematically through the columns of several London local newspapers.

Discriminatory Advertisements

The housing advertisements of the *Kensington Post*, a weekly newspaper, whose editorials oppose colour prejudice, were chosen for a detailed count because they cover a wide area which provides a great deal of furnished accommodation for all sorts of people, and which also includes several of the main clusters of West Indian settlement. In the thirteen issues which we analysed—from 7th November, 1958 to 30th January, 1959—there were altogether 3,876 advertisements of vacant furnished rooms and flats. A considerable number—1,431—had been inserted by estate agents, and most of these (1,413) were neutral: they said nothing about race, colour and nationality. Ten were 'pro-coloured'; eight were 'anti-coloured'.

Most of the 2,445 advertisements which had apparently been inserted by private householders or landlords were also neutral—2,061 were in that group. But 322—just over one in eight of the private advertisements—had an 'anti-coloured' tag; and 62 had a 'pro-coloured' one.[15]

---

[14] *The Times*, May 29, 1959. One of the short stories in *Ways of Sunlight* by Samuel Selvon (London, 1957) describes a similar situation, which also illustrates the insecurity of West Indian tenants in London.

[15] As most of the advertisements gave only a box number or a telephone number, it was not possible to tabulate them by the address of the accommodation which was vacant. In quite a number of cases it was possible, however, to take the price of the accommodation offered into account in analysing the advertisements. It was found that the incidence of 'anti-coloured' advertisements was only slightly lower for the more expensive furnished rooms (£4 per week and over) than for the cheaper ones.

The advertisers used different terms. The main kinds of 'anti-coloured' statements were these:

No coloured	. .	106
Europeans only	. .	142
White people only	.	25
English only	. .	49

TOTAL	. . .	322

There were some variations on each of these main themes; they indicate a fairly wide range of discrimination, expressed more or less crudely, and sometimes apologetically. Among the 'no coloured' advertisements were some which said: "coloured not welcome"; "not suitable coloured"; "sorry no coloured"; "regret no coloured". ("Europeans only" is a euphemism; apparently it is thought that it sounds better than "no coloured".) "English only" was also stated in slightly different ways, including "British"; "for English people"; "suit English Business lady"; "no foreigners"—which presumably refers to West Indians, who are not aliens, as well as to other groups. While the advertisers in the first three categories erect a colour bar, those in the last category do not like a whole lot of white people either. Most of them are not in fact concerned with the question of nationality, but with both race and religion. ("English only" is often used as a synonym for 'no Jews'.)

The 'pro-coloured' advertisements were divided as follows:

All nationalities	. .	30
Coloured welcome	.	23
Asians welcomed	.	7
Coloured only	. .	2

TOTAL	. . .	62

Among the first category, there were also a few with slight variants, such as "suit overseas visitors"; "no objection overseas students"; "foreigners welcome"; "Commonwealth friends welcome". And several advertisements in the second category issued a qualified invitation: they said "West Africans welcomed" or "superior coloured welcome".

A number of the "pro-coloured" advertisements were probably inserted by coloured landlords who prefer tenants of their own kind; some advertisements might have special ulterior motives; but there are certainly also a few others which are honest and sincere invitations by white owners. There is evidence that some landladies genuinely welcome coloured students.[16]

A year later, when we repeated the count of advertisements, the 'pro-coloured' ones had almost disappeared, while the proportion of the 'anti-coloured' ones had increased. (In the four issues of the *Kensington Post* from 27th November to 18th December, 1959, there were 645 advertisements for furnished accommodation inserted by private landlords. Only two of these private advertisements were 'pro-coloured'; but 102, one in six, were 'anti-coloured', as compared with one in eight in the earlier count.)

The Closed Door

The anti-coloured advertisements, numerous as they are, do not indicate the amount of prejudice which the West Indians encounter; they are merely examples of the kinds of overt discrimination displayed in reputable local newspapers, and also on the notice-boards at the windows of corner shops in or near the zones of transition. These published restrictions are only a small fraction of all those which the migrants meet when they look for lodgings. Most of the estate agents and landlords whose advertisements are 'neutral'— without reference to colour, nationality or social class—also refuse to take coloured tenants. Among the newcomers, this is a well known fact; it was obvious once again when we telephoned a sample (one in five) of all the 'neutral' private advertisers who had offered furnished accommodation in the issue of the *Kensington Post* of January 1st, 1960.

None of these people had given any hint of discrimination in their advertisements. But when we called, enquiring about a room or flat on behalf of a West Indian friend, very few (one out of every six) were prepared to consider the application. (Among this very small minority who gave a positive answer were managers of large blocks of furnished flats and rooms, and one foreign landlord: there was only one English landlord who was willing to let a room in his own house to a coloured tenant.)

There were also two slightly hesitant, though hardly encouraging replies.

"I don't think it would be possible."

---

[16] In May 1959, the coloured students of the University of Leeds gave a tea party to their landladies to indicate their appreciation of the kindness with which they had been received (as reported in the *Manchester Guardian*, May 30, 1959). Though there have been similar reports of hospitable landladies elsewhere, such examples are still very rare.

". . . If we have other applicants, I shall give preference to white people."

But the majority said quite definitely—with or without apology—that they would not accept a coloured tenant. The stock answer was: "We personally don't mind, but the other people in the house do."

This kind of statement was made irrespective of whether there had been coloured tenants in the house before or not; and also irrespective of whether white neighbours or tenants had already expressed any views on this question or not. For example:

Landlady: "I am sorry; the other residents in the house are all white and they wouldn't like it. I wouldn't like to upset any of them."

Interviewer: "Have you asked them?"

Landlady: "Well . . . I don't think they'd like it."

Interviewer: "You won't consider it then?"

Landlady: "Definitely not."

A few landlords or landladies asked: "Are your friends very coloured?" They might possibly be prepared to accept an Indian, but not a Negro.

"You see, I'm only the housekeeper here, and I work for an agent. It's really against the conditions but I have taken one or two Indian people. You know, they're not so dark. I mean, well I could get away with it if they were sort of not too obvious—well, if they are coffee-coloured, for example, or lighter."

Another conversation:

Landlady: "Is he dark? We just take Europeans; it's an all-white house—but, well is he very dark? The other people don't like it, you see."

Interviewer: "Have you ever had any coloured tenants?"

Landlady: "No, never."

Interviewer: "Then how do you know the other tenants wouldn't like it?"

Landlady: "Well, we have our way of life, and they have theirs, don't we. But how dark is he? I mean, some are jet black and some are more coffee-coloured. But if he's very dark we couldn't consider it."

There is a further variant of the stock answer: the acceptance of a coloured tenant is regarded as a threat to social status.

Landlady: "I have no objection, but my other tenants are Australians and New Zealanders and they don't mix with Indians. They don't like the smell of curry and so on. We had some Indians here."

Interviewer: "My friends are from the West Indies—Jamaica—not India."

Landlady: "Oh, they would be Negroes then? I don't think we'd like that. Also they wouldn't be the same class. My tenants are middle class people."

Occasionally the answer is offensive; more often it is quite blunt. "We don't take coloured people; it's one of the rules of the firm." But usually the refusal is stated with embarrassment, and the responsibility for it is shifted to someone else—to a nameless group or a particular person.

"I'm not the landlord actually, but this used to be my house and I show tenants over. I think it would be useless your 'phoning him; I know he's raised the price of rooms in an attempt to keep coloured people away. I am sorry."

Sometimes there are indications of genuine regret, as in the case of the elderly lady who said:

"No. I'm sorry. There are objections from the other tenants. I just run this house, but I myself have no objections. I've had every kind of tenant under the sun, but this house is run differently. I am really sorry, and I'm glad you rang up instead of your friends, because I hate to hurt people on this subject. It's all so ridiculous, the whole situation, but there it is."[17]

[17] Our experience confirms that of *The Times* correspondent who wrote (May 29, 1959): "Your Correspondent yesterday rang up the largest agency for finding furnished accommodation in London, and said that he was looking for a flat for some West Indian friends. The answer was that the agency could not help. 'None of our landladies handles West Indians.' Until recently this same big agency, which controls a substantial proportion of the market in furnished rooms and flats in all parts of London, was in the habit of giving West Indian inquirers the telephone number of an agency which would be able to help them. A few days ago, however, this agency also ceased to operate. The small agency, which did find accommodation for coloured people, proved to be in a walk-up office near Piccadilly Circus. The manager confirmed that he had stopped finding flats and rooms for West Indians. 'It wasn't worth my time,' he said. He said that he had as many as 200 West Indians a week asking him to find them a place, but he had only been able to find anything for about seven a week. . . .

Even the most educated coloured people in London normally find flats or houses in London through friends. It is not unknown for property companies to put a stipulation against coloured tenants, or against foreigners, in leases."

2. SCHOOLS

While West Indian adults can hardly escape symptoms of colour prejudice when they look for a place to live—and often even when they have found one—their children do not meet the same difficulties when they go to school. The West Indian child population in London is still rather small: there is a fairly high percentage of single young people among the migrants; many wives have not yet joined their husbands here; and it is also quite usual for parents who emigrate to leave their small children at home in the care of relatives. Thus even in the main districts of West Indian settlement (which are usually only one part of a wider school catchment area) there are so far no primary schools with a considerable proportion of coloured children. Segregation is unknown.

But this is not the sole reason for the absence of a 'colour problem' in the London primary schools. The attitudes of the local education authority, of the teachers and of the children themselves are the other significant factors. In the schools, the migrants are surrounded by the official public opinion of this country which rejects discrimination. In the sphere of a public institution, and particularly in that of education, it is 'not done' to express colour prejudice: there are some to whom it is incomprehensible; there are others who abhor it and fight it; and there are also those who are perhaps too tolerant of intolerance. But whatever the mixture, the people who set the tone usually insist on a liberal theme. In the schools, we find the outlook of the editorials, not that of the local advertisement columns.

It has not always been like that. There have been periods when Jewish children, in particular, were harassed in class rooms of the East End and elsewhere, and also in their streets. Often there was warfare between juvenile gangs of 'goys and yids'; and even the teachers were not always careful in guarding their language. But there were no signs of a similar tension, or of the slightest uneasiness in relation to coloured children, in any of the London primary schools we visited during the early summer of 1959. Even in the poorest districts—and perhaps still more in these than in others—the teachers have seen to it that the children spend their early school years in an environment that is far more civilised than it was a generation ago.

"I do not think of the coloured children as coloured," said one of the headmistresses. Her school is in an old grim building that will soon be demolished; and it is in an area in which contacts between old inhabitants and West Indian migrants have been strained. The atmosphere in the school confirmed her statement. And yet there had been considerable 'trouble' started by a West Indian girl some months ago—the sort of disturbance which in a previous period, and among people with a different frame of mind, might have easily contributed to prejudice. Not so in this case. When the headmistress described the problem, she talked of a maladjusted girl living in an unhealthy environment. To her, the colour of the child's skin was irrelevant. "All that is now cleared up," she said. "I have more trouble from the local children than from the new ones."

She was not trying to lean over backwards to avoid any criticisms of coloured people, and to demonstrate her neutrality. On the contrary, she spoke freely about difficulties which some of the migrant children have, and can cause, in their new environment. But like teachers in other schools, she also talked of the careful, often very strict, old-fashioned manner with which many West Indian children are treated by their parents. Even if their clothes are shabby, the girls wear clean dresses every day, the boys clean shirts. The headmistress could not understand how their families, almost every one of whom lived in a single room, could manage to maintain this standard.

Although West Indian children, like those of any other migrants, cannot be expected to be at home at once in a London class room, in general they seem to belong very soon after their arrival. As few of them go to school in lower middle class or middle class areas, their economic status is usually similar to that of the majority of their school fellows. In any case, there are no obvious signs of exceptional poverty in their dress and manner. And because most West Indian children are well looked after, it is hardly visible that their housing conditions are generally worse than those of their school fellows. Scholastically, too, they are so far in the middle range. "They are alert and active and very good at sports," said one headmaster. Another one told us that their parents are "keen on education".

Most important, there is of course no language barrier. Thus the great difficulty which teachers and pupils have initially with some other immigrants—from Europe and from Asia—does not exist in their relations with West Indians. "Our only problem is with the Cypriots." Two headmasters in different districts of London emphasised the same point at the beginning of the conversation. Special arrangements have to be made to teach the Cypriot children and to talk to their parents. "Otherwise they fit in all right." Similar language problems occur occasionally with Italian, Hungarian and

Polish children, and also with Indians and Pakistanis. (While we were in the headmaster's room in one school, a Punjabi labourer, in rough working clothes, brought his ten-year-old son in to be admitted. The headmaster asked a Punjabi girl in the school to interpret. "Please ask the gentleman if the boy has had measles." It was a cordial reception, but inevitably rather lame.) As West Indians can establish communication immediately, they have the advantage that they are not categorised as outsiders.

The children often give a special welcome to their new coloured school fellows just because they look different. When two Jamaican brothers, both very dark Negroes, first arrived in a London class room, there was competition among the children who all wanted to sit next to them. Similar stories were told in other places; they are certainly not exceptional. Later on, when the novelty has worn off, white children come to terms with coloured children on individual merits, just as they would with anyone else. Teachers who have known the situation of migrants in several different schools said that they had never come across any special difficulties.[18]

Still, currents from the streets outside blow into the schools. One of the headmasters whom we visited was talking of the good relations between children of different origins in his school—"the coloured children are well liked; there have been no signs of prejudice"—when a teacher came in and said that a West Indian girl had just complained of being called "blackie" by a classmate. The headmaster was dismayed. "Who was it?" It was found that the culprit was another coloured child.

The teachers in another school, in which there are more migrant children, would not have been surprised. They had noticed for some time that the West Indians tend to abuse one another in terms of colour. The greatest insult is to say "you are blacker than me". One Negro girl in this school has a colour phobia. She hates her dark skin and says that she would not mind being coloured if she were only lighter; she cannot bear being black.

Although the English children in primary schools can forget colour differences, the West Indians find it difficult to do so. Colour-consciousness, latent or acute, remains with them: they have known it in their previous homes; it is in the air in their new ones; they tend to unload it on one another.

When white boys and girls are in their teens and go to secondary schools, they, too, are no longer 'colour-blind'. At that stage, a good deal of their childhood tolerance has already been rubbed off. The

[18] The experiences of such teachers are confirmed by the observations of parents and visitors.

authority of the school has diminished; its mental climate is then only one of the many contradictory influences to which they are exposed. They may accept or reject colour prejudice; modify or emphasize it; or they might simply not be interested until a personal experience brings it to their attention. Be that as it may, at the secondary level of education, relationships between white and coloured pupils are in a new phase; they are certainly more complex than they were before. So far, however, it has been a matter of individual adjustments; generalisations cannot as yet be made because there are even fewer West Indians in the London secondary than in the primary schools, and these few are still more dispersed than the younger children.[19]

3. EMPLOYMENT

In housing, there is an overt colour bar; it is advertised; it is made plain even more often verbally when migrants knock at doors to ask for lodgings. All this is taken for granted and sanctioned by society. But it is unthinkable that there should be similar 'anti-coloured' tags in advertisements of vacant jobs. Public opinion would not allow it. The selection of tenants (other than in municipal housing) is regarded as being subject solely to the personal discretion of the landlord. It is understood that it is his privilege to bar Negroes, Sikhs, Jews, foreigners in general, cockneys, socialists, dogs, or any other species which he wants to keep away. The recruitment of workers, however, in both state and private enterprises, is a question of public policy—determined, explicitly or implicitly, by agreements between trade unions, employers' associations and government. As a landlord, Mr. Smith can practise discrimination openly; as an employer, he must

[19] However, there seems to be a definite pattern in the attitudes of white adolescents towards coloured people: though not visible in the secondary schools, it shows itself in their out-of-school hours, and when they have left school. A number of reports on such attitudes—in the Press, on radio and television and in so far unpublished surveys of particular districts of London—all confirm that the reactions of juveniles to coloured people—or to the image of coloured people—vary quite clearly with their educational and economic status. The reports also show that among adolescents who have left school at 16, who are in menial or blind-alley jobs, and who live near the zones of transition, there is considerable antipathy and even hostility to coloured migrants. When such young people meet—at street corners, in cafés and also in some youth clubs—they are liable to swap slanderous tales about the 'darkies'. Verbally, at least, they certainly do not bother to conceal their aggression. (See also Appendix C: 'Teddy Boys' at Shepherd's Bush.)

at least disguise it. In the sphere of housing, tolerance is a matter of private initiative; in the sphere of employment, it is in some respects 'nationalised'.

This is not to say that West Indians never meet intolerance when they look for work in London. On the contrary, it does exist, and it complicates their problems. But it does not dominate their immediate situation in employment as harshly as in housing. On the labour market, colour prejudice is so much interlocked with other reservations against migrants from a non-industrialised country, and with their inevitable difficulties in making a new start, that it is often a more intangible factor. In that field, discrimination is neither as crude nor as rigid as it is in housing.

On the whole, English people have, moreover, an entirely different attitude to their workmates than they have to their neighbours or would-be-neighbours. While a man is prepared to work with coloured people, or even under them, he might still be most reluctant to accept the idea that they should come to live nearby. He is far more likely to be aware of their dark skin at home than in the factory.

"They'd soon fasten down on you, wouldn't they?", said a builder's foreman. He did not want them to move into his street, because he thought that their lodgings are always overcrowded ("fourteen in one room", he kept repeating) and they, therefore, created slums. But he accepted them, and praised them, as workers. "Well, definitely, there's some good working men amongst them . . . and I've got some good working men now."[20] West Indians are well aware of this ambivalence; it is one of their complaints. But although it is bound to make them feel uneasy, it does reduce the chance of discord, at least at the place of work.

In the recent period of recession in some districts and industries, it has sometimes been even more difficult for the newcomers to find a job than to find a bed to sleep in. Nevertheless, the search for employment is less harassing than the search for lodgings, and it generally produces a more satisfactory, if often only a short term, conclusion. Once a job is found, it usually does not bring about a new chain of frictions.

The Barbadian Government Scheme

In the matter of employment, a considerable number of migrants also have help—directly or indirectly—from their official agency in

[20] From the tape records of unpublished interviews which were made by Barry Carman for the B.B.C. in several cities from October to December 1958. Some extracts from these interviews were broadcast in a symposium 'Black and White' on the Home Service on December 18, 1958.

London, from the Barbadian Government, and from British industries. The Barbadian Government is prepared to lend the passage money to migrants who have obtained jobs in Britain in advance. Under its scheme, people on the island have been, and are being, recruited by several British enterprises—the British Transport Commission, the London Transport Executive, the British Hotels and Restaurants Association, and also for domestic work in hospitals by the Regional Hospital Boards. Arrangements for direct recruitment in Barbados began in 1955, at a period when the main industries concerned—transport and catering—were suffering acutely from a shortage of labour.

At about that time the British Transport Commission proposed employing a number of Italians on the railways. (This proposal was not accepted by the National Union of Railwaymen.)[21] The London Transport Executive sent recruiting teams to Ireland, and it also turned its attention to the Caribbean. In doing so, the Executive had to consider its position as a nationalised undertaking; any decisions it took about employing coloured labour might be regarded as reflecting government policy. The Executive had, in fact, previously employed coloured people from time to time, but not many of them in operating grades. It was decided to employ them in these grades. A recruitment team went to Barbados in 1956; shortly afterwards a more elaborate organisation was set up in the island for the same purpose, together with the other industries which were interested, and with the help of the Barbadian Government.

London Transport

By the end of 1958, nearly 4,000 coloured workers had been taken on by London Transport; the majority were recruited in this country, but a considerable number (almost 1,000) have come directly from Barbados.[22] A West Indian welfare worker was appointed at the head office to assist the migrants after their arrival in London, particularly in finding accommodation. Otherwise no special arrangements were made. No announcements were made to the Press in Britain, and the monthly staff magazine (*London Transport Magazine*) has not paid special attention to the coloured workers. They appear in its pages only in photographs, usually illustrating sporting events. The migrants receive the same training as all other recruits, and also, like all non-Londoners, two extra days of training. As it is the policy

[21] *Railway Gazette*, December 23, 1955, p. 753.
[22] Thus coloured employees of London Transport, whose labour turnover is low, represent at most about four per cent of the Executive's total staff.

of London Transport not to distinguish between West Indian employees and others, and to avoid any possibility of 'segregation', the Executive does not form working groups (such as permanent-way gangs) which consist only of coloured people.

As is usual in the industry, the West Indians, like other new recruits, start in the lowest grades and are promoted in the normal way. Some have become bus drivers, train guards and booking-office clerks. Occasionally one meets a West Indian who is a station foreman; he has reached a junior supervisory post in which he is in charge of a few workers, white and coloured. West Indians earn promotion from the Executive because they stay in their jobs: it is said that their turnover at London Transport is exceptionally low.

Diversity of Experiences

But while migrants have been accepted without reservation in some places, in others they have been received with hesitation or treated with antipathy. Some employers give them excellent testimonials; others describe them as slow and sloppy workers. It is very difficult to sort out fact from fiction, and to distinguish between objective and biased tales. There are all sorts of Englishmen and all sorts of West Indians: they cannot all be expected to be reliable and hard workers. Nor is it possible to make a large-scale quantitative assessment of the migrants' employment records: employers and employment exchanges are not supposed to use the term 'colour' in their files; officially, at least, the West Indians are not classified as a separate category of workers.[23]

In any group of migrants, there are some who tell success stories; there are others who speak of hardships and failure. Indeed, their tales reflect not only the diversity of their own backgrounds and aspirations, but also the diversity of the attitudes and conditions which they meet on the London labour market. Thus any random conversations show a wide range of experiences.[24]

A Jamaican in Notting Hill

"I was a cabinet-maker in Jamaica, but here they say not good enough. I'm 45 and I get only labouring. In three years I have eleven jobs. All labouring. Every time sent away because I'm black. I work hard but always there is trouble and they say I go.

[23] Of course, this does not preclude the possibility that some firms keep an unofficial 'colour-tag'. Occasionally, however, it is possible to obtain definite proof that this is not done.

[24] The examples inserted here are extracts from our note books.

It says on my passport I'm citizen of England. But that don't help me.

I borrow money for the boat and I pay it back. I send money to my wife and five children, but there is not enough to save for the boat for them. I am a packer and I get £9. My rent is £2.15 and I send home £3. I pay tax and insurance. I not eat much. Rice, beans. I get sick in the winter. Another Jamaican and me we share a room, but he get married soon and I try to find other place. It's hard, man. Some coloured bad and make things hard for all. I was in a fight, they blame me, but was not me. The big white man start it. No one believes a black man. I'm a citizen of England. I like to go home."

A Barbadian in the Harrow Road

He was leaning against a lamp post in the Harrow Road watching the traffic. He was unshaven; his clothes were shabby. He had a sullen face, and he did not smile once, but his story contradicted his appearance.

He had come to Britain from Barbados in 1955, when he was 32, and had paid for his own passage. He had been a foreman contractor and had emigrated, not because he was badly off or unemployed, but because he wanted a change. He had worked for a short time in the building trade at Slough, and then had obtained work by his own efforts in a foundry at Southall. He had stayed at that job ever since. He worked the night shift, earning good wages on semi-skilled work.

He had been married for eleven years, and his wife and one of his six children were with him here. She worked at a food factory. The other five children were in the West Indies—"they are well cared for"—supported by money he sent home regularly. He had no plans for going home. On the contrary, he was thinking of buying a house. "No Sir, I have no complaints, not at all. No difficulties. This country is good."

A man from Antigua in Edgware Road

"No, well, you see, I come in September last year but I have no work for six months. I live on National Assistance, £2.10. My room costs £2, but I have money with me, from home, Antigua. The National Assistance people are good.

I do ordinary work. I work in a hospital. Now I work in a hotel.

I get my food there, but the money is not good. I am 44 and not married. All my friends here are from Dominica and Grenada. No one ever say things to me about coloured. I never go out after seven; too many fights. I listen to the news, and read. I share a room with a man from Grenada; the other people in the house are white and black. No trouble. You have to take what you can find, cannot pick friends, all black men together. If I have the money I go home now."

A man from British Guiana at Paddington Station

He came from British Guiana where he had been a school-teacher. Now he is a railway clerk, but, he said, he preferred to be a clerk, and did not want to be a teacher. Indeed, one reason for his coming to England three years ago was to escape from teaching. "I wanted a change."

He paid £2.10 for his room in Paddington, to which he regularly invited his friends. "I belong to the YMCA, you see. I go three or four times a week, I'm very keen on it. That's where I make my friends. Most of them are English. Real friends, I get on with them very well."

Although he lived fairly near to Notting Hill, he had not been involved in the disturbances. "I didn't see anything, not even at night, going home from work, or at the YMCA. As a matter of fact I've never met any trouble at all, all the time I've been in England."

At this several West Indians standing nearby laughed derisively. One said: "He walks around with a placard saying 'I'm not to be touched by kind permission of the High Commissioner'."

But the railway clerk insisted it was true.

Occupational Downgrading

From the confusion of many divergent accounts—by the migrants themselves, by their employers, their workmates and by observers— some general facts emerge, however. At least the outlines of the employment situation of the new minority group are clear. As shown by the records of the London Sample of West Indians, and illustrated by individual tales, the newcomers have found a fair variety of jobs in London. There is a considerable number of West Indian nurses; some men and women are employed as doctors, teachers, journalists or as black-coated workers; a few are in the entertainment world, where colour can occasionally be an asset; others have skilled manual work; and there are also self-employed people—barbers, tailors, cleaners, laundrymen, shopkeepers and café owners—who run establishments which are largely patronised by West Indians. But the group of West Indians in such middle class and skilled manual positions is small; indeed, it is considerably smaller than might be expected in view of the migrants' occupational backgrounds. Many have been unable to find jobs equivalent to their previous status at home, and thus the majority of West Indians are employed in London as semi-skilled or unskilled labourers.

Not all the newcomers who have moved down the ladder of occupational prestige since they arrived here regret their downgrading. In some cases, the change of status is more apparent than real, or it is only a minor one; in others, it is a voluntary change which the migrants wanted to make; and there are, moreover, often financial compensations: a man might earn more if he is employed as a semi-skilled manual worker than he would earn as a clerk. But there are also West Indians—and they are not a negligible group—who have had to accept positions that are very much inferior to the 'white-collar' and skilled manual occupations which they have had before; they have moved downwards—not just one or two steps, but steeply—to the lowest rank of unskilled labourers. They are bound to be bitterly disappointed; their period of re-adjustment is inevitably a rather long and difficult one.

Although both the circumstances of downward social mobility and the individual responses to them differ, occupational downgrading of some kind or other has been—and still is—so frequent an experience of West Indians in London that it has caused much concern.[25] The migrants discuss it, and so do others who watch their situation. Why are many West Indians unable to use their previous qualifications in London? Why is there, apparently, a wastage of training?

Several explanations are offered.[26] First, there is the obvious one

[25] The relevant details for the London Sample of West Indians were given in Chapter II, part 3.

[26] The most frequent one is the statement that the West Indian migrants who claim to be skilled manual or white-collar workers are not, in fact, skilled; and that quite a number are even illiterate. As was said earlier (see Chapter II, footnote 11, p. 31) this seems to be an unwarranted generalisation, and indeed this is confirmed by the only detailed study of the performance of a group of West Indian workers over a period of several years which exists—Anthony H. Richmond's *Colour Prejudice in Britain: A Study of West Indian Workers in Liverpool 1941–1951*, London, 1954. In this study, the performance of 309 West Indian workers

that certain types of skill are not readily transferable from one country to another. While some trained workers and craftsmen— motor mechanics, drivers and carpenters, for example—can, in principle at least, continue their previous occupations in this country without difficulty, there are others who may have to unlearn a good deal of what they had learnt before. An electrician, who was regarded as well qualified in Barbados, and who had been used only to putting installations in wooden houses, might not find it easy at first to tackle a task in a brick house. An engineer, who had been employed in a Trinidad sugar factory, would hardly be able to apply his expertise immediately to other industries in this country. Farmers and agricultural workers have to make a new start in any case in an urban, highly industrialised environment. And even those West Indians who have had jobs at home for which there are counterparts here may often be told that standards of qualifications and craftsmanship are very different in this country. In some types of work, they lack the apprenticeship training which is indispensable for admission into the appropriate union. In any case, they will also be told that they have still to adapt themselves to the discipline and tempo of British economic institutions.

"The West Indian or African accepts our industrial environment surprisingly quickly, if anything the men adapting themselves better than the women."[27] That is one view that can be heard. But the opposite opinion is more frequently stressed when employers and personnel managers discuss the recruitment and performance of West Indian workers. It is then said that the migrants, in general, take time to get acclimatised to British employment conditions.

---

over a period of approximately four years was assessed by the Ministry of Labour (in terms of the men's general work ability, knowledge of their particular trades and workmanship). This assessment was then compared with the men's occupational status (as stated by them). Although a perfect correlation between the two classifications could not be expected since the Ministry's assessment also took innate ability into account, a significant correlation was, in fact, found. Thus 77.5 per cent of the skilled workers (in terms of occupational status) were graded by the Ministry as being "very skilled" in their actual performance. (See Richmond, pp. 33, 34.)

On the other hand, there can be no doubt that English and West Indian definitions of skill are not necessarily alike; in particular, the English skilled worker has usually had a longer training and is far more specialised than the West Indian one. Thus the latter is liable to have difficulties in continuing his previous occupation in London, though he is also likely to be a rather versatile man who can adapt himself quickly to varying types of work.

[27] *The Times*, September 18, 1958 (in an article 'Coloured Worker in Britain' from A Special Correspondent). Similar statements have been made elsewhere as well.

Usually it is assumed that the West Indians need special instruction to take their places in British industry.[28]

Though this assumption is by no means invariably correct, as reports on West Indian employment records in several places show, its prevalence helps to explain why the migrants so often have to drift into unskilled jobs for which no particular preparation is required.[29] And as there is a high turnover in such jobs, and at a period of full employment not much competition for them, they are, of course, more readily available than those of higher grades of skill, particularly on the London labour market where there is a considerable demand for unskilled, often casual, workers in services and allied industries.[30]

There is a further explanation for the occupational downgrading which so many West Indians have experienced: it may well be at the back of some of the others; and it is the one which the migrants themselves tend to give. They say that they have to take menial jobs because of colour prejudice and discrimination. They would also agree that in the complex conditions of British industry, this is an explanation which is not easily subject to documentary proof or quantitative assessment. Though there are colour bars, and more often colour quotas, these restrictions are not publicised. Nor is it usually possible to single out colour prejudice—where it seems, or is suspected, to exist—from an intricate web of circumstances into which it may or may not be woven. Thus it is possible that some examples of alleged discrimination may be exaggerated or misinterpreted; they could be instances of other kinds of restrictive

[28] This was the common assumption in extensive discussions on the employment problems of West Indians in London at two conferences held in October 1958. One of these conferences was convened by the London Council of Social Service; the other by the Institute of Personnel Management. The people who spoke at these meetings were representative of large-scale and highly unionised industries, and it is possible that their experience differs from that of small non-union workshops. Most speakers agreed that West Indians needed special preparation for their employment in Britain. Various methods of instruction were suggested—film shows and lectures on the ships, or courses of training in this country.

[29] Another reason which is sometimes given can only be a marginal one. It is said that some skilled West Indian craftsmen have not brought their tools with them (they have sold them as a contribution to their fare to England). And they cannot, therefore, find appropriate jobs in this country.

[30] Of course, not all unskilled or semi-skilled jobs are insecure. On the contrary, there are such jobs in public authorities and public utilities which are permanent and fairly safe. Some migrants are directed to such jobs, and take them in preference to other work which is better paid and on a higher level of skill, but in industries that are subject to sharp fluctuations in employment.

practices, or of the sort of difficulties which any newcomers—white or coloured—might find.

The thorny question of promotion is a case in point. It is one of the bitter complaints of West Indians that they are not accepted for promotion. And indeed employers frequently argue that white men and women will work with coloured people, but not under them. Many white workers themselves deny this assertion: they say that it is unjustified; and their views are confirmed in those establishments (in the London Transport system, for example) where coloured people have been promoted to supervisory positions, and where no difficulties on that score have been reported.[31] While the employers' assumption plays a part in limiting the opportunities of West Indians for promotion, other factors are relevant, too. As the migrants often start in blind-alley jobs—or have to start in such jobs, perhaps also because of prejudice—their chances of improving their status are low for that reason alone. More important still is the fact that many of them have not been in their jobs long enough to qualify for promotion. Thus it is not possible as yet to assess the actual influence of colour prejudice on their careers in more precise terms.

Undoubtedly, the issues are confused and confusing. Nevertheless, there are both among workers and employers examples of behaviour that has definite connotations of prejudice; such behaviour stands out just because it is in sharp contrast to opposite tendencies of genuine tolerance.

Trade Unions

The official trade union policy is unequivocally opposed to discrimination; it was confirmed once again emphatically at the Trades Union Congress, held at the time of the disturbances in Nottingham and Notting Dale in September 1958.

"The Trade Union Movement has been forthright in its condemnation of every manifestation of racial prejudice and discrimination in any part of the world. Here in Britain, immigrants from many countries have been freely accepted into membership of trade unions and in general have been integrated into industrial life. Satisfactory housing and social integration have been more difficult to achieve. Decent people will appreciate that this is a matter which calls for understanding and that many immigrants arrive in Britain with a limited knowledge of its social and economic environment and pattern

---

[31] Nor have there been difficulties, either in London or in the provinces, in the relations between white passengers and coloured conductors, although it had been assumed, especially in provincial cities, that the public would not wish to be 'supervised' by coloured crews on the buses.

of life which is so different from their own, and to which they require to accustom themselves. Here is the field in which joint efforts in local communities can do so much to further tolerance and an appreciation of the difficult problems which are involved."[32]

This was the statement submitted by the General Council to Congress, and similar resolutions denouncing discrimination were passed, especially during that period, by many individual unions and branches.

But there is a gap, sometimes a wide one, between the policy at top level and the attitudes at other levels. While the 'high command' of a trade union passes resolutions deploring colour prejudice, the local branches may operate colour quotas. And there can also be considerable variations of opinion and practice among the local branches of any one trade union, even in the same city or metropolitan area.

> " 'The coloured people coming to England are British subjects only seeking a means of existence which is denied them in their place of birth. We implore all trade unionists to do all in their power to help them obtain employment and join their respective trade unions, thus enabling them to work and live as decent human beings.'
>
> 'It is time a stop was put to all foreign labour entering this country; they constitute a danger to the workers of this country. In the event of a slump occurring, the market would be flooded with cheap foreign labour and a serious deterrent to trade union bargaining power.'
>
> (It is understood that in this resolution 'foreign labour' was intended to include coloured workers.)"

These resolutions, which "were passed by different branches of the same craft union within two months of each other", were quoted in a report by Mr. Leslie Stephens on the *Employment of Coloured Workers in the Birmingham Area*;[33] and such examples are more likely to be found in the provinces than in London. For the contradictions in the attitudes of workers and trade union branches to the 'colour problem' are most marked in those parts of the country—in the Midlands and in the North—where memories of the depression are still vivid, and where local parochialism is strong.

In such places, outsiders are suspect; and the definition of an 'outsider' is often very broad: it is applied not only to immigrants from the Irelands, from Europe and from other continents, but sometimes also to 'out-of-towners' who come from a place that is ten miles away. And the mistrust is sharper when 'foreigners' arrive who have (or are believed to have) lower standards of living and more

---

[32] *Report of Proceedings at the 90th Annual Trades Union Congress*, Bournemouth, September 1958, p. 459.

[33] Published by the Institute of Personnel Management, Occasional Papers No. 10, 1956 (p. 17).

modest demands for wages than the local workers, and also less respect (so it is thought) for the principle of collective advancement based on trade union discipline. It is this image of outsiders which groups of migrants from Asia, Africa and from the West Indies evoke —in particular at first sight, before they have been recruited, while they are still beyond the range of personal acquaintance. It is feared that they will cut into overtime earnings and agreements; that employers will use them as a pool of cheap, sweated labour, or even as 'blacklegs' in the event of strikes.

Thus the dominant motive in disputes over the employment of coloured workers has not been open colour prejudice as such, but the fear of economic competition—a fear which is rooted strongly in the environment and traditions of some areas of Britain, though there is clearly the danger that it might also flare up elsewhere in periods of recession. Until now, such disputes have occurred mainly in the provinces, less in the cosmopolitan London region, where prosperity has been settled much longer. Indeed, the geographical contrast in attitudes has been most striking in the one industry in which the recruitment of coloured labour has been a prominent controversial subject—that of public transport services. In London, there were hardly any difficulties when coloured men and women joined the transport crews.[34] Yet in several provincial cities, there were unofficial strikes or threats of strikes when coloured people—mainly Indians, Pakistanis and West Indians—were recruited for the buses. At the very least, there were lengthy negotiations; demands were made to restrict the intake of coloured workers to a definite quota.

There are still a few cities without a single coloured conductor—or certainly without a single coloured driver. In most provincial towns, however, the troubles—at least the overt ones—were short-lived (they occurred mainly in 1955 and 1956); coloured men and women are now employed on the buses. The change in attitudes towards them was emphasised, for example, by members of the Birmingham Transport Authority in a talk with a B.B.C. interviewer in the autumn of 1958:

> "We did face the difficulty that a number of the staff thought that we should get so many coloured people and that they would cause trouble between the black and the white. It was further feared by some of our people that there was a possibility that there would be difficulty between the coloured conductor or the coloured driver and

---

[34] There is no evidence of serious objections against coloured workers in the London transport system: if there was any grumbling, it was not sufficiently outspoken and prolonged to attract much public attention. Apparently only a few problems occurred; it is said that there were incidents at three British railway depots and at two depots of the London Transport Executive.

the white passenger. I am pleased to say that we've got positive proof in our everyday working that those fears were very very largely unfounded. . . . And although on the Birmingham City Transport at the moment we've got probably more (coloured people) than on any other undertaking of a similar kind in the country anywhere, we can say with some degree of pride that they are now working with the white crews, working with the white public, and I think we can almost say that very often they're not even noticed; no one is conscious that it's a coloured driver or a coloured conductor."[35]

But although in many places the objections against the recruitment of coloured workers to provincial municipal transport systems have by now been largely forgotten, it is well worth while to recall their history. For they show how difficult it is in British industry to pin-point colour prejudice—even in a dispute which is caused by the employment of coloured workers, and in which the issue seems to be clear. Undoubtedly, colour prejudice plays a part in such disputes. Yet it is not possible to identify it precisely, nor to say exactly how large a part it plays. It is only one of many, often contradictory, attitudes which affect the situation; and once the controversy has been launched, it is pushed on and blown up by all sorts of cross-currents and considerations which are independent of the original motive. Tolerant people support discrimination—not unthinkingly and not gladly, but because they adhere to the conventions of 'patriotism' in industry. No one wants to be a renegade or a strike breaker.

Industrial Disputes

This complexity is illustrated by two disputes, in particular, which occurred in Midland towns—West Bromwich, near Birmingham, and Wolverhampton—in 1955, and which both attracted a good deal of attention at the time.

In February 1955, the employees of the West Bromwich Corporation Transport system decided to start a series of token Saturday strikes in protest against the employment of an Indian, a trainee conductor. The strikes, they said, would continue until the management and representatives of the men reached agreement on the question of coloured labour. The official union policy was opposed to discrimination on grounds of colour; the management was adamant in its intention to recruit any suitable person regardless of colour.

The first strike of the West Bromwich men took place on Saturday, February 19th. Three other municipal transport systems which ran joint services with West Bromwich—those of Birmingham, Walsall

[35] From the tape records of unpublished interviews by Barry Carman.

and Wolverhampton—became involved. These three undertakings said, as is by no means unusual in industrial relations, that they would not run their buses into West Bromwich while the strike lasted. The Licensing Authority disagreed, and refused to vary their licences accordingly, on the grounds that the public would be deprived of transport if their buses were turned back at the West Bromwich boundary. Nevertheless, the three undertakings gave orders to their drivers not to enter West Bromwich on the day of the strike.

A Conservative leader in Birmingham pointed out that the three other transport undertakings were thus giving active support to the strikers; the Labour members of the West Bromwich corporation said they were shocked by the action of the Birmingham corporation; the West Bromwich Trades Council condemned the strike and threatened to expel the branch. The Walsall and Wolverhampton undertakings then decided to run their buses into West Bromwich in any future strike. Birmingham differed and tried again to get the licence varied, although the Birmingham transport committee deprecated the action of the West Bromwich bus men. When the application to the Licensing Authority was again refused, Birmingham decided to send its buses into West Bromwich during the next strike. But the busmen of Birmingham, Walsall and Wolverhampton refused to drive into West Bromwich. They were not interested in the cause of the strike; they said that they would not be blacklegs.

Before the second strike, the Bishops of Birmingham and Lichfield appealed to the strikers to reconsider their action: ". . . efforts to enforce a colour bar are not reconcilable with Christianity".[36] The West Bromwich Transport Committee warned the bus crews that disciplinary action would be taken against the strikers. However, they did resume their strike as planned, on the next Saturday, February 26th.

That was the last strike, though not the end of the matter. A certain amount of rumbling continued. While negotiations were going on between the management and the union, a driver refused to take the Indian trainee on his bus, an action for which he apologised afterwards. But later several conductors refused to take the trainee out, and they were apparently within their normal rights in doing so. Negotiations went on for some time in a difficult atmosphere, but the trouble disappeared—from the newspapers at any rate.

There is no way of aligning these various actions in simple terms of intolerance or tolerance. It would be wrong to argue that the three outside transport undertakings were supporting a colour bar; indeed, one of them publicly opposed it. They were supporting trade union principles of loyalty, irrespective of the merits of the case. Nor

[36] *The Times*, February 25, 1955.

does it follow that the Licensing Authority was opposed to a colour bar because it refused to give the outside buses permission to turn back at the boundary; it was the Authority's task to ensure adequate facilities for the public. The general secretary of the men's union, Mr. Arthur Deakin, argued that the strike was not really a question of colour prejudice; the men were conditioned by a fear of unemployment. The strikers themselves gave contradictory reasons for their action: some spoke of a colour bar and then said later that the Indian's appointment was simply the last straw—one of a series of grievances which had accumulated.

The second dispute occurred a few months later in the neighbouring town of Wolverhampton. The Corporation transport men decided to ban all overtime from the 1st September 1955—a ban which would have reduced bus services drastically as they were kept going by the operation of overtime. The ban was called as a protest against the increase of coloured recruits. The branch secretary of the union explained: "We are not operating a colour bar. The men have made friends with the coloured men on the job, but we don't intend to have the platform staff made up to its full strength by coloured people only."[37] At that time, 68 coloured workers were employed among a total staff of just over 900. (The full complement was 1,050.) The branch secretary said that the union was originally prepared to accept 52 coloured men, but the Transport Committee of the Corporation denied that any such promise had been given.

The ban began on the 1st September and lasted until the 18th. The men wanted a five per cent quota of coloured labour, and they demanded that there should be no recruitment of coloured men while the negotiations were going on. The Transport Committee refused to accept their requests and stated that if the men were, in fact, not asking for a colour bar, as they themselves claimed, then their campaign was simply an attempt to keep the department short-staffed, and thereby to maintain overtime earnings. After much negotiation the men dropped the demand for a five per cent quota; instead a panel was set up to consider all recruits to the transport department.

On this occasion, as in other similar disputes, the official union policy was opposed to colour discrimination, and indeed the strikers said the same. It is difficult to know whether the recruitment of coloured men was merely a pretext for the ban on overtime.

Three years later, Wolverhampton was again in the news for similar reasons. This time, there were no problems on the buses; there was a prolonged controversy on the operation of a colour bar in a local dance hall. And it was a controversy which reflected the

[37] *The Times*, September 1, 1955.

conflicting views of a trade union at different levels even more clearly than other disputes in which the employment of coloured workers was the main issue.

In June 1958, the licence of the Scala ballroom in Wolverhampton came up for renewal. As it had become known that the Scala had a colour bar—the story of an Indian who had been turned away from the hall had been reported in the Press—there was considerable local opposition to the renewal of the licence. However, the licence was renewed by the local magistrates, and thus the affair of the Wolverhampton dance hall became a *cause célèbre* in this country and abroad. Questions were asked in the Parliament of India; there were echoes in the West Indies. The Labour M.P. for North-East Wolverhampton drafted a Private Member's Bill to make colour bars in dance halls and other public places illegal. The Wolverhampton Town Council unanimously proposed a by-law prohibiting discrimination in admission to fun fairs and roller-skating rinks. (Neither measure succeeded: the bill did not go far in the House of Commons; the by-law was not confirmed by the Home Secretary.)

Although there were—and probably still are—colour bars in other dance halls, public houses and similar establishments elsewhere in Britain, the Wolverhampton affair was singled out for attention—presumably because the renewal of a licence to a place which was known to practise overt discrimination had not previously been reported in any other case. The attitude of the Musicians Union, moreover, was of general interest. The 'high command' of the Union told their members not to play at the Scala ballroom until the colour bar was lifted.[38] But the local branch decided to continue to play there. As a result, the leaders of the three bands playing at the Scala were expelled from the Union. The local branch re-admitted them; the Union expelled them again. Eventually, the doors of the Scala were opened to all people—dark and white. A new management took over when the lease of the hall reverted to the landlords in February 1959, and the colour bar was lifted.

Relations between White and Coloured Workmates

Every aspect of 'race relations' in British industry shows the same kinds of ambiguities and contradictions. On some occasions, men

[38] The management then tried to get an interim injunction to restrain the Union. Their first attempt failed; the second one succeeded. The extension of this injunction was, however, refused; and the refusal was upheld by the Court of Appeal. At one stage, the management also tried to 'appease' local public opinion by proposing to operate an inverse colour bar: they offered the hall for the exclusive use of coloured people once a month. But nothing came of this proposal.

oppose the employment of coloured workers (or, for that matter, the recruitment of any outsiders); on others, men protest against the dismissal of coloured workers. The juxtaposition is obvious when by chance examples of both types of dispute—which are rather rare— are reported on the same day (as happened in October 1959). We then get a glimpse of the insecurity in the position of the coloured migrant. He does not know, nor can he know, when and how prejudice will push against him.

This was a headline in *The Guardian* (of October 24, 1959).

"COLOUR QUESTION IN TWO DISPUTES

Contrasting action

> While two hundred strikers at a factory in Derbyshire were reiterating yesterday their view that 'the coloured workers will have to go', 30 men employed by a Birmingham firm stopped work because a coloured man had been dismissed."

A report on the unofficial strike in Derbyshire had already been published two days earlier. The strike was originally called in protest against the employment of a Punjabi—a new recruit in a factory in which six other coloured men had been working for several months. The management had previously assured the men that no additional coloured workers "would be employed on work for which White labour was available."[39] As soon as the Punjabi appeared in the factory, the other men stopped work. The union instructed them to return so that negotiations with the management could start. The strike lasted, however, for several days, and in the course of it, the men extended their demand for the dismissal of the seventh coloured worker to the other six as well. The union secretary at the factory said:

> " 'We shall return to work on Monday, but we are holding a meeting on Sunday to discuss the whole affair. Talks between union and management can go on after our return, but all our members are determined that the seven Coloured men here must go. Our return makes no difference to that view.'
> The Birmingham strike lasted for only seven hours.
> It ended when the firm agreed to keep Mohammed Ghulam, aged 35, a Pakistani, in his job until the end of the tax year, when the union will try to find him fresh work.
> Ghulam, who is called 'Bill' by his workmates, had been employed as a temporary labourer for a year, but he was given three weeks' notice on Thursday. He had become one of the most popular workers

---

[39] *The Guardian*, October 22, 1959.

at the firm, even though he cannot speak English, and Mr. Thomas Budding, a Transport and General Workers' Union shop steward, said: 'We regard him as one of the most helpful and courteous of colleagues. You don't have to ask him for help; he is always there to give it.'

Ghulam was a soldier for sixteen years and one of the strikers said: 'He is a first-rate man who served his country well. . . . He endured the sufferings of a Japanese prisoner-of-war camp, and we feel we owe him something.'

A statement from the firm pointed out that there was no question of a colour bar. Ghulam had been employed on a temporary job, which had now finished. The union had agreed that the three weeks' notice with pay was 'fair and generous'."[40]

Both the union secretary in Derbyshire and the shop steward in Birmingham spoke more plainly on 'the colour question' in their factories than is usual; such test cases do not often arise. In general, the symptoms of colour consciousness and colour blindness shown by English workers are more elusive, and there is also a whole range of intermediate, inconsistent attitudes which defy classification. It is this prevalent vagueness which makes matters so difficult from the point of view of the coloured migrants themselves.

Of course, there are English workers who are opposed to discrimination on principle; there are many others who are genuinely fair, and who regard their coloured mates as individuals, not as representatives of a particular species. And there are also those who act with similar fairness, and speak with similar voices, but with undertones of aloofness and suspicion. The differences, though apparently slight, and hardly noticed by the casual observer, are detected, and sometimes even exaggerated, by the men and women with dark skins.

When English workers get together in a public house or working men's club and speak about their experiences with coloured mates, these kinds of statements can be heard.

A factory worker (who used to be a dental salesman) was asked whether there were any coloured men in his factory. He said:

"Yes . . . but they seem to be real nice pleasant chaps, you know we . . . well everyone gets on very well with them. I've never heard anyone really, you know, have anything against them at all. I've not noticed anything, they seem to do the work all right, and carry on all right, and I don't think they're too bad a lot on the whole actually."

An abrasive-wheel engineer talked about his impressions.

Engineer: "Well, this particular one that I worked with and had a

---

[40] *The Guardian*, October 24, 1959.

lot to do about, or with, he was very good. In fact, on this particular occasion they sacked some white labour to keep this coloured chap—Jamaican, he was. And he was very good at his job, and I thought he was a decent worker, in fact a decent chap all round."

Interviewer: "Did you approve of the white workers being sacked?"

Engineer: "Yes, in one respect. They was what the management call 'gypsies'; floating from one job to another, but you find the coloured worker if he is a decent chap he'll stick to his job and he'll work hard."[41]

Some faint traces of hesitation might be read into the first man's words. Yet as the interview went on, it became clear that he was, in fact, entirely unprejudiced. It was the second man who had all sorts of reservations against coloured people—not at work, he emphasised, "not as regards the working of the coloured man. I think they're just like our people, some will work and some won't." But outside the factory he saw them differently—as a category of immigrants whom he did not want "too close to home", especially in relation to white girls.

Such ambivalence exists in varying degrees: occasionally, it is unmistakable at first sight. And then there are some English workers who do not try to distinguish between pleasant and unpleasant coloured mates, but who regard them all as dark outsiders, from whom they keep apart, whom they mistrust or plainly dislike.

While accounts of relations between white and coloured workers are thus mixed, overt friction seems to be the rare exception rather than the rule. Difficulties have arisen at the recruitment stage—though less recently than a few years ago. The reports of the Nottingham and Notting Dale disturbances in the autumn of 1958 have increased vigilance against discrimination, at least at the top levels of the trade union movement. The migrants have, moreover, become far better known in industry: they are no longer merely a rather disturbing foreign image. Usually, there is at least someone in the factory who has already worked with a Jamaican John or a Barbadian George, and who has already met a coloured man from an Asian or African country. He can tell his mates about these chaps before any new coloured recruits arrive. And once the migrants are admitted into an industrial establishment, they are, in general, accepted as members of the team. This is clearly visible in those industries, like building and transport, in which there are small working groups. There is no sign of segregation when mixed coloured and white crews are on the scaffolds of a building site in the City; when they load lorries in

[41] From the tape records of Barry Carman's interviews.

St. Pancras; when they are on duty on the platform of an underground station, or when they travel together from one station to another.

Nevertheless, some serious difficulties remain, though on the whole these are not so acute for the West Indians as for other coloured migrants from India, Pakistan and Africa. The difference between the previous and the new environment is not so radical for the West Indians as it is for many of the others. By and large, the men from the Caribbean territories are already more conditioned for life and work in England than those from Asia and Africa; most important, they have no major language problem.[42] While West Indians do not speak 'local' English, and their distinct accents and phrases occasionally cause misunderstandings or mutual irritation, there is no great barrier to communication. Minor differences in speech and habits can, however, often be even more annoying to both sides than major ones—particularly when mutual strangeness is not taken for granted.

Thus the fact that West Indians on the whole are not familiar with trade union organisation is, of course, resented by English workers. As in the West Indies trade unions are still rather marginal or even slightly suspect associations, the 'green' migrant does not necessarily apply for his union card at once.[43] And so it can be easily forgotten that there are also West Indians who participate in trade union affairs in London and in the provinces; some of them have become shop stewards; a few have been elected to posts as presidents or secretaries of union branches.

The divergent interests in sports matter, too. In the larger establishments, which have their own cricket teams, the West Indians are popular because they are often good cricket players, and usually ardent cricket fans. But in many other places, they do not get on so well because they know little about 'our' favourite games (as the British workers say)—about football, snooker and darts.

Is the folklore of the coloured man's sexual behaviour, and of the white man's reactions to it, even more important? Perhaps it is. But it is so much a matter of hearsay of the most indirect kind, and so overlaid with meaningless distortions, that its significance could only be assessed through a most detailed, prolonged enquiry. There is no doubt that a tangle of sexual images about the coloured man, and of

[42] So far as we can judge, the direct cause of industrial disputes about coloured people has been more often the employment of Indians and Pakistanis than that of West Indians. This might well be a reflection of the special problems which the Asian migrants have because of their language difficulties.

[43] Sometimes, he is unable to do so because he lacks the qualifications necessary to be accepted by the craft union which he wants to join in view of his previous occupation.

sexual competition with him, strongly affects attitudes to coloured people, in general, outside the place of work. In particular, such images are reflected in the ideas of adolescents. It does not follow, however, that such attitudes are also invariably transferred to the place of employment, and spoil the relations between white and coloured workmates.[44]

Wherever there are tensions, these tend to be subdued, at least nowadays. West Indians sometimes complain that they have been slighted or insulted by their workmates. More often they tell stories of incomplete 'integration': they say that all goes well at work, but once it is done, the white workers do not mix with them in the canteen or on the way home, nor do they ask them to come along to the local pub. And indeed, it can be seen here and there that coloured factory workers sit in the canteen and walk out of the gate in groups, apart from the others. Of course, such instances are not necessarily symbols of deliberate separation: they can be the result of an unfortunate combination of circumstances. In the canteen, the long established worker does not draw up his chair at the table of the coloured newcomers because he does not realise how much such a gesture means to them; they, in turn, do not take the initiative because they are afraid of being snubbed. And so a habit is formed: one group remains insensitive; the others' thin skin gets even thinner.

It is not surprising that West Indians, or other coloured workers, are vulnerable. They are acutely aware of any signs of ambiguity, and they may even misread the signs, because they have learnt to expect inconsistent behaviour. They have certainly met it among employers.

[44] It was said in the Senior and Manley report (1955) *op. cit.*, that white workers were much more reluctant to accept coloured workers in establishments in which both men and women were employed than in those in which only men were working. This was one of the assumptions frequently held in the mid-fifties before the West Indians, and the attitudes of English workers to them, had become better known. In repeating it, Senior and Manley went on to say that white workers were more likely to object to coloured workers in job situations "where they might be thrown into contact with white women" than in others. "It was in this area of social relationship that a considerable amount of trouble arose with regard to Polish refugees, Italian miners and American soldiers." (Para. 148, p. 33.) But the analogy is hardly appropriate: the two latter groups did not work with British women in industry; and there is a considerable difference between relationships outside the factory and those inside. Attitudes from one sphere are not necessarily or directly transferred to the other—certainly not in this country. It seems, moreover, that this particular assumption, like others of the mid-fifties, has since been largely disproved. We ourselves have no evidence which confirms its validity in recent experience. There has been no difficulty on this score in municipal transport systems in London and in the provinces, nor has there been any trouble between white passengers of either sex and coloured conductors.

Attitudes of Employers

Both before and after the Second World War, many employers refused to recruit coloured workers. Such barriers were then well known; they caused considerable difficulties, particularly in the re-settlement of West Indians who had been brought to this country under an official war-time scheme for essential work in industry or for service in the Armed Forces. All was well so long as the Ministry of Labour had the powers to control the direction of labour. But as soon as these regulations were relaxed, and recruitment was again entirely at the discretion of employers, many West Indians who had been doing vital, often skilled, war work found that they were no longer wanted. Most of the doors were now closed to them.[45]

Later on, during the post-war period of full employment, there were openings again, though not throughout industry and not for all categories of occupation. When there is an acute shortage of labour, the colour of the worker's skin is no longer so visible. But even now, there are still employers who will not take on coloured workers, though they do not advertise this fact. There are also still complaints about symptoms of discrimination at some employment exchanges, although on the whole the improvement in the code of conduct of the latter has been very marked.

When employers or managers who still operate a colour bar are asked for their reasons, they tend to give the usual ones: they blame someone else. They say that they cannot employ coloured workers because their white workers would not like it; or because their customers would disapprove; or because it would lower the 'status' of their firms; or because it is their policy to recruit a labour force

---

[45] Anthony H. Richmond has described the post-war employment difficulties of coloured workers in Liverpool in his book *Colour Prejudice in Britain* (London, 1954), pp. 41–44. He wrote: "In November 1945 the Welfare Officer reported that the loosening of the provisions of the Essential Works and Control of Engagement Orders was making it hard to force employers to accept West Indians even when vacancies had been notified. The relaxation of these orders was a subject of much controversy at the time. . . . With the impending election the government was under considerable pressure to rescind these Orders. Although it subsequently became necessary to reaffirm the Orders during the economic crisis of 1947, the period of relaxation at the end of the war had a definite effect in making the placing of coloured Colonials an even more difficult problem than it might have been. Early in 1946, a number of instances were reported where men had been turned down for vacancies on the ground of their colour. The position was somewhat complicated, in certain cases, owing to claims on the part of employers that the men were not properly qualified for the work required. Although in some cases this was true, in many instances it appears to have been a rationalization of a determination not to employ coloured men in any case." (pp. 42, 43.)

that is 'representative of the local community' (presumably in terms of colour and nationality, but not of social class). And then there are also those employers (or executives) who say that they do not want any "West Indian natives": "I spent fifteen years in India, and I know what I'm talking about." It is not surprising, of course, that the colonial slang is still spoken by members of the managerial class, and that colonial images are still influential. Such attitudes affect not only the recruitment of coloured workers, but also their treatment when they are taken on after all because of labour shortages. A man who was the boss of Negro labourers and servants on the Gold Coast, or one who used to run a jute mill in Calcutta—and whose complacency was never stirred by the sight of the human kennels in the coolie lines his firm had built—such a man would hardly be an ideal employer for coloured workers in Britain.[46]

Employment exchanges are well aware of the colour bar policy of certain firms. Some of the officials, therefore, do not send the migrants to such firms when vacancies are notified, so as to avoid exposing them to rejection and humiliation. But often such precautions cannot be taken because a colour quota is far more common than a definite colour bar. Indeed, it seems that the practice of some kind of restriction in the recruitment of coloured workers—restriction of their number, in general, and also, more important still, limitation to a narrow range of occupational grades—is widespread among large firms in most industries in London. In the smaller firms, the position appears to be more varied and is also, of course, far less subject to a general assessment.

Among large firms, too, there are some exceptions. It is not the 'policy' of the public sector of industry to operate a colour quota, nor is it the practice in certain quarters of private industry to do so. Thus a considerable proportion of coloured people are employed in several branches of light engineering and food processing, and also in the catering trade, especially in works canteens. But even in such establishments, the coloured workers are usually in the 'basement' and not 'upstairs' (working, for example, as kitchen hands and not as waiters); they find it very difficult to reach highly visible, skilled or supervisory posts.

[46] Of course, this is not a new difficulty. It has been observed in previous studies of the employment situation of coloured people in Britain. For example: "It was often found that the least satisfactory type of person to set in a position of authority over the West Indian group was anyone who had experience of dealing with 'coloured labour' in the Colonies; such people tended to deal with the West Indians in Britain by methods similar to those that they had used overseas and to assume that the behaviour and conduct of West Indians was comparable with that of unsophisticated labourers fresh from the 'bush'." *Ibid*, p. 54.

In a report on "colonials" in the garment industry it was said:

'There are no colonials in the dress shops or showrooms. As one of the younger, more progressive manufacturers put it, he was quite happy to employ them in his factory, but not as sales girls in the string of shops he has built up since the war. "One is in business, after all . . . the public would not stand for it," he said with an unhappy shrug. Another retailer said: "I know it is a terrible thing to say, but colour prejudice does exist, and it is a risk we dare not take." Neither firm had actually tested public opinion to see how it would react.'[47]

The report was written early in 1957. Since then, matters have not changed in this respect. The appointment of a coloured shop assistant anywhere in London is still so rare that, when it does occur, it is featured as an event of outstanding importance on the front page of the *West Indian Gazette*.[48]

The quota system takes various forms. (The usual restriction, it seems, is that coloured staff should be no more than 5 to 10 per cent of the firm's total labour force.) The system is operated more or less 'discreetly'; and it has clearly often been adopted by agreement between the management and the union.

But there are also cases where one side or the other has taken the initiative in applying a colour quota; or where one or the other side could have taken the initiative in preventing its application (though neither side is likely to be frank in discussing their contribution to such decisions). While apparently the unions often demand a quota, the employers are by no means free from responsibility. And it is, moreover, far more likely to become known when the unions initiate or practice discrimination than when employers do the same. Employers do not pass resolutions and do not go on strike; their actions —for better or for worse—are far less noticeable in public.

The list of reasons given by employers who apply a colour quota

[47] 'Colonials in Britain: Training and Employment in the Garment Industry', *The Times British Colonies Review*, First Quarter 1957. In the catering trade, "Britain's most cosmopolitan industry", the position was (and still is) very similar, as was reported in another article—'Room for Many More in the Catering Trade'—in the same journal, Third Quarter 1957. "It would be difficult, for instance, for a Barbadian to become a doorman at an exclusive hotel. This is an English preserve. It would be idle to deny discrimination exists. Managements are often frightened of what their customers might think if they introduced coloured waiters. As yet this difficulty seldom arises because colonials still fill the unskilled ranks as kitchen porters, or *plongeurs*, who clean and polish the great copper pots with a mysterious pickle of vinegar, sand, and lemon. Some clean silver in the plateroom or assist the storekeeper or cellarman. Their wages range from £6 to £9."

[48] *West Indian Gazette*, September 1959.

is the same as that given by others who operate a colour bar. Thus it is usually said that the white workers would 'resent' it if more coloured people were recruited, or if any coloured man or woman were employed in a supervisory position. But simultaneously, it is often also said by the same management that the actual relations between their white and coloured workers are friendly. (The underlying assumption that relations are amicable so long as there is a colour quota is not necessarily a plausible one.)[49]

When employers explain their colour bar or quota policy, they do not, however, shift the responsibility only to their white workers or to their customers. It is also said that the coloured workers themselves are largely to be blamed for the restrictive practices against them. Their conduct and performance are heavily criticised—quite often by firms which have had no experience, or very little experience, of employing coloured people.

Of course, there are difficulties in the adaptation of migrants to new types of work, to unfamiliar processes, and to a faster pace in a new environment. There are inevitably problems of personal adjustment and of individual peculiarities. But all these difficulties are bound to be accentuated when the legitimate assumption that they will occur becomes an *idée fixe*: when a particular problem that does arise is immediately regarded as an instance of a general one—as an indubitable confirmation of prejudice. Thus it is impossible to disentangle the exact cause and effect sequence of such complaints against coloured people. Perhaps John McDonald from Barbados was an undisciplined and slow worker. But was he more undisciplined and slower than some John McDonald from Glasgow? And

---

[49] Employers can, of course, give a lead, and when they do so, it is effective. This has been confirmed repeatedly at conferences on the subject and in interviews with firms—for example, also in a recent, so far unpublished, survey 'On Integration of the Coloured Population of Willesden', in the course of which some 20 managers of large firms, each employing over 200 workers, were questioned. In the preliminary, duplicated report of this survey, May–June 1959 (submitted by the Citizens' Advice Bureau to the Willesden Borough Council) it was said: "Among employers questioned, all reported that they had had no serious difficulties in employing coloured workers from the point of view of racial relationships. . . . But management policy on questions of racial intolerance appeared to differ considerably as between one organisation and another. One firm, for instance, had in the past dismissed both coloured and white workers who had been involved in some kind of conflict, and seemed to think that this had not only effectively prevented any further trouble but had, in their view, helped to improve relationships in the factory. Other firms were less definite in their outlook and seemed more susceptible to the complaints of white workers. Similarly, there were those employers who upgraded coloured workers if merited, while others used coloured labour wholly or mainly on unskilled work, since they believed that this seemed to placate, or to avoid trouble with, their white workers."

did he become more difficult to work with because he thought, or knew, that he was regarded not as John, but just as a 'darkie'?

The newcomers never forget that it is the colour of their skin which exposes them to rash generalisations about their behaviour and abilities. And they do not need to read the literature of the social sciences to find out that such stereotype imagery is likely to be reinforced by the stresses and strains which it generates. But do many employers know that just as well? It seems that amongst them the inclination to look upon all coloured people as a single category, irrespective of their varied backgrounds and individual characteristics, is still very strong. Thus all West Indians are often called 'Jamaicans'; it is frequently assumed that all migrants—from India and Pakistan, from Africa and from the Caribbean territories, from villages and from towns—have the same difficulties of adjustment to the English environment. It tends to be forgotten that the West Indians have no major language problem, and that, therefore, one of the reasons which is given for relegating coloured people to menial jobs, and for keeping them apart from their workmates, is not valid in their case.[50]

The obvious 'viciously circular' dangers of such impatient generalisations—and the fact that they are just as misleading with reference to coloured people as they would be with reference to any other heterogeneous group of migrants—all this is clearly illustrated by the contradictory reports given by those firms which have employed, or are employing, coloured workers.

Some say that the migrants are not very 'robust'; others say that they are 'tough'. It is reported that 'they lack initiative', but also that 'they are ambitious and self-reliant'. 'Coloured people are slow and lazy';[51] 'coloured people work hard and quickly'. 'They are

[50] It is often assumed, for example, that it would not be possible to introduce coloured people into small piece-work gangs where quick mutual understanding is essential. But it is doubtful whether this generalisation is justified. Although lack of knowledge of local slang and special technical terms would be an initial handicap, this is one which most West Indians could presumably overcome fairly quickly.

[51] In this context, it is also often said that the piece-rate earnings of coloured workers, in general (or of West Indians, in particular), are lower than those of white workers. But statements of this kind are not supported by precise evidence. So far as we know, there has been no detailed and prolonged study of the piece-rate earnings of coloured workers, either in a particular London firm or in a group of industrial establishments. Nor have there been any recent studies of any other aspects of the migrants' performance in London industries. Most of the information given by firms is vague and inconclusive; it seems to be based on *ad hoc* impressions, not on any systematic comparison of the employment records of different groups of workers over a considerable period.

lethargic'; 'they are energetic'. 'They cannot adapt themselves'; 'they are remarkably adaptable'. Such conflicting statements can be heard whenever a group of employers and personnel managers discuss their experiences with coloured workers.

In a summary of a recent series of interviews on this subject with employers in Willesden it was said:

> "There was a variety of comment about the performance of coloured immigrants from many employers, who felt them to be slower than the equivalent white workers; others felt that with time adaptation set in; still others found them to be no different from white workers. One food firm complained that they had found coloured women workers to be dirty; another food firm, employing several hundred, stated that the coloured workers were among the cleanest of their employees. This variation in viewpoint would appear to be associated, to some extent, with the type of workers selected and with certain pre-conceptions held by management officials."[52]

No doubt, employers have, in fact, diverse experiences with coloured workers. And yet their generalisations tell us more about their own attitudes to 'colour' than about the characteristics of migrants from the West Indies, from Africa and Asia. Thus the 'success stories' are told by managers—in the public sector of industry and also in the private one—who do not regard coloured workers as a species apart, and who do not allow them to be so regarded. These employers have achieved success, as can be seen in their establishments, by the simple method of not expecting too much or too little. It is their experience which points to the main causes of friction or failure elsewhere.

[52] Preliminary Report of Willesden Survey, May–June 1959, *op. cit.*

IV

Attitudes

1. ATTITUDES OF THE NEWCOMERS

Heterogeneity

IT is just as misleading to make generalisations about the attitudes of the coloured newcomers as about those of the plural British society in which they live. West Indians are not a homogeneous group; they have little in common with one another apart from the accident of being under British control. In slightly different historical circumstances, they might have been politically independent, or ruled by France, Spain, Holland or America, as are other territories in the Caribbean. The islands of the British West Indies are widely scattered; each has its own history and traditions, its own social and racial stratification. The predominant racial group is of African Negro origin, but there are also people from Europe, the Middle East, China and India. These various groups are not distributed equally among the islands; in Trinidad and British Guiana, for example, the proportion of Indians is high. There are considerable differences, moreover, between the physical, economic and political conditions of the various territories.

Among West Indians in Britain there are, therefore, people of every shade of colour; those who look like Negroes, Mulattoes, Indians, Chinese, or like Europeans. They may have come from a small island or a large one; from one of the poorest or from one of those which are better off; from a rural or from an urban background; from a majority group or from a minority group at home. Their English dialect varies according to their origin; those who have lived in the United States, or who have been in touch with American tourists, often talk with an American accent; and there are others who speak French, Portuguese, Spanish or Indian languages.

Because of these many differences, and of the large distances between the islands, there is a great deal of inter-island rivalry. People from the big islands tend to look down on the small islanders. The latter, in turn, often say that Jamaicans are noisy and aggressive. Trinidad, the wealthiest island, competes with Jamaica, the largest one. The Barbadians are sometimes characterised as inferiors from a feudal society, who try to be more English than the English.

Although differences of opinion are occasionally expressed on apparently trivial matters—such as the conflicting claims put forward by several islands that each started the steel bands—the rivalries are important in the economic and political circumstances of the West Indies. So far, the people in the West Indies regard themselves as citizens of their territories, as Jamaicans, or Barbadians, for example, not as West Indians. The poorer islands have more to gain from Federation than the richer. The West Indian Federation, formed in 1958, is still young and restricted in its functions; it has not yet had the opportunity of generating a West Indian nationalism.

There is, however, a good deal of class consciousness tied up with 'colour snobbery'. Despite the dissimilarity between the social structure of the West Indian islands and that of the British Isles, class distinctions are of comparable importance in both societies. In the Caribbean, class distinctions are associated with gradations of skin colour.[1] Light pigmentation conveys social prestige; thus the desire to marry 'fair', so as to attain and display economic and social advance, has meant that the middle class and the intellectuals have usually been, and still often are, light skinned. Nowadays the connection between class and colour is no longer quite so close; as some of the middle class West Indians in Britain show, dark people can now advance socially. Nevertheless, class barriers are maintained. Being used to European and especially British cultural patterns, the West Indian middle classes regard the British middle class as their model. Their accent is similar to standard Southern English; in their appearance and bearing, they resemble the accepted image of the middle class in this country. Thus in many respects the West Indian middle classes have far more in common with their English counterparts than with the West Indian working class.

The awareness of differences of origin, social class and colour accompanies the West Indian migrants to Britain. Here, too, they do not form one community or a coherent, mutually compatible group of people. The distance between migrants from the various territories is often maintained in London. There have been reports of

[1] The association between class and colour distinctions in the West Indies has been well described in the anthropological and in related literature. See, for example: T. S. Simey, *Welfare and Planning in the West Indies*, Oxford, 1946; F. Henriques, *Family and Colour in Jamaica*, London, 1953; R. T. Smith, *The Negro Family in British Guiana*, London, 1956; Eric Williams, 'Race Relations in Caribbean Society', *Caribbean Studies: A Symposium* (ed. Vera Rubin), University College of the West Indies, 1957.

friction between them in factories and in public places. Occasionally, an old quarrel leads to a fight in one of the Caribbean clubs in London. During the disturbances in 1958, it was sometimes said by West Indians from the smaller islands that the 'aggressive' Jamaicans had caused trouble. More frequently, there are complaints that middle class West Indians remain aloof from working class West Indians.

It is, however, not only the West Indian middle classes who are inclined to identify themselves with the 'host society', and especially with their image of the status holders in this society—of comfortable, cricket playing, well educated hosts. West Indians, in general, and those of the Federation territories, in particular, are conscious of their 'Britishness'; they have multiple loyalties—to their own social groups and institutions; to their individual islands; and to the 'mother country'. Their education has been focussed on Britain and her history; and it is their aspiration to resemble that model of the British of which they have heard so much in their schools at home. Their status as British citizens means a great deal to them. In any group of newcomers, there is always someone who sooner or later refers to his passport: "It says here I'm a 'Citizen of the United Kingdom and Colonies'." And West Indians point out that their migration is essentially the same as internal migration within the British Isles: it means no more than that some British people from the Caribbean territories travel to the United Kingdom to live and work. In terms of the law, which makes no distinction between those born in the British and in the West Indian islands, this definition is, of course, correct.

While West Indians emphasise their British connections, many of them are proud of their Negro or Indian origins and of their own indigenous traditions. There has been, and there still is, considerable discussion of the different strains in the culture of Negroes in the West Indies and other parts of the Western hemisphere. On the one hand, it is argued that Negroes have adopted the cultural forms of their former masters, and have thus aided the dispersion of European culture in the Americas. On the other hand, attention is drawn to the African heritage in modern Negro dances, music and religion; and there are those who speak of the emergence of a characteristic West Indian culture. But there are also people who recognise 'the West Indian dilemma'. They fear that the varied and contradictory cultural elements in the British Caribbean territories might create a cultural vacuum. They ask: "What is a West Indian?"

"It has become very popular for West Indian politicians to talk about a West Indian culture, but I have heard none of them come near to defining for the mass of people what this culture is. Some people evade answering this question by saying that we are a part of western civilisation, whilst others ask, is there a West Indian culture? . . .

The descendants of the slave owners who still have an honoured place in our society have taught the great majority of educated West Indians to believe that the millions of slaves were not important, it was from the masters that all the cultural blessings flowed, they claim.

But if we accept the masters' claims we find ourselves in a dilemma for his civilisation is dying whilst ours is now being born. . . .

Because of our unique experience we find ourselves in the mid-twentieth century not knowing who we are or what we are. When a man or woman says, 'I am a West Indian', he or she knows that this envelope of life with a West Indian address is faceless, a cipher. And the West Indian will only cease to be this when through a creative representation of the smell of his earth and the dreams of his people, he can discover a true image of himself.

The images by which our middle class live today are borrowed and spurious. There is the carbon-copy Englishman type—the black, brown and high-yellow man in search of a cultural hyssop with which to wash himself white. Then there is the slave boy dressed up in a diplomat's clothes image. And going down the scale of pseudo-sophistication, there is the 'Good Negro', the cipher shaped by a mission school philosophy which equates respectable servility with being 'cultured'. . . ."[2]

Duality

There are clearly two main elements in the ideological make-up of West Indians. They regard Britain (or rather an idealised Britain) as their model; in many ways, it is the image of her institutions and customs which they follow. But there is also identification with the problems and achievements of coloured peoples in the Caribbean and elsewhere, and the desire to assert their independent status. Both attitudes are held with varying emphasis and are subject to different permutations. If the first is exaggerated, it is indistinguishable from that of the 'Good Negro'. The second, in its extreme version, becomes colour prejudice in reverse, a form of dark skin chauvinism—in particular, when the pressure of 'white supremacy' makes it difficult, or even impossible, to maintain pro-colour loyalty without anti-white militancy.

Usually, in the orientation of individual West Indians, one of the two attitudes is predominant at any one stage. But these are not necessarily alternatives; most West Indians show, so to speak, 'secondary ideological characteristics', which become more noticeable

[2] From an article on 'What is a West Indian' by Jan Carew, *West Indian Gazette*, September 1959.

as their acquaintance with this country is extended. Their own latent ambivalence is accentuated by the ambivalent behaviour towards coloured people which they meet here, and by the contradictory treatment which they get. And so it is soon apparent that the two attitudes—the 'pro-British' and the 'pro-coloured' one—are by no means incompatible. On the contrary, West Indians in Britain are compelled by their situation here to combine the ingredients of both.

Thus some West Indian intellectuals, who are dedicated to the cause of integration and give a great deal of help to inter-racial clubs, are equally active in separate coloured organisations which advocate the claims, and express the views, of coloured people as such. There are also those who argue that the ultimate aim of black and white integration can only be achieved by establishing associations for coloured people, so as to give their members the experience which will eventually enable them to join white and mixed associations with self-confidence.[3] Again, in the discussion on the participation of West Indians in British political life, the dual attitudes are shown, though in this context these also appear in opposition to one another. It is said that the special needs and wishes of coloured people can be expressed, and have a chance of being heard, only when they have their own coloured representatives in local and central government. But there are West Indians who disagree with this view. On the contrary, they reply, we should stand as representatives of existing political parties, not as representatives of coloured people as a distinct group. Their argument is based not merely on the practical necessity of party-political support, but on the principle that it is wrong for coloured people to wear a special label and to keep apart in any way.

In a sense, West Indians, like everybody else, want the best of both worlds, and in fact see, or indeed get, the worst. They expect to join British social life, formal or informal, as a matter of course. It does not always happen in that way. If British 'natives' make no particular efforts to draw them into their own societies and clubs, West Indians are liable to think that they are being slighted. But if such efforts are made, the newcomers may feel that they are being singled out as a special category. They turn to English groups. At the same time, they turn to separate West Indian organisations, established by the coloured people for themselves. Yet they are resentful, and again with justification, when white people promote such separate activities or charities. That is viewed with mistrust; it represents patronage and segregation.

[3] See also Chapter V, Part 4.

Most minority groups experience similar dilemmas. They want to merge into their new environment; they also want to maintain their own identity. But in the case of the West Indians, there are additional complications—quite apart from that of colour, which tinges all their individual and collective problems. They look in two directions at once—backwards to their Caribbean homes and forward to their new life in Britain. For while some migrants move to this country to study or to work for a limited period, many of them come with the hope to settle here for good, or at least for an indefinite period. And whatever their intentions are, the West Indians do not regard them- selves merely as transients. Unlike many other newcomers, they start from the assumption that they belong to Britain; and they also arrive here as a heterogeneous collection of people without social cohesion and a common ideological focus. And then there is bitter disappointment when they realise that they are outsiders in this country, despite their 'Britishness'.

There is no doubt that this disillusionment is a genuine and a common experience of the migrants from the Caribbean, although it is not always clear what their actual anticipations were. Did they expect to be accepted without any hesitation and delay? Many of them say they were shocked to find prejudice here; some say they were surprised not to find more. They have, of course, been used to seeing tolerance and intolerance side by side. While they often speak with pride of the multi-racial society of the West Indies, they have been brought up in an environment where there have been until recently definite colour distinctions, the traces of which can still be seen.

Mutual Strangeness

Whatever their anticipations of the existence or non-existence of colour prejudice in this country may have been, West Indian migrants soon find that their image of Britain had been incomplete and even false. They had thought of Britain as a prosperous, fairly homo-geneous, middle class society, in terms of their own glimpses of such a society and of textbook instruction. Although by now a great deal of information has been passed back to the West Indies by reports in West Indian newspapers, by broadcasts, by pamphlets, by return-ing migrants and by letters home, the newcomers still have to learn from their own experience. It is strange for them to see white people, especially white women, doing hard manual work. They can hardly believe their eyes at first when they watch women sweeping the plat-forms at tube stations or London charladies cleaning the corridors of office buildings. They are surprised to find that so few of their neighbours go to church or belong to a religious organisation. They are amazed when English people show their ignorance of the Commonwealth, in general, and of the West Indies, in particular. They are upset not only because they discover that they themselves are ill-informed about Britain, but also because the British know even less about them.

Kindly enquiries about jungle conditions in the West Indies, or questions on whether they have ever worn any clothes or lived in houses before they came to England, hurt them as much as does the common belief that West Indian migrants eat Kit-E-Kat (a tinned food for cats); or that they are heathens; or that their native language is not English. Time after time they hear the standard phrase—"You speak English very well for a foreigner"; and they get a loud answer to a quiet question because English people so often believe that they have to raise their voices to make themselves understood to anyone who looks foreign. And there is also the frequent, indeed the usual, tendency of their 'hosts' (especially in working class areas) to assume that all coloured migrants are alike—for example, that they are all primitive and uneducated; and that they all come from Africa or Jamaica. All sorts of people, including those who are not prejudiced at all, and who are well disposed towards the migrants, make the same mistake, simply because they do not know any better. But the newcomers resent it strongly: no one wants to be deprived of his individuality; and to them such deprivation has a special meaning, not only because they themselves have such diverse backgrounds and local patriotisms and stress their class distinctions, but also because they feel the lack of reciprocity. 'We have been told so much about the British. Why have they not been told anything about us?' 'They mean so much to us; we do not mean anything to them.' The West Indians soon realise that they still have to learn a great deal about the real Britain and the British people.

Nowadays all sorts of efforts are made to prepare the migrants in advance; indeed, authors of pamphlets and broadcasters, in their desire to be realistic and informative, give an almost forbidding picture of a cold, inhospitable, pedantic, gloomy Britain, without gaiety and spontaneity. (Anyone who reads these pamphlets and still wants to come must have very compelling reasons.) But still the printed word and the voice on the radio are no substitute for the actual exposure to a different world.

There are numerous warnings. They were given, for example, in a recent series of thirty-two broadcasts by the B.B.C. Caribbean Service, in which many aspects of public and private life in England were described in detail, mainly by West Indians "who have already experienced the struggle of adaptation".[4]

"Dress for the Cold!" ("Are you prepared for this kind of cold climate with its icy winds, its sleet and snow?")
"Jobs are Scarce!" (". . . bear in mind that jobs are getting scarcer and scarcer. People have been here for eight months and have not worked yet—although they have been trying very hard and spending a lot of money going up and down.")
"Costs are High". "Be Punctual." ("In England people worship the clock.") "Don't Show Off." "Watch your Step." "Quiet Please." "Trouble with Neighbours." "Prejudice against the Foreigner."

The main theme is: "You are the Stranger."

"From the time you start to live in England it is as if a sea of white faces is always around you. . . .
Even if you settle in a district where there are others like yourself, you will find that your own people are in the minority. And also, you will be mixing with West Indians from all over the Caribbean, and you don't want me to tell you how different a Jamaican can be, for instance, from a Trinidadian.
However, your greater problem will be getting on with your white neighbours. One thing you must always keep in mind is that their knowledge of your country is much less than your knowledge of theirs. Whenever you are inclined to get angry or fly off the handle at some remark—or because a person stares at you for a long time—remember that English people are ignorant of your ways and habits and they may be just displaying a natural curiosity."

About making friends at church, it was said:

"Some people will go out of their way to try to make you comfortable. Many may believe that you have never gone to a real church before and they are trying to make you like what they think is your first experience. Do not insult them for this ignorance. They will learn better in time. . . ."
"If they smile with you in church and look away from your direction in the bus, it is just one of those things. . . ."
"Sometimes they decide to give you credit for being truly converted, and then they expect big things from you simply because they may have it in their heads that coloured people are heathens who break the hearts of saintly missionaries who try to convert them.
But whatever people think, the church remains a good place to go.

---

[4] These broadcasts were also published as a booklet, with the title *Going to Britain?*, by the British Broadcasting Corporation (in 1959). There are various pamphlets of this kind. One of the earlier, a duplicated one, prepared by the British Caribbean Welfare Service, said on the title page: "With High Hopes And With Bright Visions Of Work And Prosperity You Are Considering Counting Your Fare And Applying To The Travel Agent For A Passage To Britain But—*Before You Go To Britain*—Read This Pamphlet And Try To Understand The True Position Of Life As A Worker From The Caribbean In Britain."

You may find friends there—you almost certainly will—but, if you don't, you can get there a truer picture of what you are really up against."

Another broadcast by an English employer on "An employer's point of view" in a sense gave an object lesson (though not deliberately) of 'what the migrants are up against'.

"We wanted some people in my firm, so I thought I would try and help some West Indians. . . ."
"I was amazed, never having lived with West Indians, that all those we have employed have been honest. One always understood that these uneducated peoples would see something and they would like it and they would take it. This is probably a very ignorant outlook.
We have in our factory so many very valuable articles which are so easy to put in your pocket and take away. . . . Never a month goes by when we don't have trouble in that respect, but never once have we ever had any coloured person who was even under suspicion. They have never done anything like that. It is very agreeably surprising."[5]

It is the daily routine and ordinary mores, in particular, which are so strange to the newcomers. And every false step can cause trouble. The migrants cannot visualise the claustrophobic existence of a lodger in a furnished room, somewhere in London's vastness; and so they are warned of the discomforts and prohibitions which they have to expect.[6] English shopping habits have to be explained (". . . all food-stuffs are sold by weight and buyers do not get 'make-up' or braata on what they buy. . . . You will find that fruits have Christian and surnames here"). Again and again they are told: "When in England, do as the English do"; observe the social rules—in your lodgings, in public places, at your place of work. "Eat with your mates."

"Whatever you do, for heaven's sake, whether you drink tea or not, stop working and take your break with the men. . . ."
"Joining your Trade Union is the best and surest way of identifying yourself with the boys."

---

[5] *Going to Britain?*, *op. cit.*, pp. 9, 31, 66, 67, 75, 76.
[6] For example: "You do not have a wash-basin in the room. If you want to wash you have to go to the bathroom which is shared by everybody in the house. . . . Some houses do not even have a bath, and, of course, there are no showers in England, so you have to do the best you can at the wash-basin, and in winter it's cold work. . . . You also share the toilet with the rest of the house. . . ." "Some rooms are so dark that you have to have the electric light on all day. . . ." "You can always tell a tenant by his milk bottles." ". . . try to shut the front door softly. Front doors are a bother."
The migrants are told that they must not hang their wet clothes in the bath-room (". . . many landlords do not allow this and, in any case, your clothes may be stolen . . ."); that rent has to be paid weekly in advance; that gas-fires and gas-rings have hazards; and that when kitchens are shared "you might get into a row". *Ibid.*, pp. 21, 22, 24.

"Don't laugh at anything which looks peculiar to you. By and by you will discover there is a reason for behaviour which seems strange to you."[7]

Another recent pamphlet, *Living in Nottingham*, published by the Consultative Committee for the Welfare of Coloured People in Nottingham, also indicates in concise terms the many matters with which the newcomers are unfamiliar. The pamphlet tells them:

"Do not be afraid to ask a policeman to help you if you are in any difficulty.
You have probably come from a country where you knew all of your neighbours and had many friends.
Here in Nottingham, although you may live in a house with many other people and families, you may find it difficult at first to make friends, or even to get to know your neighbours. This is because English people tend to make friends slowly.
Do not try to force a friendship. . . .
Do not play your radio or gramophone too loudly. . . .
Do not make any unnecessary noise in the passageways between the rooms or on the stairs. . . .
As soon as you arrive you must do three things:

   1. Go to the Employment Exchange.
   2. Go to the Ministry of Pensions and National Insurance.
   3. Register with a doctor."

"Do not wait for a shop steward in a factory or someone else from a trade union to approach you before trying to join.
Once you have joined a trade union do not be too shy to attend meetings and to play your part in the work of the Union."

The pamphlet describes the functions of the various social and health services and of trade unions; it lists their addresses and also those of clubs and churches. It explains the system of wage payments; income tax; how to bank money ("only keep enough money with you for your daily needs"); compulsory education; voluntary services; where to get married; the habit of queuing and the reasons for it. And on the back of the cover it asks:

"Won't
You
Join
The
Queue?"

---

[7] *Ibid.*, pp. 29, 30, 33, 59, 61, 62. Of course, the migrants are exposed to physical as well as to social hazards. Thus they have to be warned that the change of climate might cause sickness—the "common cold"; chilblains; skin troubles—and that this is likely to happen particularly during the first six months, before they are entitled to sickness benefits. (National Insurance contributions have to be paid for six months before benefits can be drawn.)

Many of these explanations are essential in view of the different institutions and folkways of the West Indies. Policemen there are regarded as people to be avoided. Trade unions in the West Indies have only recently become accepted representative organisations. The West Indian newcomer has had no previous experience of the services of the Welfare State; he has to learn to take them for granted, and to use them properly. And, of course, the minor conventions, the more intangible distinctions in manners and language, matter even more. It takes longer to become acclimatised to them; unless they are made explicit, they are bound to cause mutual annoyance and offence. It is a pity that the explanations are one-sided: it would be useful if the people of London (and other British cities) would get similar pamphlets or broadcasts on the background and customs of the coloured newcomers.

Misunderstandings

Some misunderstandings are unimportant. "No please" used by a West Indian seems merely strange; but the use of "presently" to mean "at once" has led to quarrels in factories. The migrants are told: "You have got to get accustomed to hearing certain expressions like 'I work like a black' or 'Nigger in the wood pile'. These are . . . not meant to be insulting, so do not be over-sensitive. . . ." Are they getting used to these terms? It is easier to follow the advice not to use West Indian swear words. "If you have to swear, use the English ones. West Indian ones are not popular."[8]

Learie Constantine, the well-known West Indian cricketer, in his book *Colour Bar*, written after he had lived in Britain for twenty-five years, says:

> "Like most other coloured people, if I am introduced to a white person, I have learned now to keep my hand at my side until a white hand is plainly offered to me; a good many times of holding my hand out and having it ignored has taught me what I must call 'Negro-in-England' manners. At first, when that happened, I used to feel very hurt, but now I understand that it is often no more than a mark of *gaucherie* on the part of the person who will not shake hands, not a deliberate affront at all."[9]

No doubt he did meet affronts, deliberate and thoughtless ones, but it is also true that handshaking is not common in this country. Indeed, some people in Britain now make a point of shaking hands

[8] *Ibid.*, p. 59.
[9] Learie Constantine, *Colour Bar*, London, 1954, p. 67.

with the coloured people they meet, though they would not do so when they greet white acquaintances.

West Indians note that however friendly they may be with their mates at work, they are usually not invited to their homes. Although habits vary in different parts of the country, in most areas in Britain it is not a working class custom to entertain friends at home. The front parlour is reserved for the visits of relatives.

Some migrants complain that they are stared at; others say that they are ignored—their neighbours on the same landing may never say a word to them. When a coloured man sees that white passengers remain standing on a tube train although there is an empty seat next to him, he suspects that he is being shunned. Occasionally, this may be so. But in any case, it is usual for people on London tube trains to remain standing (for short journeys) while seats are free, irrespective of the colour of seated passengers.

As West Indians are bound to be unaware of the whole range and diversity of British mores, and in particular of class and local differences in behaviour, they may imagine that they are treated coldly or snubbed because of their colour, when this was not intended, or when they were treated like other foreigners in Britain, or like members of another social class. Despite all warnings, they have come here with visions of the 'mother country', of a closely knit, friendly society of gentlefolk. They are unprepared for the symptoms of alienation, found in any large city in an advanced industrialised economy, and also for the peculiar distinctions and contradictions in British institutions and manners. Moving about from one social group to another, or even from one working class district to another, they expect similarities of social forms and can so easily draw the wrong conclusion when the differences are obvious. Mr. Jones, the grocer, may seem curt simply because his expression of friendliness is unlike that of Mr. O'Connell, the building worker. The ways of life of the working classes of Poplar and Shepherd's Bush are not identical; Notting Dale and nearby Bayswater are two worlds apart. And then there is the quick, to the outsider incomprehensible, transition—of which most Englishmen are capable—from a warm personal approach to a cold impersonal withdrawal. There is also the characteristic English talent for maintaining social distance between themselves and people from another social class or another country. The West Indian, like other newcomers, must often ask himself: "The English, are they human?"

It is all very baffling. But unlike other foreigners, the West Indian regards himself as British; he wants to adapt himself; and he is supposed to conform wherever he goes, travelling from the Mile End

Road to Paddington, and from there to Marble Arch. A great deal is expected from him, and far less is given in return. He makes far more effort in understanding the British than the British make in understanding him and his background. They are easily irritated by his voice and his clothes—especially when both are loud—by his love of music and dancing and by his sociability. They are even more upset because many London girls (of all kinds) like these very qualities —a welcome contrast to the drab monotony of brown brick and grey sky. It is not surprising that West Indian Londoners find genuine comradeship with white Londoners more freely in the 'shady' streets of North Kensington than in the respectable working class quarters.

When the East Ender goes to the West End, his manner is taken for granted as a matter of class distinction. But when the West Indian from the East End goes to the West End, his similar working class manner appears far more peculiar and alien: he is a coloured man without a cockney accent. When he is poor—or when he lives frugally, as he tends to do, and saves his money so that he can send it home—he is regarded as a liability. When he spends his money freely, or when he has become prosperous and rides around in his motor car, he is scorned as a dark *nouveau riche*. It is very difficult for him to do anything right. It is even more difficult for him to know whether he is doing anything right.

As he seldom knows what to expect in any particular situation, he may tend to aggregate all the minor frictions and suspect everyone of being prejudiced. An African, an Indian or a Pakistani in this country can find refuge in his own community, in his own religion and language. The West Indian, who has no distinct culture of his own, can easily develop a nagging anxiety complex which works itself out in a series of complaints. When he 'gets his cards', he is inclined to attribute his dismissal to discrimination. When a shopkeeper takes a long time to serve him, this, too, is regarded as a sign of prejudice. When anyone is gruff or abrupt, the dark man assumes that this is a reaction to his colour. And, of course, his anxiety complex gets worse according to the amount of misunderstanding, unmistakable coldness and prejudice which he meets. The migrants know very well that they have a chip on the shoulder; they talk about it; they try to get rid of it; but there are not many who are able to do so.

'Integration'

"You've never seen a chip as big as the one I had on my shoulder", said the man from Trinidad. "I was at the Labour

Exchange, I'd just been demobbed, and I saw that my file was marked *Coloured*, and I went mad. I got out my Air Force Pay Book and threw it at the clerk. 'This isn't marked coloured', I shouted. 'No one in the Air Force cared whether I was coloured or not, why should you?' That sort of thing kept on happening. I went for a job once at a factory, and when I walked towards the personnel office I heard some music, Ole Man River. I remember humming it, because I thought I'd get the job. But I didn't, and later I heard that when coloured people came there for jobs they'd play that tune to warn everybody.

Then I went to Tiger Bay and Liverpool. There were some race riots in Liverpool in 1948; everyone has forgotten them. We all got pushed around by the police. Ex-Palestine Police. I did all sorts of odd jobs, living in rotten rooms, and I used to write home to say how well I was doing. They're lower middle class and respectable. Then I did some welfare work with coloured people, and after that I managed to do a social science course.

That's when I lost the chip on my shoulder. I don't mean just being a student and all that. It was afterwards when I couldn't get a job and I should have been frustrated and fed up. I went to the N.A.B. and the chap was very curt. He offered me some money; it wasn't enough, so I said, 'Look here', very politely, 'you're supposed to come to my house and see my conditions.' And I quoted the National Assistance Act and all the regulations. That shook him. It all ended happily. We became quite friendly.

Of course the ordinary migrant isn't in that position. I got a welfare job, meeting parties of migrants and fixing them up with jobs. Then I got married to an English girl. I'd read all the reports about the horrors of mixed marriages in England, and when I went to meet her family that old chip came back again. I was expecting to be snubbed or thrown out or something. But nothing happened. You know man, I was almost disappointed. All tensed up for a fight, and nothing. Or rather they made me welcome.

When my wife had a baby none of them asked was it black. Nowadays I don't even notice if people stare at me in the street when I'm out with her. I mean, I don't know if they do or not. Yes Sir, I'm integrated."[10]

[10] An extract from one of our interviews. Although this is not an unusual story, its 'happy ending' is not necessarily a typical one. The life of coloured professional people, of intellectuals and of students in Britain is by no means free from problems, as shown, for example, in A. T. Carey's book, *Colonial Students*, London, 1956. Even so, the hardships of the coloured middle class in this country are far more limited in scope, and less likely to have cumulative results, than those of the coloured working class. Moreover, within most professional circles and especially

Our friend from Trinidad knows the score. For it seems that on the whole middle class West Indians are comparatively fortunate: they live here in a fairly homogeneous, protected environment. Working class West Indians—or rather those who have working class occupations and lodgings in this country—have greater difficulty in becoming 'integrated' and—perhaps for that reason—they also tend to retain a stronger patriotic attachment to their territories of birth.[11]

A West Indian doctor or social worker, a journalist, a jazz player or a student spends at least a part of his day in London among people who are not strange to him, and to whom he is neither a novelty nor an alien. (It is when he goes outside his immediate group that he becomes colour conscious again.) His colleagues do not regard him *a priori* as a threat to their status. He shares their interests; he speaks their 'language'; his manners, his clothes and his routine are the same as theirs (or just as varied as theirs). And if he does seem different, he may be accepted for that very reason. He is often in a circle where it is the non-conformists who conform; where individuality or eccentricity (if only of a particular kind) is welcome.

It is not so with the West Indian manual labourer. The people among whom he lives and works do not correspond to his previous image—an idealised image—of the well-to-do British. To them, he is a foreigner. The sense of mutual strangeness is acute and harassing; and it persists. For in an atmosphere of insecurity, any outsider is a competitor. In the confined quarters of working class districts, there is not much room for any deviation from the norm; codes of behaviour have to be precise and tend to be parochial; work and home are kept in separate compartments. The newcomer is expected to obey the varying specific rules: if he adjusts to one group (or one district), he is regarded as maladjusted in another.

In any case, it is often difficult for him to identify himself readily with the folk and folkways around him. As most West Indians who migrate do not belong to the lowest ranks in their own society, many

---

in the universities, there do not appear to be nowadays any serious difficulties in the social relationships between coloured and white people. In that respect, recent experience certainly does not tally with the circumstances reported in an unpublished, but frequently quoted, study by Miss V. E. Junod on the "Coloured 'Social Elite' in London" in 1952.

[11] Of course, these generalisations need to be qualified: there are working class migrants who participate freely in British activities; among the middle class there are also those who emphasise first and foremost the separate identity of Negroes or West Indians *per se*. Moreover, as has been said already, the various loyalties—to coloured people, to the home territories and to Britain—cannot be sharply separated from one another. They are fluid; and they tend to coalesce.

of them had never thought of themselves as members of the working
class before they arrived in this country. Men who were employers
in Port of Spain have become factory hands in London; women who
had their own servants have become kitchenmaids. Although their
incomes in this country are higher than before, their standards of
living have deteriorated in some respects. If they are looked down
upon here—and it is said, for example, that they were probably used
to living in pigsties[12]—they might well be inclined to look down
upon those who regard them as inferior.

It does not take the migrants long to discard their optimistic text-
book notions of the British. Apparently, however, it takes many
British people far longer to discard their pessimistic, though ambivalent, stereotype notions of coloured people—or at least to make it
plain that they have done so. In response, the West Indians adopt
new images of the British, which are far less complimentary than
their previous ones. Thus they, too, tend to withdraw behind a screen
of uncertainty. Here and there, mutual strangeness has been modified by personal acquaintance, but it has been an uneasy *rapproche-
ment*. In general, the barriers between 'natives' and newcomers,
erected by the stereotypes on both sides, are still maintained. And
wherever that happens, both sets of *idées fixes* (or suspicions of *idées
fixes*) become, in turn, still more rigid, and thus the barriers between
white and coloured become still higher. It is an unhappily familiar
sequence.

2. ATTITUDES TOWARDS COLOURED PEOPLE

In a recent novel, a long-established West Indian explains the facts
of life in Britain to a newcomer:

> "Since I come 'ere I never met a single English person who 'ad any
> colour prejudice. Once, I walked the whole length of a street looking
> for a room, and everyone told me that he or she 'ad no prejudice
> against coloured people. It was the neighbour who was stupid. If we
> could only find the 'neighbour' we could solve the entire problem.
> But to find 'im is the trouble! Neighbours are the worst people to live
> beside in this country."[13]

---

[12] This kind of remark can be heard also in places where it would not be expected. It was reported, for example, that at a meeting of the Kensington Borough Council, at which the conditions of a 'slum' street with white and coloured
tenants in North Kensington were discussed, one of the aldermen had said: "If
the standards of these coloured people were low there were no standards by which
they could judge—they probably accepted a pigsty as usual and they were des-
perate for homes." *The Kensington News*, April 8th, 1960.

[13] A. G. Bennett, *Because They Know Not*, London, 1959, p. 22.

Ambivalence

The observation that English people are hypocrites in matters of race relations is commonly made by West Indians living in this country. Those who shut doors to them often do so with a smile and an apology. West Indians cannot understand why newspapers, which are liberal in their editorial attitude towards coloured people, still accept and print discriminatory housing advertisements. Nor does it make sense to them when a firm which employs coloured people with success nevertheless adopts a quota system; or when men who are glad to work with them reject them as neighbours; or when it is said that the 'public' would not like to be in close contact with coloured people—white customers would not wish to be served by coloured shop assistants—though white patients are glad to be looked after by coloured nurses. Such inconsistent behaviour can be regarded as examples of hypocrisy, but this is only a short-hand description, not an explanation of its causes and symptoms.

As colour prejudice needs to be viewed in relation to the history and changing traditions of the society in which it occurs, it is not especially helpful to measure British tolerance or intolerance by the yardstick of apartheid in South Africa or segregation in the United States, North and South. Britain has not had a large coloured population whose history has conditioned both black and white; attitudes towards people of a different pigment have not been institutionalised and hardened, either negatively or positively. Britain's colonial and colour problems have been abroad; and to most citizens, they have been very remote. There has been, and there still is, a dichotomy between attitudes towards 'colour' in the United Kingdom itself and in its territories overseas.

In the past, the treatment of an Indian, an African or a West Indian in this country was determined less by his colour *per se* than by his social status. It was the Sikh pedlar, the Lascar seaman or the West Indian labourer who was regarded by those who had colonial experience and associations as a 'coloured alien'. The Indian Brahmin or the African Prince was accepted in white 'high society' in England. But the Indian or African who was welcome at Harrow, Cambridge and the Inns of Court (and who noticed less colour prejudice than antisemitism in such circles) was not admitted to the white men's clubs in India or Africa. The same class of people (sometimes even the same individuals) who were his schoolmates and colleagues in England were his masters and his gaolers in his own country.[14]

[14] These well known contradictions are very clearly illustrated, for example, in several passages of Jawaharlal Nehru's *An Autobiography*, London, 1936.

Nowadays this contradiction is beginning to be reversed, just as the flow of migration is reversed. Fewer white Englishmen make their careers as administrators of dependent territories; more coloured people arrive to work in England. The old ideology of colonialism with its connotations of prejudice, on its way out in the new Commonwealth, is becoming more noticeable in the 'mother country': multi-racial harmony is more a theme for export than for import. While denunciation of apartheid in South Africa is universal in Britain, denunciation of symptoms of discrimination next door is rather sporadic and equivocal. And there are also those who say that they abhor segregation of coloured people abroad, but do not wish to practise integration at home.

It is this dichotomy in British attitudes towards coloured people which helps to explain the ambiguities in race relations in this country. And as the old and the new version of the dichotomy still co-exist to some extent, confusion is worse confounded. Most Englishmen and women are not as yet used to regarding 'racial harmony' as their own personal problem, but they are used to 'passing the buck'—in the earlier period, they were inclined to disregard the problem elsewhere; more recently, they tend to ask someone else overseas to solve it. This was not so obvious so long as contacts with coloured people in this country were infrequent. But in the changed situation in Britain and in the world, it has become very evident that responsibility for prejudice and discrimination is shifted from the self to others—from the landlady to her lodgers or neighbours; from the employer to his workers or customers; from the opinion leaders to the 'teddy boys'; from the white to the coloured.

The equivocal approach to race relations (the frequent statement—'I dislike discrimination but I am obliged to practise it') is so common just because it is by no means simply an alibi. It contains an element of sincerity. British ambivalence towards coloured people, minority groups and foreigners, in general, is not merely a product of the conflicting attitudes of different social groups; it exists within each group, in official and in unofficial public opinion; and it is also reflected in the minds of individuals. Of course, most societies and individuals have 'split' minds of some kind or another. But the British blend of tolerance and intolerance is a special one; and there is the difficulty, moreover, that neither the society as a whole nor the individuals are by and large as yet clearly aware of this ambivalence; its serious moral and political consequences tend to be ignored.

Ambivalence on matters of race relations is another heritage of British imperial history. For the role of empire builders and administrators was not, and could not have been, merely one of harsh impersonal authority over colonials, of master to servant; it also had to include—in varying doses—some ingredients of a family relationship in order to be maintained. This latter attitude, especially, was noticeable when people from distant countries of the Empire came to Britain. Here at home they were regarded as a special species of dark visitors—strange, exotic, intriguing, sometimes comic or even sinister. But they were also looked upon with pride as being members of the Empire, as symbols of its far-reaching power—with a pride which sometimes developed into affection, paternalistic or fraternal.

Most coloured visitors remained foreigners nevertheless. And in general, the British attitude to foreigners tends to be one of superiority towards an inferior being. A person with an unusual name or accent may in law be a British subject, who has all the rights of equal citizenship. But he is not really regarded as British; he does not in fact belong.

While there is this British aloofness towards foreigners, there is also a tradition of tolerance towards deviant or minority groups—religious, racial and political. Tolerance has increasingly become more explicit; nowadays it is supposed to be an integral part of the official outlook of British society. This was shown clearly in the reactions to the 'riots' in 1958, and to the murder of a West Indian in 1959. 'How could it happen here? It must not happen here!'[15] That was the theme of most responsible spokesmen. (Perhaps they had forgotten that it had happened before and not so long before.)

There are thus contradictory elements in the attitudes of British people towards coloured people living in this country. There is the widespread assumption of the inferiority of foreigners; there is also widespread tolerance. And coloured foreigners, in particular, evoke emotions both of animosity and friendliness. They are rejected in one place and accepted in another—sometimes by the same person. (Or they might be barred one day and admitted on the next.)

Guilt Feelings

Indeed, colour prejudice has two faces: discrimination works both ways. While there are apparently few people in any social stratum in Britain who are genuinely free from prejudice, there is also, so far, only a minority who are dogmatic and self-righteous in demanding

---

[15] These actual words, or similar ones, became almost a cliché in this context. For example, it was said by the Government speaker, the Earl of Perth, in a House of Lords debate: "The recent disturbances have shocked us all out of a spirit of complacency and led us to examine what we are doing on the problem of colour prejudice. Broadly, I think we felt that such things could not happen here." *Parliamentary Debates*, H.o.L., 19th November, 1958, col. 674.

'Keep Britain White'. Just because colour prejudice is not quite proper and yet so diffused, it tends to get reversed. It evokes individual and social guilt feelings: the desire to make amends; to compensate for anti-colour discrimination by using terms of pro-colour guardianship. Prejudiced tendencies set off overprotective tendencies; coloured people are pushed aside or treated with kid gloves; and sometimes they are pushed aside with kid gloves.

But while the antibodies engendered by colour prejudice soften the symptoms of the malady, they do not cure it: in fact, in some respects, they aggravate it and prolong it. The coloured people are blamed, consciously or sub-consciously, for the guilt feelings which follow from prejudice and discrimination. And any suspicions of pro-colour bias accentuate anti-colour bias. Indeed, such suspicions are the core of a new rapidly growing folklore: time after time one can hear, especially in blighted districts and among grumbling adolescents, that it is the 'blacks' who are allowed to jump the housing queue, who work less, earn more and are subject to far fewer criticisms than 'our own people'; who are not rebuked for their misdemeanours; and who are, in general, the coddled favourites of all those in authority. Time after time, the same theme is played up in fascist and semi-fascist propaganda. Any explanation of the actual facts—any attempt to clarify the folklore and to oppose the racist agitation—is regarded merely as another example of unfair preferential treatment of the 'darkies'.

It is unlikely that this vicious circle sequence will be broken so long as the whole subject of multi-racialism in Britain is treated like a 'security risk'; so long as the all-pervasive ambivalence towards colour is kept concealed behind a parade of polite phrases and manners.

The Law

The operation of the law reflects, and accentuates, the current confusion on this subject. In some respects, the law is quite clear: Commonwealth citizens have all the rights of British subjects; they are not second-class citizens before the law.[16] Coloured people do not have to report changes of address to any authority. They can become established civil servants on the same terms as other British citizens.[17] Like the others, too, subject to the same qualifications,

[16] The West Indian's status as "a citizen of the United Kingdom and Colonies" was defined in the British Nationality Act, 1948.

[17] There are some established Civil Service posts—mainly in the Service departments and also in some other branches where security is involved—to which

they can vote, and they can—and do—stand as candidates at local and Parliamentary elections. There was a coloured candidate in a London metropolitan borough at the municipal elections in May 1959; a coloured West Indian was the Labour Party's candidate in a London constituency at the Parliamentary elections in October 1959.

There is, of course, no legal bar to a mixed marriage. Nor is there a definite taboo. (A dance scene on television, in which a white girl had a coloured partner, has provoked a spate of hostile comments. But in London, a white girl and a coloured man can appear on the stage together in love scenes without attracting special attention—as has happened in two plays produced in 1959, *Hot Summer's Night*, by Ted Willis, and *A Taste of Honey*, by Shelagh Delaney.)

But while the law does not single out coloured people for special treatment, it leaves the way open to expressions of prejudice and to some forms of discrimination.[18] There is no law which allows discrimination; there is also no law which defines it and prohibits it explicitly. It is not an offence, for example, to publish discriminatory advertisements; to deny employment or promotion to coloured people; or to refuse to let accommodation to them. In fact, one common type of restrictive practice—that of covenants in leases which prohibit the sub-letting or assignment of property to coloured persons—could apparently in certain circumstances be upheld by the courts. It seems that such prohibitions may be enforceable in law if they are quite explicit and precisely define the class of persons against whom they are directed.[19]

It is not illegal, moreover, to make abusive statements about coloured people—verbally or in print. The law, as it stands now, is concerned with defamation of individuals, but not, except in very

people born outside the United Kingdom are not generally appointed. The admission rules vary: in some cases, the nationality and birthplace of the applicant's parents and the length of his residence in the United Kingdom are also taken into account. Colour and race, however, are not relevant criteria. While a coloured migrant would not be admitted to one of the more exclusive posts—and would for this purpose be in the same position as a naturalised British subject—a coloured man born in the United Kingdom would be eligible if he had the appropriate qualifications.

[18] See also Chapter V, Part 1, on proposals to introduce legislation against discrimination and group defamation.

[19] However, a restrictive covenant which bans not only coloured sub-tenants but also all coloured visitors to the premises could probably not be enforced. (An example of a prohibition of the latter kind was reported in an article in *The Guardian*, May 17, 1960, in which the law relating to such matters was discussed. In this particular case, the clause was later withdrawn by the landlord.)

rare cases of seditious libel, with defamation of groups.[20] The current position, and the reasons for the reluctance to make group defamation illegal, were summarised by the Committee on the Law of Defamation in 1948.

> "A considerable body of evidence has been tendered to us dealing with what may conveniently be described as Group Defamation—that is to say, false statements vilifying not identifiable individuals, but groups or classes of persons distinguishable by race, colour, creed or vocation. Under the existing law, such statements cannot form the subject of civil proceedings for libel or slander. If they are made with intent to incite persons to commit any crime, to create a disturbance, to raise discontent or disaffection among His Majesty's subjects, or to promote ill-will and hostility between different classes of such subjects, they may amount to the crime of seditious libel; but prosecutions for seditious libel, save in the most flagrant cases, may easily present the appearance of political prosecutions which the English tradition tends to view with disfavour.
> The most widespread and deplorable examples of Group Defamation at the date at which we commenced our sittings were directed against the Jews; but complaints were also made to us of unfounded vilification of particular trades. It is, we think, symptomatic of Group Defamation that the subject matter varies with current internal and external political trends. Much as we deplore all provocation to hatred or contempt for bodies or groups of persons with its attendant incitement to violence, we cannot fail to be impressed by the danger of curtailing free and frank—albeit, hot and hasty—political discussion and criticism. No suggestion has been made to us for altering the existing law which would avoid the prohibition of perfectly proper criticisms of particular groups or classes of persons. The law of seditious libel still exists as an ultimate sanction and we consider that the law as it stands affords as much protection as can safely be given.
> We do not, therefore, recommend any general change in the existing law to deal with Group Defamation."[21]

Legal sanctions can be invoked against those whose words or behaviour in public places are intended, or are likely, to provoke a

[20] "A class of persons cannot be defamed as a class, nor can an individual be defamed by a general reference to the class to which he belongs. A plaintiff may be able to show, however, that, though the statement reflected on a class of persons, he was the person aimed at and defamed; in such a case an action will lie at his instance. If the judge holds that the words complained of are reasonably capable of being understood to refer to the plaintiff, the further question, whether they do refer to the plaintiff, is a question for the jury." Halsbury's *The Laws of England*, 3rd Edition, Vol. 24, London, 1958, p. 5.

[21] *Report of the Committee on the Law of Defamation*, Cmd. 7536, London, H.M.S.O., 1948, paras. 30–32. The Committee had a rather long lifetime: it was appointed in March 1939; its meetings were suspended during the war and resumed in May 1945. The evidence on group defamation was collected before coloured people had become one of the main targets of racialism in England.

breach of the peace;[22] and also against those who deny or violate any rights founded in the common law. But apparently the context and motives of such offences are largely irrelevant in the eyes of the law: colour prejudice is not necessarily a material or an 'unreasonable' factor. It does not matter much, it seems, whether an innkeeper says: 'Get out, nigger'; or 'So sorry Sir, we have no room.' The law is concerned with the questions whether the hotel had an obligation to provide accommodation or not; whether it had any reasonable ground for not doing so; and also whether the 'nigger' or 'Sir' who was turned away suffered inconvenience or damage as the result of the refusal to give him a room. It is not clear whether colour prejudice could be regarded by the courts as a 'reasonable' ground for such a refusal.

Thus the famous case of Constantine v. Imperial London Hotels Ltd in 1944, which arose when the plaintiff, the well known West Indian cricketer, was refused accommodation, provided no definite precedent for the illegality of colour discrimination, despite the fact that there were aggravating circumstances—at least in terms of commonsense, if not of common law.

Learie Constantine was at that time a civil servant, the local welfare officer of the Ministry of Labour on Merseyside. He came to London to play in an international cricket match at Lords.

> "When rooms were booked at the . . hotel for Mr. Constantine and his wife and daughter, the question was asked: 'Have you any objection to coloured people?' and the answer received was 'No'."

It is depressing enough to learn that this question had to be asked. But that was only the prelude. When Mr. Constantine arrived at the hotel, with his superior officer from the Ministry of Labour and the manager of the cricket match, objections were raised in an abusive manner. In reviewing the evidence in the High Court, Mr. Justice Birkett, who gave judgment, was reported to have said:

> "He was satisfied that the manageress of the hotel was grossly insulting in her references to Mr. Constantine. It was enough to say that from the outset the manageress made it clear . . . that Mr. Constantine could not stay in the hotel; that she used the word 'nigger' and was very offensive; and that she declined to receive the party and refused to listen to reason."

Mr. Constantine and his party went to another hotel. The defendants conceded ". . . that *although*[23] he was a man of colour no ground existed on which [they] were entitled to refuse to receive and lodge him."

[22] Public Order Act, 1936, Section 5.
[23] My italics.

N.—9

The plaintiff won his case on the facts that the innkeepers had refused to receive and lodge him "without any just cause or excuse". Mr. Justice Birkett ". . . reviewed the authorities at length, and said that there was no express authority to guide him. He held that the action was maintainable without proof of special damage, since the plaintiff's right, founded in the common law, had been violated and denied, and in those circumstances the law afforded him a remedy. He (his Lordship) had been urged to award exemplary damages because of the circumstances in which the denial of the plaintiff's rights took place. He did not feel on the authorities that he could do that, having regard to the exact nature of the action, and he therefore gave judgment for Mr. Constantine for nominal damages only, which he assessed at five guineas."[24]

Although the High Court has rebuked one hotel, there is apparently still "no express authority" to guide the conduct of those innkeepers, publicans and managers of dance halls who are inclined to practise discrimination. The judgment in the Constantine case has not prevented hotels from turning away coloured people: such incidents are occasionally reported in the Press.[25]

As the law ignores the existence of discrimination, there has been a good deal of uncertainty about its application to colour bars imposed by dance halls and public houses. Uncertainty, however, diminished to some extent when it became known, in the summer of 1958, that the licence of a ballroom in Wolverhampton had been

[24] *The Times*, Law Report, June 29, 1944.

[25] There was, for example, a report on a similar incident in July 1958 when a London hotel refused to accept three American coloured ladies, who had booked their rooms several months in advance, and asked them to take alternative accommodation. This case was the subject of two questions in the House of Commons. The President of the Board of Trade was asked whether, as "the Minister responsible for tourism", he did not feel "that he should take some steps to prevent the colour bar spreading to London hotels or, at any rate, express his personal detestation of the practice". The President of the Board of Trade replied that he very much deplored discrimination on grounds of colour. The Attorney-General was asked what action he proposed to take "against the management of a London hotel from breach of its common law duty to provide accommodation for travellers . . .?". The written reply was "None". (*Parliamentary Debates*, H.o.C., 31st July 1958, cols. 1584 and 197.) A more general question on the same subject was raised a few months later when the President of the Board of Trade was asked why he had advised the British Travel and Holidays Association to reject a motion condemning the colour bar in British hotels. The President of the Board of Trade repeated his previous statement that "Her Majesty's Government strongly deplores the practice of racial discrimination" and added "but this does not seem to be a matter in which hotels should be disciplined in the manner suggested. An hotel keeper has certain obligations under common law to receive guests, and it is for the courts to decide whether he fulfils them". (*Parliamentary Debates*, H.o.C., 13th November 1958, cols. 547, 48.)

renewed, despite local objections to the ballroom's colour bar.[26] Whilst previously many publicans and managers of similar establishments had thought that it was illegal to refuse admission to coloured people or to segregate them, they then realised that this was not necessarily so. In fact, the licensing justices can take complaints about discriminatory practices into account when they consider the renewal of a licence, but their interpretations of the importance of such complaints for their decision is varied; and there are, moreover, no specific rules of conduct for the managers of licensed premises. The latter have considerable discretion in their dealings with customers, white and coloured. Thus there are managers of licensed premises who have maintained an open colour bar for a number of years without interference or penalty.[27] On the other hand, when a licensing authority has quite plainly expressed its disapproval of discriminatory practices, this has a 'deterrent' effect. Thus occasionally one hears of a public house where tolerance was introduced because the publican had good reason to assume, or was told, that his licence would not be renewed if he continued to close his doors to coloured people.[28]

[26] At the session of the licensing justices, at which the renewal of the ballroom's licence was considered, the licensee was reported to have said that "he had been instructed by the management to refuse admission to coloured people as a matter of policy". The application for renewal was opposed by a number of people. Among them were the M.P. for North East Wolverhampton, a member of the Wolverhampton Town Council, the Secretary of the Wolverhampton Branch of the International Friendship League, and the Secretary of the Wolverhampton Free Church Council. The chairman of the licensing justices, in announcing the decision to renew the licence, was reported to have stated that "some intelligent things had been said in the witness-box and [that] he hoped the management would take notice." (*The Times*, June 18, 1958.) The new management which took over the ballroom in February 1959 lifted the colour bar. (See also p. 81.)

[27] A case in point is a public house in St. Pancras.

[28] Although—or just because—the law with respect to such matters is uncertain and customs are so varied, it is often argued that no special legal ban against discrimination in inns and licensed premises is needed. This argument was again expressed, and the current legal position was summarised, by the Government spokesman in a lengthy debate on this subject in the House of Lords in 1958. "Innkeepers are under a Common Law obligation (expressly preserved by the Act) to provide refreshment and accommodation for travellers unless there are reasonable grounds in any instance for not doing so . . . whether any particular refusal to provide refreshment and accommodation is reasonable can only be decided by the courts. However, the licensee of a public house, or other premises (not being an inn) licensed for the sale of intoxicating liquor is entitled, if he wishes, to refuse to serve anyone—so the courts have held. Similarly he has an occupier's ordinary Common Law right of arbitrarily requesting any person to leave and of ejecting him upon refusal. When the renewal of a licence is being considered, however, the licensing justices are entitled to, and do, take into

Occasionally, a coloured man nominally breaks the law because he protests against a colour bar, which is not illegal. This anomaly was brought out sharply in one judgment that should be remembered. It was given in a case which happened in Liverpool in 1943. A West Indian (Mr. George Alexander McGuire Roberts) had twice been refused admission to a dance hall—first, when he was in mufti, and again later when he wore his Home Guard uniform. In protest, he stayed away from Home Guard parades—because, as he said, he had been insulted while wearing the uniform. He was fined £5 for failing to attend Home Guard duties without reasonable excuse and appealed against the fine.

In giving judgment on appeal, the Recorder of Liverpool, Mr. E. G. Hemmerde, K.C., said that:

> ". . . the case raised in an acute form a question they would have to face hereafter . . . he did not understand how in the British Empire, with so many coloured people as its citizens, anything in the way of a colour bar could exist or ever be allowed to exist by any Government that was worth the name of Government. People came over here to risk their lives on behalf of what they proudly call the Mother Country, and he considered it impertinence for any country to accept the aid of coloured people from any part of the world and then to say 'Our laws do not enable us to deal with you on terms of complete equality'."

The Judge continued:

> "Mr. Roberts is breaking the law when, having come here to serve his country, he refuses to be insulted. The fact that he is guilty should be more the subject for laughter than anything else. I cannot allow Mr. Roberts' appeal on the question of principle, because the law was against him. But where the law is ridiculous one might as well draw attention to the fact. The fine of £5 will be reduced to one farthing and Mr. Roberts will be allowed the costs of the appeal."[29]

While the law is in a sense 'colour blind', the courts are not. Pronouncements from the bench are varied, and indeed on occasion in sharp contrast to one another.

---

account the manner in which the premises serve the public, and it is open to anyone interested to object to the renewal on the ground of the licensee's conduct towards some of his customers. Therefore, so far as the general conduct of licensed premises is concerned, there seems to be no need for amendment of the law. For the rest of the establishments mentioned . . . restaurants, dance halls, music halls and the like, cases of discrimination are not very frequent, and when they do happen public opinion is apt to be aroused and to condemn the action. Such acts really classify as individual acts of discrimination." *Parliamentary Debates*, H.o.L., 19th November 1958, cols. 718, 719.

[29] *The Times*, August 2, 1944. (See also Anthony H. Richmond, *Colour Prejudice in Britain*, *op. cit.*, p. 90.)

"*Colour Saves Man From Prison*" was the heading of a report on the case of a West Indian who was accused of having damaged a police car by hitting it with a milk bottle during the disturbances in Notting Dale in September 1958. The man was told by the Magistrate (as quoted in *The Times*):

> "Some of you coloured men think there is a prejudice against coloured men. Let me tell you this: if you were a white man you would be sent to prison here and now. It is only because you are a coloured man and were subjected to some provocation by a lot of hooligans that I am not dealing with you in that way."

In another case, one coloured man was sent to prison for four months and seven others were fined (the fines ranging from £15 to £40 each) for "unlawfully possessing offensive weapons" during the same period of disorders in Notting Dale. (None of these men was described as unemployed. They had varied occupations: three were painters; two were labourers; one was a cabinet maker, and one a club proprietor.) The Judge is reported to have said to them:

> "Some of you are what might be called undesirable or misplaced persons. I have no power to send you back to your place of origin. The social problem that you reveal is no business of mine. Although perhaps the legislature might give us power to guard against such misplaced persons all I have to do is to protect the public."[30]

The Range of Attitudes

Although the coloured migrant is a British citizen by law, it is still true that he is set apart in this society—officially and privately; subtly or crudely; positively or negatively. Moreover, law and public opinion writ large give only a bare indication of the actual range, complexity and diversity of British attitudes towards the coloured minority in this country. Parliament, the spokesmen for political parties and trade unions and all the other voices of authority do not speak the language of the urban byways of physical and social blight. Indeed, they hardly know that language, even less the conditions in which it is spoken. *Hansard* and *The Times* are not read in the basements and at the street corners of Notting Dale, Brixton, Liverpool and Cardiff. While the coloured newcomers meet ambivalence everywhere, it takes many different forms and is derived from varied motivations. It is that which makes mutual understanding and adaptation so difficult and so slow.

[30] *The Times*, September 16, 1958. *Manchester Guardian*, November 11, 1958. These are not isolated examples of pronouncements by judges or magistrates. Similar statements—of both kinds—are reported from time to time; and statements of the second kind are occasionally sharper than the one here quoted.

To coloured men and women, every encounter with white British people is a new hazard. At one extreme they are met by plain prejudice, foul language and even violence; at the other, they may be welcomed with enthusiasm. They may be regarded with indifference, curiosity or concern. There are English people—particularly in rural areas—to whom the subject of black and white in this country has hardly as yet any meaning. There are some others everywhere—old and young; poor and rich; Left, Right and outside party politics—who are allergic to reports of prejudice and discrimination of any kind, and who express their opposition passionately, although they themselves have no personal reason (other than their innate principles) or political obligation to do so.[31] And there is also the kind of person who was reported to have said: "Actually, I often bump coloured people with my shopping bag. Then I can smile and say 'sorry' just to show them that we aren't all rude."[32]

Coloured people are feared as competitive intruders; they are thought of as promoters of crime and as carriers of disease; they are resented when they are poor; they are envied when they are resourceful and thrifty. They are looked down upon; they are patronised; occasionally they are treated just like everyone else. They will be addressed as 'Sir' or 'Madam' and greeted with unstinted courtesy. But they are also afraid that someone might shout after them 'Where's your tail?' (That is the stock example of abuse which coloured people always quote.) Indeed, courteous and offensive remarks might well be made to them simultaneously by the same people.

When a Negro wants to marry an English girl, he may find that her family accept him without regard to his colour, or he may be turned out because of it. People may stare at him in the street when he walks along with a white girl, or, more often, they may take no notice at all. Usually there is only one thing of which he is sure in British society—that he cannot know what to expect. Some West Indians, bewildered and hurt by British ambiguity, have been heard to say, ironically or seriously, that they would prefer the definite colour bar of the South of the United States (though few of the people who speak in these terms have, in fact, experienced the Southern system of segregation). At least, they argue, in those places a coloured person

---

[31] When one meets people of this kind, usually women, at meetings and in other public places, it is evident that they do not belong to any one social or political group. Conversations with them indicate, moreover, that their vehement dislike of prejudice and discrimination is not necessarily derived from any particular personal experience or from direct involvement with the affairs of coloured individuals or associations.   [32] *Manchester Guardian*, January 7, 1959.

knows where he stands. He does not have to fight an often elusive enemy.[33]

British attitudes towards colour are so ambiguous that they invite misunderstandings. In observing the experiences of West Indians, and in hearing about them, it is, therefore, often difficult to identify prejudice or discrimination. A particular incident might be an example of unbiased or of biased behaviour. Or it might contain an element of both: native aloofness is emphasised in contacts with dark skinned 'foreigners'. And for the coloured man it is far more difficult still, if not impossible, to make such distinctions. In his extreme uncertainty, he is bound to attach positive or negative meanings to neutral white conduct—meanings which were not intended or implied at all. It is just because he is delighted to be greeted with sympathy in one place that antipathy in another pains him so much. Thus in his mind the ambivalent white responses tend to be exaggerated. Hopes are raised; disappointment follows.[34]

There are some migrants who say that they themselves have never met any prejudice; there are many more who see it in everybody's face and in everybody's actions. Every dark skinned person knows

[33] It seems that British ambivalence has been maintained and that thus coloured people in this country feel hardly any more secure now than they did some years ago. In that respect, there seems to have been very little improvement. For the same kind of remarks which are made by recent migrants were made by West Indians who lived in England in the forties and early fifties. Anthony H. Richmond quoted several typical comments of this kind. "Over here you never know what to do. You get to expect the worst." And again: "In America you know where you stand; in England the people say they have no prejudice or colour bar, but in practice we know that it is there. But because it is not out in the open we cannot fight it. In America you can either avoid trouble, or you know where to go, and what to do, if you want to fight against it." Richmond commented: "The ambiguity of the racial situation in England is therefore a source of anxiety to the Negro, and this in its turn produces inevitable personal maladjustment. This varies in degree from a slight feeling of uneasiness and not quite 'belonging' to more serious symptoms of mental breakdown, which in two cases led to suicide. One man jumped from a high window and another died of coal-gas poisoning." *Colour Prejudice in Britain, op. cit.*, pp. 99 and 122.

[34] One of the recent novels, which deals with the experiences of a West Indian newcomer to England, gives a concentrated portrait of the uncertainty from which the coloured man suffers. At one stage he "was like a man waking from a nightmare. Now he knew the English, it was obvious that the colour bar was something the blacks had fashioned for themselves, creating it out of memory and fear. . . . The prejudice was only English shyness, a gentle reluctance to intrude on another man's privacy." But at the end he feels differently. "How could he condemn his son . . . to grow up in England, civilised, enlightened England whose secret prejudice was deeper and more bitter than anywhere on Earth; England, where a coloured man was tolerated only if he stayed at the bottom?" G. R. Fazakerley, *A Stranger Here*, London, 1959, pp. 192, 222.

of other dark skinned persons who have experienced discrimination. Stories of slights, insults and hardships pass rapidly around the coloured communities.[35] And in the current climate of Britain, this is inevitable. For while a coloured man may be unnecessarily 'touchy' at one moment, half an hour later he may be confronted with the very kind of incident which has an obvious prejudiced connotation, and which perpetuates his touchiness.[36] It does not take long to hear and see actual examples of the anti-coloured phrases and situations which the newcomers report to one another.

Expressions of Prejudice

Indeed, although the varied permutations of British ambivalence towards colour do not fall into simple categories of prejudice *per se*, they do have a definite pattern. The same ignorant clichés about and against coloured people are repeated every day—politely or crudely, unintentionally or deliberately.[37] And even the rather superficial methods of public opinion surveys reveal the pattern of bias.

It was shown, in particular, by one nation-wide Gallup poll on race relations, carried out on September 3rd and 4th, 1958, while the disorders in London were still going on.[38] In this survey, nine questions were asked—on who was to be blamed for the disturbances; on control of immigration; and on attitudes towards coloured people

[35] As might be expected, some of these stories are told out of context. We heard, for example, of a public house in North Kensington where coloured people were not served. The publican invariably told them to get their drinks at a nearby West Indian club. But apparently the pub and the club had an agreement whereby the club bought drink from the pub on the understanding that coloured people would be sent to the club. Again, allegations that a particular establishment operates a colour bar, though correct at one time, are occasionally out-of-date. On the other hand, there are managers of licensed premises who definitely refuse to admit coloured customers.

[36] We have seen several, rather striking illustrations of this kind of sequence during our own investigations.

[37] These clichés have been remarkably persistent. They are still very similar to those quoted in earlier literature on race relations in this country—for example, to the stereotypes listed by Anthony H. Richmond in *The Colour Problem*, London, 1955, p. 243. Apparently, the stereotype images of coloured 'strangers' have so far hardly been modified either by the growth of the coloured minority (although this has had some influence on individual attitudes) or by changes in the general political climate and in educational curricula. These latter changes have not as yet been sufficiently thorough to dispel the widespread ignorance and to substitute new realistic, versatile notions of coloured people in this country and abroad for the old *idées fixes*.

[38] The following paragraphs give a brief summary of the results. For a more detailed report, based on our re-tabulation and analysis of Gallup poll material, see Appendix B.

with respect to housing, employment, schools and inter-marriage. While comparable material from other polls is also available, the September 1958 survey provides an opportunity of examining not only the answers to individual questions, but also—and more important—the interrelations between the answers.

Of course, *ad hoc* surveys of this kind cannot reflect the complexity of British attitudes on matters of race relations, quite apart from the fact that expressions of opinion on coloured people are frequently inconsistent with behaviour towards them. And yet the verbal reflexes prompted by the poll indicate the same tendencies which are observed in other surveys and accounts of the experiences of coloured migrants.

The results show that the veneer of racial tolerance is a rather thin one. On the one hand, verbal disapproval of the principle of discrimination was widespread—and not only at that time, but also on the occasion of earlier and later polls.[39] Thus comparatively few people—one in six—thought that a 'colour quota' should be applied to immigration of Commonwealth citizens into Britain, though almost two-fifths said that the number of both white and coloured Commonwealth immigrants should be restricted. Less than one in ten said that the coloured people were chiefly to blame for the disturbances in Nottingham and London. And it has to be remembered that they gave their answers to that question spontaneously—before the public indictment of the disturbances had gathered momentum, and before the leaders of opinion had expressed their condemnation of white 'hooligans' in the Press, on radio and television.

On the other hand, there was far less disapproval of discrimination in practice. Symptoms of bias were increasingly obvious the nearer the questions came to issues of direct personal relevance. Just under half of all those in the national sample said that coloured people should have equality of opportunity on the labour market; about one third said the same with reference to municipal housing. (But it seems that many of those who gave an altruistic reply to the latter question were not themselves on council housing lists.) In general, replies to questions on aspects of the housing situation were divergent: however, the dichotomy in British attitudes towards coloured workmates and coloured neighbours—especially to considerable numbers of coloured neighbours—was clearly visible. And, as might be expected, the question which evoked the strongest segregationist

[39] This was shown also, for example, in the reactions to the affair of the Wolverhampton dance hall, which was in the news in June 1958. In a nation-wide poll at that time, 62 per cent expressed their disapproval of the colour bar at the Wolverhampton dance hall.

tendency was that on intermarriage: 71 per cent said that they dis-
approved of marriages between white and coloured people.

Answers to questions on other personal issues were apparently
influenced by a distinction between attitudes towards coloured people collectively and individually. Thus the majority—61 per cent—
said that they would definitely, or might possibly, move "if coloured
people came to live in great numbers" in their district. But a minority—30 per cent—said that they would or might move "if coloured
people came to live next door". In this context, the respondents presumably thought of a few coloured neighbours.[40] An even smaller
group—7 per cent—were against integration at school. (They said
"Yes" when they were asked: "Would you object if there were
coloured children in the same class as your children at school?") It
can be assumed that the majority gave a tolerant reply largely because
the principle of segregation is particularly ugly in this respect, though
the fact that there is so far hardly anywhere in Britain a considerable
proportion of coloured schoolchildren was perhaps also relevant.

The verbal 'reflexes' on different issues of race relations are not
necessarily coherent; there could be a number of people who give
their answers haphazardly, without an apparent interconnection;
and also without giving an indication of ever having thought about
such questions before. But in fact less than one in four (23 per cent)
of the people questioned gave a haphazard series of replies. The proportion of 'Don't Know' answers, too, was lower than is usual in
public opinion polls on general, fairly new political subjects.

Among the majority whose replies showed varied degrees of
coherence, there were four groups, in terms of an 'anti-colour bias'
rating: a strongly biased group; an unbiased (or almost unbiased)
group; and two intermediate ones. Both the size and the characteristics of these four groups confirm general observations of the
distribution of prejudice in British society.

---

[40] The assumption that residential segregation is closely connected with, or
even largely derived from, prejudice against sexual relations and intermarriage
between white and coloured people has been made in several American studies of
prejudice, and a fairly high correlation between these two aspects of prejudice has
occasionally been found. But in this particular British opinion survey, the
association was not a close one: there was far more explicit objection to inter-
marriage than to *individual* coloured neighbours. The results are, however, not
sufficiently detailed to be conclusive. In general, resentment of coloured people in
Britain is shown most openly and clearly in the field of housing (where the
coloured are most likely to be thought of collectively—as intruders, competitors
and 'invaders'); and also with respect to sexual relations. British segregationist
tendencies in housing are apparently derived from a compound of economic and
sexual motives, and also from actual social frictions between English people and
newcomers in the early stages of mutual adjustment.

A small minority—one in ten of the total sample—expressed prejudice in an outspoken and rather stubborn manner; they gave biased answers to all or most of the relevant questions. At the other end of the scale there was a slightly larger group—about one in seven—who were apparently free (or almost free) from prejudice: their answers were consistently (or fairly consistently) unbiased or non-committal. But the majority were ambivalent (though not incoherently ambivalent); they showed stronger or weaker leanings towards prejudice; and it was in these intermediate groups that the British 'split mind' on issues of race relations could be most clearly seen.

It seems, moreover, that there is no section of the population which has a prerogative of tolerance or intolerance: the differences between the social characteristics of the four groups on the bias scale were not very marked. It is true that both young men and old women had a particularly strong anti-colour bias;[41] supporters of the Conservative party were slightly more inclined towards bias than supporters of the Labour and Liberal parties; and there were also some regional variations in the pattern of attitudes. (Apparently, the most biased region is the Midlands.) But there was no social class difference in the responses to questions on colour: the distribution of consistently biased, unbiased and ambivalent answers was alike among non-manual and manual workers. There was, however, one clear-cut distinction—that between respondents who knew coloured people personally and those who did not. The former—almost one half of the sample—were definitely more tolerant than the latter.[42] No doubt, the old recipe for the improvement of social relations, which has worked elsewhere and with reference to other minority groups, is also applicable to the situation of the coloured newcomers in Britain.

Indeed, this recipe might be applicable especially in this country—just because there is, apparently, only a minority whose predisposition towards colour is a rigidly negative one. The majority have a

[41] Conversely, old men and young women showed a strong and very similar tendency towards tolerance. (The 'young' category in this classification was that of people aged 16 to 34; the 'old' category that of those aged 65 or over.)

[42] It is possible, of course, that personal acquaintance with coloured people is a symptom of tolerance, rather than a cure for intolerance. In other words, those who have a predisposition towards tolerance may know coloured people, while those who are prejudiced avoid contacts with coloured people. But it is unlikely that this is a sufficient explanation of the difference between the attitudes of the two groups, as reflected in this survey. In general, coloured people are not segregated in Britain and therefore contacts with them—at work and in public places—occur largely by chance and not by choice. In many circumstances, those who wished to avoid coloured people would not be able to do so. In others, those who wished to meet coloured people would not have an opportunity of doing so.

'secret' prejudice. Their attitudes are ambivalent, and therefore presumably also plastic.

There seems to be a three-fold split: there is far less overt approval of discrimination in principle than in practice. And in the latter respect, there is a tendency to differentiate between rules of behaviour towards a coloured individual in a particular situation and those which are applied to the anonymous coloured, thought of as a collective category. This is shown in various ways; and it can be interpreted in various ways. Such a differentiation (especially just a verbal one) is compatible with acute, irrationally fixed prejudice. Even the most dogmatic antisemite in Germany or segregationist in the Deep South was (and is) willing to admit that he knows a 'good' Jew or a 'white' Negro; and the antisemite or segregationist is occasionally prepared to make exceptions and to associate with Jews or Negroes on his own terms. He is not prepared, however, to regard the 'good' Jew or 'white' Negro as anything but exceptional; he does not change his generalisations about Jews or Negroes on the basis of his experience with individuals from these groups.

In some cases, the fairly typical British distinction between a particular coloured individual and the anonymous category might be of a similar kind. But, in general, in Britain this distinction is more likely to be associated with the widely held view that it is improper to state explicitly the principle of colour bars. Thus it is also improper to admit that all coloured people are regarded as being alike, and that they should all be treated alike. What happens in practice—as soon as it is necessary to step out of a particular situation in which only a few coloured individuals are involved—is quite a different matter. It is quite possible for the worker to say: 'one coloured mate is acceptable; but five are too many'; or for the employer to say: 'I will accept a coloured labourer, but not a coloured clerk'; or for the landlady to comment: 'I know there are good and bad coloured people, but I do not want to have any coloured lodgers.'

Nevertheless, the British worker, the employer and the landlady who speak and act in this way might take account of their personal experiences. Their prejudice, vacillating, uneasy and fed on misinformation, does not appear to be immutable; it might be amenable to rational clarification. Sooner or later, they might be prepared to compare their preconceived notions of the coloured as a category with their own knowledge of coloured individuals. The positive elements in their attitudes and behaviour towards coloured people could thus become more pronounced.

But this is a slow and an uncertain process. Personal contacts with coloured people do not necessarily have a positive effect; and in any

case they are a matter of chance. So long as there is prejudice—
however ambiguous and concealed—it tends to lead to discrimination and thus to be self-perpetuating. It is unlikely that British tolerance will exorcise British intolerance unless other social influences—
quite apart from peripheral encounters with coloured people—work
decidedly and unequivocally towards that end.

3. NOTTINGHAM AND NOTTING DALE

'Explosive Matter'

The British twilight situation of anti-colour bias has seldom been
illuminated. In such a situation, self-awareness of tendencies towards
prejudice is a prerequisite of ideological progress. But British society
—with its apparent social unity and strict class divisions; with its
mixture of tolerance and intolerance—has found it particularly difficult to recognise the fissures of its mind. They are so imbedded in the
social structure that they are taken for granted. They are an integral
part of a traditional pattern of contradictory attitudes towards
'foreigners' from another class, another place or country, with
another language, religion or colour. For long the biases seemed to
be no more than the defects of national virtues, and were therefore
largely ignored. Thus it was possible to believe that the virtues were
almost universal, but that the defects, if they ever proved to be
troublesome, were highly localised—that the source of the disorder
existed in a marginal social group but not 'at home'. As the different
social classes 'keep themselves to themselves', they are not well-
informed about one another, nor are they inclined to be intro-
spective. And there were always shock absorbers. Primitive prejudice can be thought to be harmless so long as it seems to be offset by
a civilised dislike of formal discrimination.

"... there cannot be an explosion unless there is explosive matter
around; and surely the explosive matter is race prejudice ... nearly
all of us have colour prejudice." This was one comment, an exceptionally frank one, made in a House of Lords debate on the disturbances in the autumn of 1958.[43] Similar debates could well have been
held before 1958: there had been sufficient warnings of pathological
symptoms; there had also been explosions before.

After the First World War, in the early summer of 1919, there were
dramatic race riots in Cardiff and Liverpool; and at the same time,

---

[43] It was made by the Earl of Lucan in discussing the causes of the riots.
Parliamentary Debates, H.o.L., 19th November 1958, col. 685.

there were disturbances in most dock areas which had coloured 'colonies'—in Newport, on Tyneside, in Glasgow and in the East End of London (in Canning Town and Stepney).[44] During the Second World War, in 1943, there were several ugly brawls in some of the dance halls in Liverpool. A few years later, similar incidents occurred in several places; and at least four more large-scale outbreaks of violence were reported.[45]

In Birmingham, in May 1948, a crowd of white men (variously estimated to have been 100 to 250 strong) besieged and stoned a house where a number of Indians were staying. In Liverpool, a fight outside an Anglo-Indian café on the Saturday night of the August Bank Holiday in 1948 sparked off a series of violent crowd scenes and attacks, which continued for another two nights.[46] In London, a fight between white and coloured people in Deptford

[44] The disturbances in Cardiff and Liverpool in June 1919 were indeed race riots—in the extreme sense of this term. There were simultaneous battles of great violence in various parts of the two cities for several days. In Cardiff, they were mainly in 'Nigger Town', as *The Times* reported at that time. Several people were killed; many were injured; there were widespread arrests. Houses of coloured people were raided; all furniture, windows and doors were broken; the occupants were beaten up. There was shooting and knifing. Other houses were set on fire, while crowds waited outside to attack the coloured occupants when they had to come out. ". . . immediately a negro showed himself in the centre of the city he was molested." (*The Times*, June 14, 1919.) In Liverpool, over 700 Negroes were removed to Bridewell prison "for their own safety" even before the riots were over. But although these prolonged violent battles were referred to as "race riots" at the time, they did not attract a great deal of public attention; and the comments on them were generally 'anti-coloured'. Indeed, many of them (including some by senior police officers and retired colonial administrators) would nowadays be classified as racialist propaganda. A measure of the prevailing prejudice can be found in a statement that was tolerant by 1919 standards. "Some of the more sober-minded citizens of Cardiff consider that the coloured men are not alone to blame for the disturbances, although, at the same time, they deplore the familiar association between white women and negroes, which is a provocative cause. There are over a thousand coloured men out of work in Cardiff, most of them sailors, and it has to be remembered to their credit that during the war they faced the perils of the submarine campaign with all the gallantry of the British seaman. The negro is almost pathetically loyal to the British Empire and he is always proud to acclaim himself a Briton. His chief failing is his fondness for white women, and American naval officers stationed at the American naval base at Cardiff have often expressed their disgust at the laxity of the British law in this connexion." (*The Times*, June 13, 1919.) A description of the Cardiff riots is given in K. L. Little's book, *Negroes in Britain*, London, 1948, pp. 57–60.

[45] There might have been other disturbances as well. It is difficult to know because during the inter-war and early post-war period such disorders were scarcely reported in the national Press.

[46] The Liverpool disturbances in 1948 are described by Anthony H. Richmond in *Colour Prejudice in Britain, op. cit.*, pp. 102–107.

Broadway in July 1949 was the start of an evening of rioting. There had been sporadic fighting for several nights before. The police escorted the coloured men to their hostel and kept them indoors. Meanwhile, a hostile crowd—of 800 to 1,000 people—had gathered outside the hostel, and although a police cordon was put across the road, the crowd continued their siege and made repeated attempts to break in. The coloured men threw bottles and crockery from their windows. Two coloured men were seriously injured; three policemen were hurt. (Seven white men and eight coloured men were later tried on various charges.) The disturbance lasted from 8 p.m. to midnight.

In August 1954, there was racial warfare for two days in another part of London, in a small street of terrace houses in Camden Town. Both white and coloured were militant; crowds collected; there were skirmishes with bottles and axes, and a number of ugly incidents; one coloured man was pursued by a crowd on to a bus, where the fighting continued; two coloured men were set upon by white youths and beaten up. On the evening of the second day the atmosphere was so thick with hostility that fifty policemen stood by and cordoned off the street at both ends. Firemen had been drafted in, for apparently there had been threats of incendiarism. As the evening went on, it became quieter, and the firemen went back to their station. Shortly afterwards, a petrol torch or bomb was thrown into a house occupied by coloured men and two white women (as was said). The house burst into flames.

The scenes in that street in Camden Town were repeated on a larger scale four years later. The 1954 disorders were not front-page news; they were quickly forgotten, except by the few who were directly or professionally concerned. Nor did any of the subsequent sporadic brawls and fights in several provincial cities, in Nottingham and in London attract much attention. The coloured people themselves and their immediate neighbours, social workers and anthropologists were well aware of these troubles. But public opinion, in general, did not take much notice.

Quite apart from the fact that social introspection is liable to be rather harassing, there were two main reasons for the lack of interest in manifestations of racial tension. First, in the early fifties the "new Commonwealth, which has grown up since 1945," had only just begun to be thought of as "the greatest multi-racial association the world has ever seen". Thus the concept of the United Kingdom as "the heart and centre of a great multi-racial Commonwealth"[47] had

[47] Labour Party, *Racial Discrimination*, September 1958, p. 2. Conservative Commonwealth Council, West Indies Group, Memorandum (duplicated) on 'Race Relations in Britain', 15th April, 1959.

only just become one of the first articles in the national credo from Right to Left, from Oxbridge to Redbrick. Second, until the mid-fifties, the number of coloured migrants in Britain was so small that few people here needed to be concerned with their existence and their problems. Even when the coloured minority group grew, it was still for some time quite easy to ignore the 'explosive matter'—to remain unaware of the British split mind. When the headlines on the Nottingham 'race riots' appeared in late August 1958, it was no longer so easy. And at that stage, there had to be headlines: in Britain's new situation, an event which previously might have been dismissed as a minor disorder was seen as a disturbance of dramatic significance. Thus the 1958 riots had a cathartic effect, though neither a thorough nor a lasting one.

The shock of recognition was too sharp: in shame, almost in self-defence, many of the previous illusions of the united, civilised, liberal British society were maintained. Surely, it was thought, British reputation had merely been wronged by a few hooligans?

> "Suddenly, on a small scale, we are faced with these ugly, frightening, primitive emotions . . . in Britain, which has hitherto always been regarded as the very cradle of liberty and tolerance, the most law-abiding country in the world."[48]

But was the display of ugly, primitive emotions in Britain really so sudden and unprecedented? It seems that it was not. If we look back not only on the experiences of coloured migrants, but also on those of other minority groups, we see previous symptoms of prejudice, latent and acute. And was the scale so small—as measured by the standard of this country, and not by that of one in which apartheid is the ruling system? What happened in fact?

A folklore developed almost at once about the 'race riots'; they have been both magnified and minimised. They were not race riots in the extreme sense of the term—the actual damage done by physical violence was less extensive than the threats. But nor were they merely minor isolated brawls, set off by sheer accident.

Turmoil in Nottingham

On Saturday, August 23rd 1958, a fight between a coloured and a white man started just at closing time, around 10 p.m., outside a public house in The Chase, a decaying Nottingham district, where a

---

[48] *Parliamentary Debates*, H.o.C., 30th October 1958, col. 418. (This statement, made by Mr. Nigel Fisher, was later repeated in the memorandum issued by the Conservative Commonwealth Council, *op. cit.*)

considerable number of coloured people are concentrated.[49] The exact cause of the fight is obscure; various versions have been told, publicly and privately. But it is clear that the fighting spread within a few minutes. Several white men were stabbed by coloured men. Their attacks—and the immediate rush of rumours of their attacks—caused counter-attacks and threats against the coloured, in general. ". . . dozens of men and women were injured by knives, razors, palings and bottles." A hostile shouting crowd of about 1,500 people gathered. At first, no more than two or three policemen were standing by; and apparently it took some time for police reinforcements to arrive. The fire brigade was called in. "It was an ugly riotous crowd and fires could have been started," said the Assistant Chief Constable of Nottingham later to the Press. "Several coloured men were removed by the police for their own safety. A number of them had cuts and bruises."[50] Eight white people—including a policeman—were taken to hospital. It took 90 minutes to restore order: by midnight, the crowds were dispersed.

But that was neither the end of the matter, nor had the events of that night been a case of spontaneous combustion. Those who knew the district and the situation had been aware of growing tension for some time before. Coloured people had been molested, humiliated and beaten up by white men (". . . vaguely known as 'teddy boys', though their age range seems to run from over 20 to at least over 30."). There had been frequent assaults of that kind, particularly during the fortnight preceding the riotous Saturday; and there had been widespread rumours that further warfare was imminent. The police thought that the initial fights of coloured against white on the Saturday night had been a reprisal for the previous attacks on coloured people.

> ". . . the Assistant Chief Constable [of Nottingham] confirmed that there had been assaults. He said that two white men were on remand charged with robbery with violence against a coloured man. The attacks made by 'teddy boys' in the past fourteen days were responsible for Saturday night's outbursts. The coloured community, he said, apart from a few isolated cases, was 'very well behaved'."[51]

On Monday, August 26th, *The Times* reported "*All Quiet Again in Nottingham*", but many of the other national newspapers were less optimistic—and less restrained. Some of them had picked up the 'teddy boys' story in a distorted form. Real boys—perhaps teddies, but certainly adventure-hunting or aggressive youths—from near and

[49] It was estimated that about 2,000 to 3,000 coloured people were living in Nottingham at that time. The total population of the city was 313,000.
[50] *The Times*, August 26, 1958; *Manchester Guardian*, August 25, 1958.
[51] *Manchester Guardian*, August 26, 1958.

far took the cue and invaded the district.[52] It was not quiet in The Chase; there was mounting tension. Everyone was waiting for the next Saturday night.

The rendezvous was kept on the following Saturday evening, August 30th. In St. Anne's Well Road, the scene of the previous week's disturbances, there was a large mixed crowd—'teddy boys'; sightseers in cars and on foot; reporters; some local white people, but hardly any coloured ones: they had been advised to stay indoors and were anxious to do so. And there were police patrols who kept the crowds moving. It was reported that there was a "milling mob" which grew to about 4,000 people during the evening. A car with three West Indians in it passed through and was stopped.

> "Cries of 'Let's lynch them', and 'Let's get at them', went up as the crowd, many of them teddy boys who had poured from public houses, tried to smash their way into the car. Beating on the windows, they tried to overturn it. . . . Finally police forced a path through them and told the coloured men in the car to 'go like hell'. They did."

Later on, there was more trouble; it started, so it was said, when a cameraman lit a magnesium flare to "film a scuffle between a small party of youths". The crowds, which had begun to disperse, rushed back, thinking there was a fire. There was great agitation and shouting—for example, as was said subsequently in the Magistrate's Court, "Find some niggers". "By this time all coloured people appeared to have left the streets . . . an ugly white *versus* white clash developed as police vans came into the area." Some of the fighting was directed against the police, but no policeman was injured. More than fifty people were taken to police headquarters, and 24 boys and men (whose ages ranged from 16 to 45) were charged under the Public Order Act.

Next day the Chief Constable held a Press conference and said:

> "This was not a racial riot. The coloured people behaved in an exemplary way by keeping out of the way. Indeed, they were an example to some of our rougher elements. The people primarily concerned were irresponsible teddy boys and persons who had had a lot to drink."[53]

---

[52] Some came from a considerable distance. For example, one 18-year-old London boy, who had travelled to Nottingham with two others, was arrested at Nottingham Midland Station early in September. 'Offensive weapons'—a rubber cosh with lead inside and a length of bicycle chain—were found in his suitcase; and he had a piece of glass in his pocket. (*Manchester Guardian*, September 5, 1958.)

[53] *Manchester Guardian* and *The Times*, September 1, 1958. The reports on the Court proceedings appeared on September 2, 1958. Five men were sentenced to three months' imprisonment each (among these were the 'nigger-chasing' men, aged 24 and 45 years respectively); fifteen men were fined; one was remitted to the

On the following Saturday evening, September 6th, there was again a crowd in the district, though a much smaller one than previously. Again there were 'nigger-baiting' incidents. A siege of some coloured people's houses developed into a missile battle between the tenants who threw milk bottles from the upper floors and the crowd below who bombarded the houses with bricks and bottles and broke windows. In a dark side street coloured men were chased; five were assaulted. But the police vans arrived quickly, and the fighting was stopped.

There was no further news of anti-colour mass hysteria in Nottingham. But there was a footnote. A bus company in an adjacent town advertised coach tours to see "the terror spots of Nottingham".[54]

Rioting in London

The importance of the events in Nottingham was both accentuated and overshadowed by the simultaneous, far more serious outbursts of violence in London. The London disorders were not just a Saturday evening pastime; they continued without interruption for several days; and they were also spread over a much wider area than the Nottingham turmoil. The short-hand newspaper description—of the 'Notting Hill' riots—was incorrect. In fact, the disturbances fanned out from Shepherd's Bush and adjacent Notting Dale to several pockets in Notting Hill, Kensal New Town, Paddington and Maida Vale. And while in Nottingham the troubles occurred in the centre of a district densely settled with coloured people, this was not so in London. On the contrary, the main explosions took place beyond the fringes of relatively concentrated coloured settlements or even further away; and the worst offenders came from housing estates and districts which were—and still are—almost wholly white. One of the most sordid zones of transition in North Kensington, which

---

Juvenile Court; and three were acquitted. An uproar broke out on the public benches of the Court when the prison sentences were announced. There were shouts and screams; several people had to be ejected, some with difficulty. It was said that the cameraman, who had lit the magnesium flare, had staged a mock fight in order to film it: and that the 'real' fighting broke out afterwards. He himself denied this strongly and said that he had lit the flare after the disturbance had started.

[54] Apparently similar tours were advertised in other places as well. The Sheriff of Nottingham was reported to have said: "I am horrified by this latest development. It comes at a time when we are striving to eliminate racial conflict. I understand that chalked notices have been displayed outside bus garage booking offices in Leicester . . . giving full details of the trips. It is rumoured that the same thing is being done in other cities and towns." The police were asked to intervene and to request the trips to be withdrawn. (*The Times*, September 16, 1958.)

has a considerable cluster of coloured people, was comparatively quiet—though it is a zone where 'marginal men', white and coloured, live side by side; which has generally a shady reputation; and where trouble was, therefore, expected by local officials when it broke out elsewhere.

However, as in Nottingham, the large-scale disturbances in London, too, were preceded by a series of apparently sporadic assaults on coloured people. But in London it was not the retaliation of a few coloured men which sparked off the crowd outbursts, nor was there a definite chain of incidents during the turbulent days. 'Nigger-hunting' simply spread and collected an increasing number of partisans—active forces and passive spectators—simultaneously in several districts. And although no one was killed, the actual violence, and even more the cumulative threats of violence, produced an atmosphere of menace and fear which closely resembled that of a text-book race riot.

In July and early August 1958, there were several attacks by gangs of white youths on coloured people, quite apart from the 'normal' fights between individuals. In mid-July, a gang of about fifteen 'teddy boys' raided a café, owned by a coloured man, in Shepherd's Bush. (It was said that they came from a large housing estate, the White City estate, in that district.) They damaged the place and ran away before the police arrived. Twelve days later, about twenty or thirty youths attacked the same café; six (from Shepherd's Bush, Fulham and Notting Hill, whose ages ranged from 18 to 23) were arrested; and five of them were found guilty of "causing malicious damage" and were fined. The café owner said in court that the raid "was just like an earthquake. . . . I didn't try to stop them because I would have been killed if I had."[55] Just over three weeks later (on Saturday, August 17th) another gang of 'teddy boys' besieged a 'coloured' house in Shepherd's Bush. Windows were broken; a crowd gathered outside.

On Saturday night, August 23rd, during and shortly after the hours of the disturbances in Nottingham, there was an air of acute tension, and a display of aggression in various places in West London. The incidents which occurred could not be regarded simply as the usual Saturday evening fighting: they had a particularly ugly, deliberate twist. Coloured people had already become afraid of one weekend sport—attempts by drivers of cars to run them down at night. (Apparently, in the weeks preceding the late August crisis, such drivers had not been teddy boys, but older 'respectably' dressed men.) And at that time, too, the slogans and scrawls of

[55] *The Times*, August 27, 1958.

fascist agitation—"Keep Britain White"; "People of Kensington Act Now"—had become part of the scene, especially in and around Notting Hill. (The White Defence League had been busy; the Union Movement had been active, holding meetings and distributing a new set of leaflets.)

Before and after closing time on that Saturday evening, there were several attacks on coloured people and houses.[56] And in the small hours of the morning, a gang of nine white youths aged between 17 and 20, most of whom came from Shepherd's Bush, toured their district and the adjacent ones in a car. They were, as they said, "nigger-hunting"; and they were armed with iron bars, torn from street railings, starting handles, table legs, pieces of wood and a knife. Once in a while, when they saw a coloured man walking on his own, or no more than a couple, they stopped to attack. Five coloured men whom they had assaulted were taken into hospital; three of them were seriously injured. One was wheeled into the Magistrate's court to give evidence. Another, with a chest wound, was carried in on a stretcher.[57]

This was the notorious case of the 'nigger-hunting' youths, who were tried at the Old Bailey three weeks later and sentenced to four years' imprisonment each. In giving the verdict, Mr. Justice Salmon said to them:

> "You stand convicted on your own confessions of a series of extremely grave and brutal crimes . . . you nine men formed yourselves into a gang and set out on a cruel and vicious manhunt. You armed yourselves with iron bars and other weapons. Your quarry was any man, providing there were not more than two of them together, whose skin happened to be a different colour from your own. Your object was to instil stark terror and inflict as much pain and grievous injury as you could.
>
> During that night you savagely attacked five peaceful, law-abiding citizens without any shadow of an excuse. None of them had done you any harm. None of them had given you the slightest provocation. Indeed, you knew nothing about them, except that their skin happened to be of a colour of which you apparently did not approve. Two of them were lucky enough to escape before you were able to inflict other than comparatively minor injuries. The other three you left bleeding and senseless on the pavement. . . .
>
> Everyone, irrespective of the colour of their skin, is entitled to walk

---

[56] One of the incidents during that night occurred in Bramley Road, Notting Dale (not far from Shepherd's Bush). This was one of the main scenes of the later violent disturbances. But there were—and are—very few coloured people in this street and in the immediate vicinity.

[57] The Magistrate said: "I have never before seen a man in that state brought into court. I don't think he is fit to give evidence." (*The Times*, September 1, 1958.)

through our streets in peace, with their heads erect, and free from fear. That is a right which these courts will always unfailingly uphold.

As far as the law is concerned you are entitled to think what you like, however foul your thoughts; to feel what you like, however brutal and debased your emotions; to say what you like providing you do not infringe the rights of others or imperil the Queen's peace, but once you translate your dark thoughts and brutal feelings into savage acts such as these the law will be swift to punish you, the guilty, and to protect your victims. . . ."[58]

This judgment became known all over the world. For both its tenor and its significance were associated with the events that happened in the interval between the 'savage acts' of which Mr. Justice Salmon spoke and the trial at the Old Bailey. But in the days which followed the ominous weekend of August 23rd and 24th, there were few who recognised the signs of growing disorder. The newspapers were still preoccupied with the Nottingham events. The heading of a report on the situation in several cities with coloured minorities in the *Manchester Guardian* of August 27th was:

"OTHER CITIES NOT PERTURBED ABOUT NOTTINGHAM IT COULDN'T HAPPEN HERE FEELING."

However, this article (which was more realistic than most other anticipations in the Press) did also say that the "Notting Hill Gate—Shepherd's Bush area" had been "unsettled for the last three weeks" and mentioned some of the incidents which had occurred.

"Police have shown in this area that they are determined to be firm and have arrested some of those believed to have been involved in the incidents with complete impartiality. This, they believe, may prevent future outbreaks of violence."

Three days later, shortly before midnight on Saturday, August 30th, violence did break out on a larger scale than before. Again the place of the disturbances was Bramley Road and the vicinity in Notting Dale, where few coloured people live. The houses of several of them were attacked: one house was set on fire; two others were bombarded with bricks and milk bottles; a bicycle was thrown through the window of a fourth. A noisy aggressive crowd of about 200 people filled the streets; there was fighting—"iron railings, choppers and in some cases bicycle chains were displayed."[59] Two policemen were slightly injured and thirty were needed to clear the streets.

Next day, there were similar scenes in Bramley Road, but larger

[58] *The Times*, September 16, 1958. On the subsequent repercussions of this sentence, see pp. 142–43.
[59] *The Times*, September 1, 1958.

crowds of about 400 to 700 were involved; the fighting was more furious; there were shouts, "We will kill the black . . ." and "We will get the blacks"; at times the crowd behaved like a "lynch mob" (as was said later in the court proceedings); there were battles with iron bars, dustbin lids, knives and bottles between white and coloured, and between the "mob" and the police. Several people were injured and taken to hospital; two police cars were damaged. (All this happened although the police had taken precautions and were patrolling the area in pairs.)[60] And there were disturbances in several places. ". . . A gang of 100 youths armed with sticks, iron bars and knives gathered under the railway arches near Latimer Road Underground Station."[61] Some distance away, there were fights, too, in the Harrow Road and in Kensal Rise.

From then on, there was an uninterrupted, chaotic and yet repetitive sequence of rioting, day and night, over a wider area. The crowds were swollen; tempers were sharper; the threats more insistent; the fears greater. The infection spread, and so did curiosity: more combatants arrived and sightseers, too. Most coloured people stayed indoors; but some came out to fight; others collected milk bottles to retaliate if and when their houses were bombarded with petrol bombs and bricks. There were attacks and counter-attacks.

Monday and Tuesday, September 1st and 2nd, were the days of climax, when the disturbances broke out at all hours and were most widespread. But they continued in various places for several days; there were sporadic outbursts—similar to the late August incidents—until mid-September in Notting Hill, Notting Dale, Paddington and also in a few scattered, more distant London districts.

Some of the newspaper headlines in the first days of September were sensational. But in fact, the restrained accounts in small print,

[60] Thirteen of the men involved in the fighting in Bramley Road on that evening (ten white and three coloured men) were later charged with making an 'affray' and tried at the Central Criminal Court. Five men were sentenced to terms of imprisonment ranging from eighteen months to two years; eight others, including the three coloured men, were found not guilty. A charge of making an affray has been seldom brought in the recent period. (There was one previous case in February 1957.) An affray is an ancient misdemeanour at common law, defined as "a fight of two or more persons in a public place to the terror of her Majesty's subjects". The Recorder in sentencing the men said: "By your conduct you have put the clock back nearly three hundred years and disgraced yourselves and your families. As a growing menace, street warfare has made it necessary to revive the law and it must be sternly enforced if society is to be rescued from the miseries of the Middle Ages." He characterised their case as one of "street brawling sharpened and intensified by racial jealousy". (*Manchester Guardian*, September 20, 1958.)

[61] *The Times*, September 1, 1958.

and in particular the stories of the experiences of some individuals, were more dramatic.

This was one incident that occurred on September 1st:

"It comes as a shock to hear the ugly phrase 'lynch him!' on English lips in an English city. But it must be reported that these words were used not once but a dozen times yesterday afternoon. . . .

The object of this venom, a young West African student, was running for his life down Bramley Road, followed by a gang of young toughs who had set upon him, kicked him and twisted his leg before he could escape. Dashing into a greengrocer's shop he persuaded the owner's wife to bolt the door and hid himself in a back room until the police came and rescued him. By that time a crowd of two hundred white people had gathered on the pavements and in the roadway, and it took the combined efforts of police on horseback, in radio squad cars, and twenty constables on foot to disperse them.

The incident took place not fifty yards from the scenes of the worst fighting in the so-called 'race riots' at the week-end. . . .

Long before trouble actually broke out in Bramley Road yesterday afternoon there had been an unhealthy mood in the streets of Notting Hill. It was not a normal Monday, for there was hardly a black-skinned person to be seen in the shops or on the pavements. . . . At the street corners, knots of young men could be seen gathering and occasionally being dispersed by constables on foot patrol.

Into this ugly situation stepped an outsider who had no inkling of what was in store for him. Mr. Seymour Manning is a 26-year-old African student who is at present living in Derby. He had come down for the day to see friends in Notting Hill, and though he did not know it he was under close observation from hostile eyes from the moment he stepped out of the Latimer Road Underground Station.

In the four hours that I had been in this area he was only the third coloured person that I had seen venture out of doors. I watched him disappear up Bramley Road. A few minutes later there was an outburst of screams and jeering and I saw Mr. Manning sprinting back towards the Underground, his tie and blazer streaming out behind him. As his three pursuers closed in, he turned in desperation and flung himself into the doorway of a greengrocer's shop, turned, and slammed it shut. A moment later the shopkeeper's wife . . . appeared in the doorway, locked the door behind her, and turned to face the trio of toughs. She had two friends with her—a housewife of her own age and a boy in his teens.

She kept them at bay until the police arrived a few minutes later. Soon after the first two constables came to her rescue, a radio car arrived, and after that came full reinforcements. It was during the interim period, before it was clear that the police were on their way in force, that people on the opposite pavement called out for a lynching. I went up to one of the young men, who looked to be about 25, and asked him what he had against the African in the shop. 'Just tell your readers that Little Rock learned us a lesson,' was the reply.

Another youth, who had also been calling for a lynching, turned to me and said: 'Tell them we've got a bad enough housing shortage around here without them moving in. Keep Britain White.'

Half an hour after he had taken refuge in the store, Mr. Manning was rescued by a squad of policemen who held back the crowd and escorted him to a car. He was taken off to the home of his friends, where he was treated for bruises and shock."[62]

On that day, many similar incidents were reported:

". . . a crowd of youths went through Oxford Gardens . . . smashing windows in houses where coloured people live. 'They didn't miss a house,' said one white resident. . . .
A police official said earlier: 'There are thousands of people milling around the Notting Hill area. All available reserves are either on duty or standing by. . . .'
In Ladbroke Grove a well-dressed coloured man was kicked in the back as he was leaving the Underground station. At once crowds started to gather and groups of youths 50 to 100 strong rushed from the streets near by where they had been marching, shouting and throwing stones.
It appeared they had been called to the scene by the occupants of large cars, some of them containing eight or ten people, which were cruising round the area. . . .
Coloured people were being advised to go home and some were escorted by policemen.
A coloured man with a girl companion walking down Lancaster Road were chased by a crowd of screaming youths and girls. Saucers, cups, and bottles were thrown. The couple took to their heels pursued by the crowd crying 'Let's get the blacks'."[63]

The M.P. for North Kensington, Mr. George Rogers, toured the area in a loudspeaker van, appealing "for common sense, decency and tolerance in this matter of race relations". He asked people "to remain calm, to stay indoors in your homes tonight, and to obey the police".[64] But while he was touring, there were 'nigger-hunting' tours as well. Five white men, for example, who were later fined, were said to have driven around, shouting from their car, "Stir them up", and other unprintable exhortations.[65] When the evening came, the Union Movement set up a stand outside Latimer Road Underground station.[66]

[62] *Manchester Guardian*, September 2, 1958. In the same issue was the report of another 'small' incident which gives an idea of the atmosphere of those days. A boy of 15 appeared before the Juvenile Court. He was said ". . . to have approached a coloured man in a railway compartment at Liverpool Street Station and shouted: 'Here's one of them—you black knave. We have complained to the Government about you people. You come here, you take our women and do all sorts of things free of charge. They won't hang you, so we will have to do it.' The coloured man was frightened and moved to the other end of the compartment. . . . Another passenger called the guard and the boy was put in the guard's van."
[63] *The Times*, September 2, 1958.   [64] *Ibid*.
[65] *Manchester Guardian*, September 17, 1958.
[66] The Union Movement were particularly active in various parts of the district during those days. On September 4th, one of its members (aged 27) was

On the next day, September 2nd, Scotland Yard issued an appeal to the public, saying that the Metropolitan Police "will continue to carry out their duty to preserve the Queen's peace without fear, favour or discrimination". They pointed out that "at incidents of unrest the situation is seriously worsened by the presence of sight-seers". However, the 'incidents of unrest' of the previous day were repeated. Most coloured people stayed hidden; some were militant. Coloured bus conductors who lived in the North Kensington area were escorted home by police at the end of their journeys.

"A dark face against the light of a lamp-post in Bramley Road went by. 'Look, that's a wog going along,' said one of the many pale boys that stood about hawking *Action*, the Union Movement paper. But nobody stirred. Too many police were hovering about in the still warm air. The man went out of sight, the only dark face I saw."[67]

"A big crowd of youths chanting 'Down with the Niggers' as-sembled in Lancaster Road and a youth leading one group held up a banner with the slogan: 'Deport all Niggers'."

". . . racial feeling is not confined to the gangs of youths, many of them from the Elephant and Castle and other distant tough districts, who cause the trouble in the evenings. In one street where some of the ugliest fighting has taken place your Correspondent found a group of men in a public house singing 'Old Man River' and 'Bye Bye Blackbird', and punctuating the songs with vicious anti-Negro slogans. The men said that their motto was 'Keep Britain White', and they made all sorts of wild charges against their coloured neighbours."[68]

Altogether at least 55 people were arrested on that day, more than on each of the previous days. The charges varied—the usual ones were using insulting or threatening behaviour, obstructing the police, or possessing offensive weapons. Broken milk bottles, dustbin lids, iron bars, bicycle chains and loaded leather belts were most popular; firearms were not used. The collection of 'offensive weapons' put into a box in the Magistrate's court during one of these hearings indicates the range. The box was "gradually filled with flick knives, stilettos, razors, a bicycle chain, choppers, a club, and a carving knife".[69]

---

arrested in Ladbroke Grove while distributing pamphlets. He was accused of using insulting behaviour. Another man, accused of the same charge and fined, was said by a police sergeant to have been trying "to stir up trouble against coloured people". He was marching down the Harrow Road on September 6th, shouting, among other things, "Achtung, Achtung, Heil Hitler."

[67] *Manchester Guardian*, September 3, 1958.
[68] *The Times*, September 3, 1958.
[69] *Ibid.*

It was reported that about 140 people were arrested in the London 'riot' areas during the main days of the disturbances from August 30th to September 4th, 1958. (In addition, there were some arrests both before and after these

The police and the peaceful public were hoping for rain to 'damp the trouble'. And when the rain did come on September 3rd—after four of the most turbulent days that London had seen for a long time—it did help to disperse the crowds; unrest was more localised.[70] But the next day was hot and tense again, though the scope of the disturbances was more restricted than before. Petrol bombs were flung into the houses of coloured people in Notting Hill and Paddington. There was the by then usual 'anti-nigger' shouting and bottle throwing. Even the most ordinary encounter between white and coloured could still set off new turmoil. When a coloured mother's perambulator brushed against, and became entangled with, a white mother's push chair at a road junction in North Kensington, a crowd of about 150 people collected instantly, and the police had to be called to restore order.[71]

On September 5th, two West Indian Ministers arrived in London— Mr. Norman Manley, the Chief Minister of Jamaica and Dr. Carl Lacorbinière, the Deputy Prime Minister in the Federal Government of the West Indies. A third, Dr. Hugh Cummins, the Prime Minister of Barbados, followed shortly afterwards. They held talks with the Government, addressed meetings of their countrymen and visited the critical areas in London and Nottingham. Gradually the coloured people in the troubled districts of London went outside again. But unrest and fear were still acute until mid-September.[72] During that

---

dates.) Most of those arrested during the six critical days were fined; some got prison sentences and some were discharged.

The majority of the people who were arrested during the disturbances were white; one in four were coloured. A high proportion of the white people arrested (about 60 per cent) were under twenty years of age; but one in seven were over thirty; and the remainder in the intermediate age groups. Most of the white 'offenders' (about two-thirds) lived in the districts in and around Notting Dale in which the disorders occurred, but comparatively few came from streets in which coloured people are densely clustered. Over two-thirds of the white people arrested (those for whom all the relevant details are available from Press reports) had their addresses in streets or districts in which hardly any or no West Indians live (as shown by the data for the London Sample, referred to in chapter II).

[70] It did rain on that day steadily from the early afternoon until the mid-morning of the next day. And there was also a heavy, thundery shower in the evening at the critical time, just when the public houses were closing.

[71] *Manchester Guardian*, September 5, 1960.

[72] The police were still patrolling the area in force and dispersing any groups that formed in the streets. Thus when Mr. Manley was touring Paddington on September 8th with his colleagues, he was told by the police to "move along" while he was talking to four other West Indians in the street. Mr. Manley was rather irritated by this incident, and was reported to have said: "As there were fifteen to twenty people at the time on the opposite side of the street, I felt it was a discriminating act and indicative of the attitude of the people in the area to our people, which I can only hope is not general anywhere else." *Manchester Guardian*, September 9, 1958.

period, attacks on coloured people and houses were still reported, not only from the Shepherd's Bush to Paddington belt, but also from other places in Greater London.

Whose Disorder?

On September 15th, Mr. Justice Salmon gave judgment in the trial of the nine 'nigger-hunting' youths. It was an exceptionally severe sentence, and it has, therefore, become a very controversial one.[73] It was meant to have a deterrent effect, and it probably had that effect, at least for a time.[74] For after September 17th, it could be said that the temperature in and around North Kensington had become normal again. Standards of normalcy had, however, changed. Since the 'riots' sporadic aggression against coloured people in those marginal parts of West London has become routine, though it does not follow a regular curve. It has been an uneasy truce.

Mr. Justice Salmon told the nine offenders:

"It was you men who started the whole of this violence in Notting Hill. You are a minute and insignificant section of the population who

[73] In many quarters, Right and Left, the view was taken that, as Mr. Fenner Brockway put it (after having asked the Home Secretary to recommend the exercise of the Royal Prerogative to reduce the sentences): "These youths were as much the victims of the hysteria which swept over Notting Hill as the West Indians." (*Manchester Guardian*, August 19, 1959.) Moreover, the general concept of punishment was discussed at length in this context. And there was not only reasoned discussion. Mr. Justice Salmon was henceforth referred to as that "Jewish Judge" by the fascist papers. (It was also reported that he had received a threatening letter.) The boys appealed against the sentence, but without success. Nevertheless, the controversy is still continuing. The Labour M.P. for the boys' constituency (Hammersmith North) raised the question again in the House of Commons in February 1960, and asked that "further consideration . . . be given to a reduction of these sentences if it is not possible to quash them altogether". He said that the boys had found themselves in the "trouble cauldron" of a district "where justice is swift". He was supported by several members on both sides of the House. A Conservative Member argued that the boys "should be punished surely only for the violence of which they were guilty, and not for the nature of the persons against whom it was directed". He went on: ". . . I was postulating the case of the same degree of violence used by similar boys against not coloured people . . . but against, say white people, possibly on the other side of the controversy, perhaps *too strong* advocates of race discrimination." (My italics.) He suggested that in those latter circumstances "much lighter sentences would have been inflicted". The Government spokesman (for the Home Department) replied that he was "unable to indicate a prospect that the Home Secretary will find it possible to recommend any remission of the sentences which the court considered right and which were upheld on appeal". *Parliamentary Debates*, H.o.C., 23rd February, 1960, cols. 331–339.

[74] It is probable that the prison sentences passed in Nottingham on September 1st had a similar effect in that city. for subsequently the disturbances petered out.

have brought shame upon the district in which you lived, and have filled the whole nation with horror, indignation, and disgust."[75]

The Judge expressed a view current at the time. The upsurge of aggression in West London was so disturbing that everyone wanted to be reassured. 'Why had it happened?' 'Who was guilty?' 'Is it over now?' It is perhaps not surprising that the answers were circumscribed; they tended to simplify rather than to clarify the search for causes and culprits.

Thus there was widespread agreement that it was a 'minute' group of young hooligans or 'teddy boys' who were responsible for the troubles in Nottingham, and even more for those in Notting Hill.[76] Some sections of the Press were blamed. It was said that their sensational treatment of the news had had a snowball effect: it had excited young 'ruffians'; and it had also attracted the 'morbidly curious' sightseers, whose presence had made it so difficult to restore order. There was talk of the influence of fascist agitators, who were, however, regarded as another 'insignificant' lunatic fringe by many commentators. And there was even some straightforward 'witchhunting': a well-known American columnist explained (in the *New York Herald Tribune*) that the disturbances in Nottingham and London were the result of a Communist conspiracy—indeed, of the same conspiracy that had accentuated racial friction in Little Rock, and fomented riots in the Southern states of his own country. This was the one theory that—as the *Manchester Guardian* said—"had not occurred even to the most Right-minded commentators in Fleet Street".[77] Nevertheless, as the point had been made, some people thought it appropriate to add it to their repertoire.[78]

Another parallel set of explanations was sought not only in the problem of white trouble makers, but also—or even more—in the 'Colour Problem'. There were those whose instinctive first reaction

[75] *The Times*, September 16, 1958. (This was an additional paragraph in the speech previously quoted.) The Judge ended by saying: ". . . I am determined that you and anyone anywhere who may be tempted to follow your example shall clearly understand that crimes such as this will not be tolerated in this country, but will inevitably meet in these courts with the stern punishment which they so justly deserve."

[76] The very fact that the events were referred to, and are remembered, as the 'Notting Hill' disturbances, despite the fact that they were spread over a much wider area, is also consistent with the general desire to regard them as an isolated disorder.

[77] *Manchester Guardian*, September 11, 1958.

[78] For example, the Bow Group wrote in a 'Memorandum on Coloured Peoples in Britain' (October 1958): "The Communist Party and the Union Movement (and, to a lesser degree, the Irish Republicans), each with an axe to grind, are anxious to see their ends furthered by fermenting unrest."

to the disturbances was to argue, explicitly or implicitly, that there would be no racial friction if there were no coloured minority in this country; or that the quantity of friction is determined by the number of coloured migrants. Hence it was their contribution to the discussion to ask for immigration control.[79] There were others who adopted a more sophisticated approach: they probed the characteristics and habits of coloured newcomers. This was done with diverse intentions—positively and negatively, on the basis of more or less scanty information. But however the probing was done, there was still far more dissection of the coloured minority group than of British society.

Thus although there were other lines of thought as well, the predominant accounts of the causes of disorder tended to be evasive and tautological. Stripped of the verbiage, they said not much more than that it is the coloured people who represent a colour problem; or that a small irresponsible section of the population had acted irresponsibly. This was a typical summary:

> "Those involved in the recent outbreaks invariably appear to have been ill-educated, unskilled and irresponsible. Few white participants have been other than teen-age hooligans. Most of the coloured people have been West Indian labourers, frequently from Jamaica."[80]

It was a deceptively simple sum of disorder, and while many of the items were correctly noted, something went wrong in the addition.[81]

[79] The course of discussions on this subject is described in Chapter V, part 1.

Another version of a similar attitude was expressed in a long letter by a titled gentleman to the *Daily Telegraph*, September 19, 1958, headed "Peoples at Peace—An Example from the Deep South". The writer said that he had recently stayed in Georgia and the Southern states. "I found, in Savannah and elsewhere, the coloured folk far happier than in the great Northern Cities, living naturally in their own quarters, earning all the wages they needed, driving cars that white people might envy and enjoying all that civilisation which they would never have reached had they been left to develop in Africa and where they should have been returned after the American Civil War. . . . They [the 'old ruling race' of the South] tell me they do not want to be rushed by Washington and also that they do not want the coloured in their hotels, theatres, clubs or churches. Incidentally, the coloured prefer their own churches. . . . I found the coloured in the South the happiest community in America. . . . Experience shows that new towns and suburbs should be erected for the coloured in England."

[80] Bow Group Memorandum, *op. cit.*

[81] Although there were many news items on the disturbances and a great deal of commentary, a general detailed account of the events is not available. A brief one (some points of which I have been unable to confirm) is included in James Wickenden's pamphlet, *Colour in Britain*, London, 1958, pp. 30–34, 38–42. This pamphlet was written immediately after the disturbances and completed on September 30th. However, a realistic description, derived from a great deal of personal observation, can be found in the last chapter of Colin MacInnes's

It is true that there were many young people involved in the disturbances—in London even more than in Nottingham; but not everyone who took part, actively or passively, was young. And the young live in an adult society. The 'youthful thugs' were roaming around in an environment in which their actions were not discouraged; indeed, it seems that they were definitely encouraged by some of their elders and betters. They rarely met white opposition. While there were many people who preserved their sense of decency in the turmoil of Notting Dale—some white housewives did the shopping for their coloured neighbours who dared not go outside—active defiance of 'nigger-hunting' was rare. There were not many who had the determination of the greengrocer's wife who stood outside her door facing a violent crowd.

The 'teddy boys' had the sanction of their own back street society; more important still, they were operating in terms of their own social code—in deliberate opposition to the region of remote official authority beyond their back streets. 'Nigger-baiting' was their new form of social protest, a particularly convenient form because it was, apparently, tacitly accepted by some sections of both worlds; indeed it combined the worst of both worlds—the worst of their inside and of the outside world.[82]

Was that not made clear by the sightseers who came to watch aggression? And were the many hundreds who stood by as mere spectators any less to blame than the few young 'hooligans' who acted in the performance? It is unlikely that the actors would have continued without the spectators.

It is probable, too, that the more sensational accounts in some sections of the Press intensified the pathological excitement. But they did not create it; it was there to be intensified. And in general, the Press played a positive role—not only by acknowledging the impor-

---

novel, *Absolute Beginners*, London, 1959. This chapter gives a vivid impression of the atmosphere and situation in the critical districts of London during those turbulent days.

[82] The protest theme—against the 'establishment'—was expressed also in the fact that the gangs which roamed the streets included abusive remarks about the Queen in their repertoire of hostile shouts. And one remark of this kind, in particular (reported in *The Observer*, September 7, 1958) showed better than any lengthy treatise on colour prejudice in Britain how the lack of positive influences from the official world, however unintentionally, combines with the negative influences in the back street world. One of the boys told *The Observer* reporter: "It's all the . . . Queen's fault. She goes to all the black countries and they do their war dances for her and then they think that they can come over here and take our jobs."

The image of the savage, primitive Negro, still communicated from 'above', becomes explosive within the zones of transition.

tance of the events, but also by the critical editorial comments on them.

Objective difficulties accentuated the tension between coloured and white at that time. There was a minor recession—and thus increased competition for unskilled jobs—in Nottingham. Both there and in London, the housing problems in the zones of transition were acute. And the latter, in turn, contribute to the awareness of social and cultural differences between 'natives' and newcomers. But such problems exist at other times and in other places without causing an explosion. Indeed some of them exist more strikingly in the districts of fairly dense coloured settlement than in the actual foci of disorder in London.

Moreover, the widespread assumption that Notting Hill is a 'coloured quarter', and that it was the ghetto-style mode of living of the new minority which largely explains the disturbances, is not confirmed. There are as yet no coloured ghettoes in London; there are only a few streets with clusters of coloured people, and these streets were not the main scenes of violence.

Why then did the 'riots' break out in the Shepherd's Bush-Notting Dale-Paddington belt? Why there and not elsewhere? The actual concrete frictions between white and coloured were not most intense in these places. It is the friction between white and white which is symbolised in these districts and for which outlets have to be found. All the current unrests are rolled into one in these streets. They are a panorama of the schisms in British society which cause disturbance, singular and plural. And once the turmoil starts, it is bound to spread because it is not self-contained. The 'trouble makers of Notting Hill' acted out tendencies which were latent in all social strata. They were shouting what others were whispering.

That was the lesson of the 1958 disturbances. They revealed that there are in mid-twentieth century Britain not 'two nations' but several, which are estranged from one another. And both the disorders and the comments on them also showed more clearly than any previous events the all-pervasive British ambivalence towards colour. Most important, they proved that in so ambiguous a situation, aggressive fringe groups, though 'minute', are not 'insignificant'.

V

Disharmony and Harmony

1. REACTIONS TO THE EVENTS OF 1958 AND 1959

SINCE August 1958, the distinction between official opinion and private opinions on matters of race relations in this country has become increasingly marked, though it is by no means as yet quite plain. Previously, the growing number of West Indian newcomers had not attracted a great deal of attention. Then suddenly—but not unexpectedly in some quarters—the 'colour problem' in Britain became nation-wide and world-wide news. Public opinion was challenged.

The First Impact

The flood of reports and comments caused by the disturbances in the early autumn of 1958, at its most intense in September, lasted until the end of the year. At least the views of official institutions and their spokesmen began to be clarified—and also in some respects to coalesce. The Press was almost unanimous in its censure of the 'hooligans of Notting Hill'; and in its concern with the 'race riots', 'outbreaks of racial violence' or 'racial disturbances', as the events were variously called. (It was the last term, without the adjective, which became the accepted one.) *The Times* came out (on September 4th) with a classic first leader on 'A Family of Nations'. For several weeks, almost every issue of a newspaper and journal contained items, articles or editorials on questions of race relations. There were radio and television programmes; national and local conferences. Many individuals and organisations—the political parties, trade unions and voluntary associations at the national and local levels—felt impelled to state their position on the subject of 'White and Black' in Britain. It is true that there were some—in particular, the 'Lords Spiritual'—who remained silent at that time.[1] Nevertheless, the

---

[1] In the House of Lords Debate on 'Colour Prejudice and Violence', the Earl of Lucan said: ". . . there seemed to me some noticeable gaps among those public figures who denounced the rioting. Certainly there was a statement by the

British Council of Churches and many ministers and congregations spoke plainly; and there was certainly no scarcity of rebuke for the 'dastardly attacks'.

New organisations were formed in response to the events. Special pamphlets and memoranda were issued—for example, by the Labour Party, the Fabian Society, the Bow Group, the Conservative Commonwealth Council, and by Mosley's Union Movement.[2]

The Labour Party, in its statement on *Racial Discrimination*, said:

> "The Labour Party utterly abhors every manifestation of racial prejudice, and particularly condemns those instances which have recently occurred in this country."

The Bow Group spoke:

> "The foreign reputation of the United States has suffered severely as a result of Little Rock. For the U.K. to be laid open to similar charges would disillusion many who look upon Britain as a tolerant corner in an intolerant world."

The Conservative Commonwealth Council gave a warning:

> "We cannot retain the integrity or the cohesion of the Commonwealth unless we can solve and eradicate colour prejudice here in Britain."[3]

---

late Pope Pius XII denouncing racialism, and a number of ministers of religion in this country, of various sects and denominations, also did fine work; but, unless I missed something, there was a notable absence of statements by the official religious leaders in this country of the main Christian and other sects". During the same debate, Lord Silkin commented: "The other category of person—I hope I may say this with all delicacy—from whom we have not had a word, is the Lords Spiritual. We have had one or two present for part of the debate, but I think this House would have been enriched if it had had some expression of opinion from the Lords Spiritual in this House." *Parliamentary Debates*, H.o.L., 19th November 1958, cols. 684, 685, 703.

[2] The Labour Party's Statement on *Racial Discrimination* was published very soon after the disturbances, in September 1958. The Fabian Society pamphlet was written by K. L. Little, *Colour and Common Sense* (Fabian Tract 315, 1958). The Bow Group ("an independent research society of younger Conservatives") and the West Indies Group of the Conservative Commonwealth Council issued duplicated statements on 'Coloured Peoples in Britain' in October 1958; and on 'Race Relations in the United Kingdom' in April 1959, respectively. The Union Movement's pamphlet, by Robert Row, was: *The Colour Question in Britain: Causes and Solution*, 1959 (see Chapter V, part 2). The Institute of Race Relations also issued a pamphlet: James Wickenden, *Colour in Britain*, *op. cit.* Several other publications, written before the disturbances, were published just at the period when race relations was the topic of general interest. Among these were books by the Rev. C. S. Hill and by E. R. Braithwait, *To Sir, With Love* (London, 1959) and a pamphlet which is apprehensive of 'miscegenation': G. C. L. Bertram, *West Indian Immigration*, Eugenics Society (London, 1958).

[3] These are quotations from the statements referred to in footnote 2 above.

Although there were variations—and not only slight ones—in the tenor and emphasis of the numerous pronouncements made at that time by 'opinion leaders', the public statements—apart from those coming from the extreme right-wing fringes, and from some odd men out—all had one common denominator: 'racial discrimination is un-British'. It was on that basis that the discussion about the reasons and remedies for racial tension continued. The disturbances occurred in the middle of a Parliamentary recess. But soon after the new sessio⟩ had begun, debates were held in both Houses of Parliament. Questions on the subject were included in opinion polls. In the Queen's broadcast on Christmas Day 1958 was a friendly reference to people from the Commonwealth living in Britain.

In many public places, though not in all, the first reaction to the events of the late summer was one of acute shock. The revelation of aggressive racial prejudice was startling; it aroused shame and anger. Lord Pakenham expressed this feeling when he opened a debate on 'Colour Prejudice and Violence' in the House of Lords in November 1958:

> ". . . I think most of us felt during those crucial weeks that we were standing on the edge of a precipice and that we were looking into an abyss from which we must draw back, and draw back at once. If that sort of thing was going to continue, it might be an exaggeration to say that our survival was at stake, but it would be no exaggeration whatever to say that our British traditions and the ideals that we most prize and pride ourselves on in the face of the world would be placed in extreme jeopardy."[4]

The general social climate—international and national—at the moment of the disturbances in 1958 largely explains the intense and widespread public response to them. They became in a sense a focus of general uneasiness amid the cold peace of the late fifties; a symbol of social ills, already much discussed; an image of the threats to individual and national self-respect in a segmented society and in a changing Commonwealth. 'Colour' was in any case already in the daily news from Africa and America. In particular, the 'uncivil war' between the defenders and opponents of white supremacy in the South of the United States had been followed closely in Britain. Little Rock had become a dishonourable term; Governor Faubus had no declared friends in this country. And then suddenly it appeared that there was a number of them after all—right next door. Numerous, though inappropriate, comparisons between Little Rock and Notting Hill were made.[5]

---

[4] *Parliamentary Debates*, H.o.L., 19th November 1958, col. 633.
[5] These comparisons were made not only on this side of the Atlantic. The American newspapers—North and South—gave a great deal of space and

In the background, there was also the danger of growing unemployment in Britain at that period; it was emphasised as a source of friction between white and coloured people. There was the chronic housing problem, aggravated by fairly recent changes in the policy and finance of municipal housing which had made the scarcity of new accommodation for low income groups even more acute. Various symptoms of urban social pathology had just then caused a good deal of concern: crime and violence (in words and deeds); 'teddy boys'; prostitutes; licensed drinking clubs. All these symptoms are visible especially in the zones of transition in large cities where coloured newcomers tend to live. Prostitution, in particular, was much talked about because of the contemporaneous proposals for changes in the law relating to homosexuality and prostitution. The stereotype of the coloured man, who induces white girls to become prostitutes and who lives on their earnings, was frequently mentioned. And it was one of the charges against coloured people that their clubs—usually dingy basements in residential streets—were noisy nuisances, and also centres of drug-peddling and vice. It was said, moreover, that there were altogether too many "dens of iniquity" of this kind —white or coloured—and that they were places of general lawlessness.

Thus the disorders in Nottingham and Notting Hill were in fact part and parcel of many others. Most commentators put the immediate blame for the disturbances on white fringe groups—teddy boys and trouble makers; or on general social problems, more or less vaguely defined. Some held different views. After Mr. George Rogers, the Labour M.P. for Kensington North (which includes Notting Hill and Notting Dale), had visited the Home Office to discuss the events, he said to the Press that he had told the Junior Minister: ". . . it was wrong to say this trouble had been started by hooligans. It was the reaction of people, very sorely tried by some sections of the coloured population."[6]

Among official spokesmen, Mr. Rogers was in a minority; indeed this part of his statement was severely criticised and not easily forgotten.

As the debates—public and private—continued, there was much

---

prominence to the English 'race riots'; indeed, so much that, by and large, it was not possible to get a realistic picture of the actual events in Nottingham and Notting Hill from these reports. At that time (as I myself know), it was also a rather trying experience for a British citizen to answer questions in the Deep South, where it was generally thought—with satisfaction by the segregationists, with dismay by the Negroes and their friends—that Notting Hill had, in fact, become an outpost of Alabama.   [6] *Manchester Guardian*, September 4, 1958.

speculation about causes and cures; and consequently a polarisation of opinion. There were those who regarded the problem of racial tension as a British responsibility, and who said that new measures were needed to counteract it—in particular, more housing for low income groups; improved education for citizenship; a better mutual exchange of information on British and Commonwealth affairs; legislation against racial discrimination and group defamation. But there were others who talked primarily, as they said, in 'practical' terms. They argued that as it was a 'colour problem', it was aggravated by the growth of the coloured minority, and especially by 'undesirable' coloured immigrants. They demanded, therefore, that immigration into Britain should be controlled; or that migrants from the Commonwealth who were convicted of criminal offences should be deported; or that both policies should be adopted. During the autumn, it was this issue—of the 'quantity' and 'quality' of immigrants—on which the controversy was focussed.

Control of Immigration

It was not a new idea to restrict the number of immigrants from Commonwealth countries. There had been similar occasional suggestions and discussions before the 'riots'. A few months earlier, on April 3rd 1958, the Commons had debated a back bench motion on the adjournment:

> "That in the opinion of this House, the time has come for reconsideration of the arrangements whereby British subjects from other parts of the Commonwealth are allowed to enter this country without restriction."

Although the terms of the motion (signed by three Labour members, two Conservatives and one Independent) were rather wide, the discussion in the House was mostly concerned with coloured immigrants. The Government speaker, Miss Hornsby Smith, said:

> ". . . we cannot ignore the rising potential of this immigration. In view of the size of the populations of the countries from which these people are coming, we have to take stock of the position as it now presents itself, and to realise that it could in the future possibly constitute a very grave burden on this country if the trend were to increase, or if the numbers arriving in this country were to become out of proportion to those that the country can reasonably absorb."

She mentioned enquiries made by government departments into rates of unemployment, sickness and crime among coloured people in Britain. "Although the coloured immigrants are not, on the whole, being assimilated into the country", in general, they did not cause any 'special' employment, health or police problems. There had been discussions with the governments of the West Indian territories, of India and of Pakistan on the question of discouraging "unsuitable immigrants".

> ". . . we are certainly not complacent . . . but we remain reluctant to contemplate any departure from our traditional readiness to receive all citizens who have the status of a British subject."[7]

Shortly afterwards, for reasons of their own, the governments of India and Pakistan did in fact impose a stricter control on intending emigrants to Britain.

Immediately after the first outbreak of violence in Nottingham, two Nottingham M.P.s—one Conservative and one Labour—asked for a partial closing of the 'open door' to Britain. They were sharply criticised: ". . . it is deplorable", said the *Manchester Guardian*, that they "should have spoken as though the entire onus rested on the coloured community and talked of restricting immigration to this country as if this might be the prime remedy."[8] But there was also no lack of support for their views. Indeed, the events of Notting Dale intensified the demand for curbing immigration; it was made by several other M.P.s and elder statesmen, and in particular by some of the previous advocates of a 'quota'. This pressure was reflected in the Government's statement issued on September 3rd 1958.

> "As regards the wider aspects of policy, Her Majesty's Government has for some little time been examining the results of this country's time-honoured practice to allow free entry of immigrants from Commonwealth and colonial countries. While this study of major policy and its implications and effects on employment will continue, Her Majesty's Government do not think it right to take long-term decisions, except after careful consideration of the problem as a whole."[9]

---

[7] *Parliamentary Debates*, H.o.C., 3rd April 1958, cols. 1426 to 1430. In May, a similar, more strongly worded, motion was tabled, for which the signatures of 31 Conservatives, two Labour members and one Independent had been obtained before the Parliamentary recess. The question was not again raised by the same group of signatories in the next session after the disturbances, though some of them maintained their demand for restricting immigration of coloured people. A new motion was tabled and discussed (as mentioned on pp. 156–57).

[8] *Manchester Guardian*, August 28, 1958. The two M.P.s were the Labour Member for Nottingham North and the Conservative Member for Nottingham Central.

[9] This was the last paragraph of the Government's statement. Its full text was important, no less for the omissions than for the content. The preceding paragraphs read:

> "The Home Secretary, Mr. Butler, has reported to the Prime Minister on the incidents involved in racial disturbance in Nottingham and Notting Hill. These incidents have an immediate and a long-term importance.

However, the implicit suggestion in the Government's statement of the possibility of limiting immigration from the Commonwealth was soon modified—doubtless because the opposition to such a major change of policy, coming from influential quarters in this country and from the Commonwealth, was by no means silent. And it could hardly be denied, moreover, that the demand for restrictions did not refer to the majority of immigrants from the Commonwealth— to those who are white—but to the minority, those who are coloured.[10] Immigration control was a polite term for some sort of colour bar.

The Government's view, after considering the expressions of public opinion, was given by Mr. R. A. Butler, the Home Secretary, at the Conservative Party Conference in the second week of October 1958. He said: "We should maintain the long and respected tradition of allowing citizens of the Commonwealth to come here." But he added that the Government would in the next session probably seek power to deport criminals. The Conference, however, passed a resolution asking that the immigration laws should be revised "irrespective of race, colour or creed" on the basis of reciprocity with respective Commonwealth and colonial countries, and that "immigrants who are convicted of serious criminal offences should be subject to deportation".[11] According to the Government spokesman in the House of Lords debate of November 19th on 'Colour Prejudice and Violence', the question of legislation to deport criminals was then still under consideration. Two weeks later, on December 5th, when the Commons debated a back bench motion on 'Immigration (Control)', the Government speaker concluded:

"Both the Government and, I am glad to record, the Opposition Front Bench do not see the necessity for any general control of immigration. The Government are considering very carefully the

---

The immediate aspect involves the maintenance of law and order. The Government and the authorities concerned wish to make it clear that the utmost strictness will be observed in the impartial enforcement of the law and in preventing the illegal carrying of offensive weapons.

Meanwhile, it is important that the significance of these incidents should not be exaggerated at home or oversea.

The general public can best contribute by the exercise of the utmost discretion in avoiding situations in which they may become unwittingly involved." (*The Times*, September 4, 1958.)

[10] It was estimated from official sources that in 1956 about one in four of all immigrants from Commonwealth countries in the U.K. were coloured. Though the official statistics are by no means precise, and the ratio of coloured migrants has presumably increased since then, they are undoubtedly still a minority of Commonwealth immigrants.

[11] *The Times*, October 12, 1958.

possibility of legislation to deport criminals, but, as I have pointed out, that gives rise to great complexities."[12]

There were thus two main shifts in the Government's position. The idea of controlling immigration by statute was quickly discarded, and attention was concentrated on the possibility of deporting 'undesirable' people and criminals. By the beginning of December, when the issue had been further discussed, the Government was adopting a cool attitude towards suggestions to deport criminals. But this was not the end of the matter; since then discussions with Commonwealth countries have continued.

Although there were notable differences in the dominant attitudes of the three major parties—as shown by their annual conferences in October—the debate on immigration tended to cut across party lines. There were some Labour Party people who supported the idea of controlling immigration; there were others who only went so far as to support proposals to deport criminals. But the Labour Party's official view was not hesitant:

"We are firmly convinced that any form of British legislation limiting Commonwealth immigration to this country would be disastrous to our status in the Commonwealth and to the confidence of the Commonwealth peoples."[13]

The Liberal Party Conference spoke in similar straightforward terms. An executive emergency motion was passed, denouncing racial discrimination and rejecting any restriction of immigration.[14] The Conservative Party Conference, on the other hand, demanded such restriction (though on the basis of mutual agreement with Commonwealth countries); and it also asked for deportation of criminals. And yet there were Conservatives—frontbenchers and backbenchers —who were strongly opposed to the first proposal, if not always to the latter. Indeed, it was on the question of the deportation of criminals that there was most uncertainty, and that party lines got tangled most often.

The Conservative Commonwealth Council, speaking for the considerable wing of Conservatives who were decidedly 'liberal' in their attitude to immigration, said that it would be wrong to "deny Commonwealth citizens their traditional right to come to Britain".

"It is our view that if we were to legislate against colour we would in the end bring about the disintegration of the Commonwealth."[15]

---

[12] *Parliamentary Debates*, H.o.C., 5th December 1958, col. 1588.

[13] Labour Party Statement on *Racial Discrimination*, *op. cit.*, p. 4.

[14] The Communist Party and all the extreme left-wing associations were no less emphatic.

[15] Memorandum by the West Indies Group of the Conservative Commonwealth Council, April 1959, *op. cit*.

The Stigma of Prejudice

However, most people—Conservative and Labour—who advocated immigration control were very anxious to start off by saying that they did not intend "to legislate against colour". There was no doubt about it: as the public debate went on, the words 'colour prejudice' increasingly became 'dirty'; they denoted a stigma to be shunned, the traces of which had to be avoided in making responsible policy proposals. By the end of 1958, political etiquette with regard to such matters had become stricter.

When Mr. Cyril Osborne, a Conservative Member who had for some time been concerned with immigration control and similar questions, spoke in the Commons after the recess during the debate on the Queen's Speech in October 1958, he referred to "the urgent need for a restriction upon immigration into this country, particularly of coloured immigrants". (In this category he put all those who are "loosely termed coloured people, including Maltese and Cypriots".) He said:

"I realise that our motives might be misinterpreted overseas, but it is time someone spoke for this country and for the white man who lives here, and I propose so to do."

Mr. Osborne then went on to talk of the dangers—actual and potential—which the coloured people bring to this country because, as he alleged, of their propensity for idleness, sickness (especially tuberculosis and leprosy) and crime; and also because of the alarming growth of their numbers. (He estimated that at the current rate of immigration "we should have 6,000,000 coloured people in this country after the next two decades".)[16]

Mr. Osborne's speech was received on both sides of the House with embarrassment, dismay and anger. It was plain that there was no sympathy with his views, certainly not with their presentation, although a number of Members were inclined to support the idea of deporting criminals. A Labour M.P., Dr. Horace King, had an opportunity to reply to Mr. Osborne immediately.

"Having just returned from the deep South, I may be pardoned if . . . I make an observation or two on the distasteful remarks we have heard . . . remarks which almost made me feel I was in the South again. . . . I believe it is almost a sin against the Holy Ghost to equate crime with the colour of the skin."[17]

Next day, a Conservative Member, Mr. Nigel Fisher, rebuked his hon. Friend, Mr. Osborne.

[16] *Parliamentary Debates*, H.o.C., 29th October 1958, cols. 195–205.
[17] *Ibid.*, cols. 204, 205.

"I hope I am right in saying that probably 99 per cent of the House
of Commons would be opposed to discrimination on grounds of
colour as such."

Mr. Fisher went on to talk of the nature of colour prejudice, in
relation to the recent disturbances.

". . . the deeper side of it, the twisted, distorted racial hatred and
bitterness which sparked off these breaches of the peace, is deeper
rooted and immensely complicated in source and character. . . . I
think the 'nigger haters'—of course, I do not include my hon. Friend
among those—are not normally people of very high intelligence or
very high education. They are generally the least secure economically
and socially. . . ."[18]

Nevertheless, Mr. Osborne raised the question again, though his
private Member's motion, which the Commons debated a few weeks
later, was then—in his view—"restrained, moderate and limited".
The motion read:

"That, whilst this House deplores all forms of colour bar or race
discrimination, it nevertheless feels that some control, similar to that
exercised by every other Government in the Commonwealth, is now
necessary, and urges Her Majesty's Government to take immediate
steps to restrict the immigration of all persons, irrespective of race,
colour, or creed, who are unfit, idle or criminal; and to repatriate all
immigrants who are found guilty of a serious criminal offence in the
United Kingdom."

This time, Mr. Osborne started his speech differently. "I recognise
that this subject is political dynamite. . . . I shall try to say nothing
at all that will increase the difficulties either of the Colonial Secretary
or of the Home Secretary." He stressed that his previous speeches
(in the House and on television) might have been misunderstood. He
himself had "no racial hatreds or antipathies" and "no colour bar
sympathies". And yet he went on very quickly to talk about coloured
immigrants, and continued to do so despite an intervention: "The
hon. Gentleman is spoiling the case".[19]

Mr. Martin Lindsay (a Conservative) who seconded the motion
might have had some chance to repair the damage, for he was quite
frank. He said:

"The Motion uses the words: 'irrespective of race, colour or creed'
but we cannot discuss this matter in such a general context. We all
know perfectly well that the whole core of the problem of immigration
is coloured immigration. We would do much better to face that and
to discuss it realistically in this context."
"We must ask ourselves to what extent we want Great Britain to

---

[18] *Parliamentary Debates*, H.o.C., 30th October 1958, cols. 416 and 418.
[19] *Parliamentary Debates*, H.o.C., 5th December 1958, cols. 1552–1561.

become a multi-racial community. . . . One of the difficulties about discussing this problem is that we are all a little scared of being thought to be illiberal. I frankly admit that that is not a charge which I should like to have laid at my door. . . . I could not find any excuses whatever for anyone who believed in a colour bar in any community where black and white have to co-exist. That, however, is altogether different from changing the nature of a community. . . ."[20]

Still, it was no good. In spite of "the pious wrappings of this motion" (of which one of the speakers in the debate complained) there were very few in the House—and certainly none on the Government and Opposition front benches—who were prepared to take the risk of supporting it. Any talk of legislative action to restrict immigration from the Commonwealth "irrespective of race, colour or creed" had that undertone of colour prejudice which was no longer politically wise—at least not in the sphere of influence of Westminster at that stage.[21]

This had been quite plain, too, in the course of a slightly earlier debate in "another place". Those noble Lords who had previously sympathised with proposals for statutory immigration control no longer wanted—as Lord Salisbury said—to "press Her Majesty's Government on this matter". He added:

"I know that it would only embarrass them if we were to do that at the present time, and . . . the last thing we want to do is to embarrass the Government on this particular issue . . . it would be far better, if possible, to settle this matter by agreement."[22]

Thus the idea of restrictive legislation was shelved for the time being; instead, the suggestion was made to explore the possibility of

[20] *Ibid*, cols. 1562, 1563. The Government speaker rejected the motion (see p. 153) and also pointed out that Mr. Osborne had now quoted an estimate of 800,000 coloured people in the U.K. in 1978—"a very big change from the figure of 6 million which my hon. Friend quoted in the debate on the Address". (Col. 1588.)

[21] This particular shift of attitude was noticeable not only in Parliament, but also in some sections of the Press, and in public discussions generally. Thus immediately after the first outbreak in Nottingham (on August 27th 1958) the Liberal *News Chronicle* had an editorial, 'Too Many Immigrants', in which it was said that "some form of immigration control—distasteful though that is" seemed to be necessary. The next editorial (on September 4th), 'Remain on Guard', was less certain: "The Government is right to consider immigration control with great caution." Five days later (on September 11th), in a leader on 'Deportation', the editors stated that although "in the first hours of dismay" they had advocated immigration control, "applied without discrimination of colour or race", they had now changed their minds. "A restrictive policy must be abandoned"; it would have "a tragic effect throughout the Commonwealth countries". But "undesirables" should be deported.

[22] *Parliamentary Debates*, H.o.L., 19th November 1958, cols. 672, 673.

informal agreements with Commonwealth countries. When Lord
Elton supported this latter policy—which has been officially accepted
since 1958—he expressed the gist of the difficulty:

> "We should not seek to exclude, but rather should wish to be able
> to exercise some power of selection and regulation. And in that way
> we should not be exposing ourselves to the invidious and everdreaded
> charge of colour prejudice. . . ."[23]

Anti-Discrimination Bills

"We are all against discrimination, just as, in theory, we are all
against sin", said Lord Silkin in the Lords.[24] But how should disapproval be shown? There was far less unanimity in answering this
question. Should sin be punished? Should any bars against coloured
people or religious minorities—in employment and housing, in hotels,
restaurants and other public places—be made illegal?

This was the second main theme of public controversy at the time,
and like the first—the issue of immigration control—it was not a
novel one. The fact that here and there overt discrimination against
Negroes and Jews was practised—even before the emergence of a
considerable coloured minority group—was well known. Complaints
were heard especially during the Second World War, after the influx
of American troops. West Indians and other coloured British people
were turned away from dance halls and cafés which had previously
been open to them. The owners introduced colour bars—in defer-
ence to the wishes of their new American customers[25]. At that time
and subsequently, there had been several *causes célèbres*; some sections of the Press, right and left, had been alert both in bringing
such cases to public attention, and in subjecting them to public
rebuke. Thus already in the late forties and early fifties, questions
on the legal aspects of discrimination had been asked in Parliament
on various occasions; and there had been several Private Members'
bills to make discrimination a punishable offence. But none of those
had been enacted.

Neither the post-war Labour governments nor the successive
Conservative governments agreed to introduce such legislation. Then
—as later—three main arguments were put forward against it. First,
it was unnecessary: some of the sanctions implicit in existing

[23] *Ibid.*, col. 659.

[24] *Ibid.*, col. 706.

[25] On the deterioration of race relations in the North of England as a result
of the arrival of American troops in 1943, see Anthony H. Richmond, *Colour
Prejudice in Britain, op. cit.*, pp. 86–90.

common and criminal law were relevant and adequate.[26] Second, discrimination was not a fit subject for legislation because it was difficult to draft an Act, defining the offences, and to enforce it; and to do so, moreover, without interfering with certain common law privileges of individual freedom. Third—and this was the dominant argument —discrimination could only be eradicated through the influence of "enlightened public opinion", not through the majesty of the law.

After the disturbances in Nottingham and Notting Dale, these arguments seemed threadbare to some of their previous supporters. Even before then, as the coloured minority group became larger, complaints about 'colour bars' had been more frequently heard. Thus there had been since the autumn of 1958 a growing body of 'enlightened public opinion' which thought that its own example could not be sufficient; that public education and legislation on matters of intolerance were not incompatible but complementary; and that censure of discrimination should, therefore, be written into the law.

The Labour Party held this view. Their statement, issued soon after the disturbances in September 1958, said:

> "The Labour Party urges Her Majesty's Government now to introduce legislation, making illegal the public practice of discrimination. In any case, it pledges the next Labour Government to take an early opportunity of introducing such legislation. . . . It will use the full weight of Government influence against all such discrimination."[27]

The Conservative Party and the Government disagreed. The arguments previously put forward against legislative proposals of this kind were repeated, though more elaborately in view of the increasing number of protagonists on the other side, and another variant was added—the warning that discrimination might be increased rather than diminished by a formal prohibition against it.

> "The Act of Parliament would run a risk of recognising the existence of discrimination in a way which might draw attention to it and would tend rather to foster it than to do away with it."[28]

---

[26] For example, in November 1949 the Attorney General of the Labour Government, Sir Hartley Shawcross, argued that it was unnecessary to legislate against restrictive covenants in leases which exclude coloured tenants. He thought that such covenants ". . . may well be void under the existing law as being contrary to the rules of public policy upheld by English courts" (*Parliamentary Debates*, H.o.C., 21st November 1949, cols. 2–3). However, there seems to be some doubt in this matter. (See p. 113.)

[27] *Racial Discrimination, op. cit.*, p. 4.

[28] This was said by one of the Government spokesmen, Lord Chesham, in the most extensive House of Lords debate on the subject. (*Parliamentary Debates*, H.o.L., 19th November 1958, col. 718.) The same argument was produced at length in all the controversies on this question.

In this context, frequent references were also made to state legislation against discriminatory restrictive practices in the North of the United States—usually on the assumption either that such American law had not been very effective, or that its experience was hardly relevant to the consideration of similar issues in this country.[29]

While in the 'post-riots' debates on immigration control party lines had been blurred, and bi-partisan agreement had been quickly reached on rejecting not only legislative action but also further public discussion of this "embarrassing" subject, the controversy on proposals to outlaw discrimination followed a different course. It was never quite so prominent, but it was more persistent. To begin with, in the shadow of the Nottingham and Notting Dale events, party lines on this question were sharply drawn; and they remained clearly visible, though some Conservative spokesmen were in sympathy with the idea of prohibiting discrimination, and a few later supported it. Moreover, this idea—unlike the other on immigration control—became more respectable, not less so, as time went on. Prejudice and discrimination had become news; public opinion, in general, had become more perceptive in reacting to the symptoms, both positively and negatively; and as the back street agitation for racial animosity became more noisy, the advocacy of counter-measures gained strength.

In April 1958, a group of twelve Labour M.P.s, headed by Mr. Fenner Brockway, had once again sponsored a Private Member's Bill "to make illegal discrimination to the detriment of any person on the grounds of colour, race and religion in the United Kingdom". (This was Mr. Brockway's third attempt to introduce such legislation.) The Bill defined 'discrimination':

> ". . . a person exercises discrimination where he refuses, withholds from or denies to any other person facilities or advantages on the ground of the colour, race or religion of that other person."

It then specified the public places (such as lodging houses, restaurants and dance halls) in which discrimination should be prohibited. It proposed that restrictive covenants or provisions in leases, relating to the use or occupation of premises, should be void; and that restrictive practices in employment should not be allowed.[30] The

[29] Both assumptions are rather tenuous; the former even more than the latter. (See Chapter VI, pp. 234-5.)

[30] Clauses 4 and 5 of this Race Discrimination Bill (Bill 105, 6 & 7 Eliz. 2, 30th April 1958) read:

"No person who employs any persons in any industry, trade or business shall be entitled on any such ground as aforesaid to refuse to employ or to promote or to terminate the employment or promotion of any person, and

Bill was designed so that, if enacted, it would have an educational rather than a punitive purpose. The suggested penalties were rather slight: a maximum fine of five pounds in the case of the first offence; and a maximum fine of twenty-five pounds in the case of a subsequent conviction. It was also stipulated that anyone in charge of a licensed (or registered) public establishment who practised discrimination (as defined) "may be refused a renewal of or deprived of his licence or registration". Although this provision is not an obligatory one, it was added because public policy on this question is rather vague and can, under existing arrangements, be variously interpreted by the licensing or registration authority. Thus it can happen that the licence of a 'colour bar' establishment is renewed.[31]

This Bill, like many Private Members' bills on all sorts of subjects, did not get a second reading in the Commons. After the disturbances, the same group of M.P.s introduced it once more; again without success, though this was not an indication of lack of support for their views at that time—at least not on their side of the House.

Since then, similar proposals have been made—formally and informally—from time to time. In the summer of 1959, a deputation of Labour and Conservative M.P.s discussed their suggestions for 'anti-colour bar' legislation with Mr. R. A. Butler, the Home Secretary.[32] In the Commons, a few days earlier, Mr. Butler had, by implication, repeated the Government's view that such legislation was unnecessary:

> "Racial discrimination has no place in our law and responsible opinion everywhere will unhesitatingly condemn any attempt to foment it."

A Labour Member (Mr. S. Silverman) then asked:

---

no persons shall be entitled on any such ground to act in consort to secure these purposes.

No person shall be entitled on any such grounds as aforesaid to employ any person at less than the standard rate of wages and conditions for his grade of work."

The same Bill was introduced by Mr. Brockway twice in 1956. When it finally reached a second reading (on 10th and 24th May 1957), the debate was stopped for lack of a quorum. (The Bill was again presented by Mr. Brockway in November 1958, and for the fifth time on 12th April 1960.) A similar, less controversial Bill—referring to discrimination in admissions to public places, but not to employment—was introduced by Mr. John Baird, the Labour Member for North-East Wolverhampton, in July 1958. It did not get a second reading.

[31] See Chapter IV, pp. 116–17.

[32] The deputation, headed by the chairmen of the British-Caribbean Association, is referred to below see p. 199.

"Will the right hon. Gentleman bear in mind that while it is perfectly true, as he said, that racial discrimination forms no part of our
law, there is nothing in our law to make racial discrimination itself
illegal? Does he not think that the time is rapidly approaching when
there ought to be?"[33]

Tension in the Air

Just at that moment, this question was certainly asked by many
people. For the murder of a West Indian in the mean streets of North
Kensington on Whit Sunday 1959 had once more brought the words
'colour', 'discrimination', 'prejudice', 'violence' into the daily
vocabulary. Once more there were black headlines.

During the early months of 1959, the memories of Nottingham and
Notting Hill had begun to fade—in the places of public debate. Discussions on the life and future of the new minority in Britain were
no longer so prominently in the news, though there were articles and
statements drawing attention to the activities of anti-coloured
organisations. Warnings of potential violence were given; everyone
who walked around some parts of North Kensington, in particular,
could hardly fail to see the signs.

This was a note on an ordinary Saturday afternoon's visit to the
market in the Portobello Road.

There is a climate of conflict. I got a whiff of it quite unexpectedly. In Colville Square, one of the most unfortunate examples of Victorianism one can find, there is an atmosphere both
of vitality and decay. Even here, there is a new block of flats at the
corner—just opposite the tall, decrepit, amazingly ugly houses. At
first sight, it seems that there is mixed occupancy of most houses,
and certainly of the side streets here. Mixed groups at the doorsteps; mixed couples—dark men, light women—several with a
definite married look, carrying their shopping baskets, pushing
their prams.

Around the corner in Talbot Road, there was a Negro wedding
party outside the Church; they were just being photographed (by

[33] *Parliamentary Debates*, H.o.C., 4th June 1959, cols. 369, 371. At that time,
the Press also drew attention to the fact that the Government had not ratified an
International Labour Office Convention "to pursue a national policy designed to
eliminate any discrimination on the basis of race, colour, sex, religion, political
opinion, national extraction or social origin in respect of employment or occupation" and to introduce appropriate legislation "where necessary". The Government issued a White Paper (Cmnd 783, June 1959) saying that "while fully
sympathetic to the spirit of the two Instruments", they did "not propose to ratify
the Convention or to accept the supplementary Recommendation".

a white photographer). A charming sight—a pretty bride; a delighted bridegroom; a score of guests (two white ones among them); many children; a rainbow of colour in a grimy street. A lot of onlookers—mostly Negroes, but also some whites.

A few steps along is Talbot Tabernacle; opposite a pub and club (then closed)—a West Indian meeting place; quite a number were still standing outside and talking. Many more dark people were passing by, rapidly, as though time were short; a few were driving along, or were polishing their rather aged cars.

So far all was ordinary. Going back into the Portobello Road—very busy and crowded at 3 p.m. on Saturday—I saw a knot of people at the opposite corner—a knot distinguishable from the other crowds by its size, its density and its gestures.

Is there a row going on? As I walked towards the corner, I saw two policemen walking towards it, too—and before I could reach the group, part of it had already been dispersed by the police. Several coloured men—tall, straight, bright shirts—who had been in that knot came along, shouting, laughing, but obviously in a fury. "White man"; "blood"; "cutting his hand"; "I'm as good as any one of them".

What was it all about? An Irishman had got into an argument with a number of Negroes and white bystanders. He had pulled out a knife and then cut his hand—to show that 'white blood was thicker', and he dared them to do the same to themselves. (So I was told.)

There was still a number of pale, mean looking characters standing around at that corner—not 'teddy boys', but middle-aged sour and aggressive types. And there were also some old ladies with their shopping baskets and two younger ones who did not at all like what they had just seen. They were frightened; they said: "It happens all the time." And this was obviously one of a series of 'normal' incidents.

The whispers among the white women, the tension of the other bystanders, the grins of the toughs, the anger of the Negroes —and most of all the re-grouping of the group broken up by the police—all these were signs of unmistakable animosity. The Negroes had moved off a few paces, and then remained—still in a cluster— in the side street. The women and the other white 'pacifists' had gone back to the market stalls. But a small group of tough whites stayed around the two policemen at the 'conflict corner', some muttering, some slightly apart, just waiting. And there was another group of Negroes at the opposite corner of the Portobello Road, watching the white bunch around the policemen; they were waiting, too.

There was not much doubt about it: these groups looked like the sentries of hostile camps, engaged in the awareness of mutual hostility.[34]

There was a routine of minor rows and incidents: "Keep Britain White" notices stuck up on walls and lamp posts, and pushed through letter boxes; street corner agitation; Mosley meetings; rumours; occasional fights—no big explosion, but a lot of rumbling, sparks and flickers, in an environment of physical decay and social discontent. Altogether, there was a smell of tension in the air. And tension is cumulative, of course. The autumn events in Nottingham and Notting Dale came as an unexpected shock to the British public—and also to many coloured people themselves. Once these disturbances had occurred, the climate was different: apprehension and animosity were growing. The image of the relations between coloured and white became much sharper, and as a result, it also tended to be distorted, in terms of disharmony and harmony alike. In such circumstances, a new dramatic event can easily have far more than intrinsic and local significance. Emotions and attitudes will again be rapidly intensified; apprehension becomes fear; antipathy turns into hostility; indignation into anger. Ill will and good will both are accentuated. The meaning of everyday personal experiences seems to have changed, and may indeed have changed just because these experiences are loaded with new connotations.

The Murder

This is what happened when Kelso Cochrane, a 32 year old West Indian carpenter, was murdered near the railway bridge at a sordid street corner in Kensal New Town on the night of May 17th 1959. No one had been killed during the autumn riots but now a coloured man had been stabbed to death. The many previous warnings given by prominent local citizens, foreign observers, responsible journalists and associations—none of them scaremongers—now had a new alarming sound.[35] And alarm was greater still because the murder

[34] An extract from our notebooks, November 1958. During the following months, the symptoms of conflict became more frequent and obvious, and although there were some exaggerated news stories, by and large the reports of responsible observers, and their diagnoses, were certainly correct.

[35] Among those who issued such warnings were the Conservative M.P. for South Kensington; the British-Caribbean Association; the Conservative Commonwealth Council; and the Labour Secretary of the American National Association for the Advancement of Coloured People, who visited the area. (See also pp. 174, 175.) There was also a number of reports in newspapers and periodicals.

remained an unsolved case. No one has been arrested and brought to trial for the killing of Kelso Cochrane.[36]

There is thus no precise judicial evidence for the circumstances of the murder, though—judging from the newspaper reports and the inquest—they did not seem to be particularly obscure. On his last Saturday night, Cochrane, who had a thumb injury, had gone for treatment to a hospital in Paddington. He was on his way home, walking by himself. At 1 a.m. he had reached the corner of Southam Street and Golborne Road, three streets away from his house. It was there that he was stabbed in a 'scuffle' (or 'fight') with five or six white youths (some said six or seven). There were several eye witnesses. Two of them (a mother and daughter, who were sitting up late sewing at a window overlooking Southam Street) said the youths had walked after Cochrane; one of them had called 'Hi, Jim'. (In another version, they are alleged to have called 'Jim Crow'.) Cochrane turned round.

> "Suddenly the gang of five or six and him appeared to be involved in a scuffle and he fell. Before the fight one of the youths tried to rip away an iron railing as a weapon. Neither of us saw any knife. After the youths had run away the coloured man pulled himself up and walked towards the railway bridge."[37]

He did not get far. Two coloured men came to his assistance, and so did a taxi driver who had noticed a 'scrimmage' going on at the opposite corner. (He said at the inquest: "The whole thing took about a minute.") The taxi driver took Cochrane to the nearest hospital, where he died. He was killed by a single stab wound in the chest, made apparently by a stiletto type of knife.[38]

Was Cochrane killed because he was black, as all the coloured people far and wide firmly and persistently believed? Or was robbery the likely motive, as the police announced two days later? (It was said that Cochrane had told detectives before he died that his assailants had asked him for money, but that he had had nothing to give to them.) Or was the attack just "wanton, aimless and very cowardly", as the Coroner assumed, after hearing the inquest? No doubt, all sorts of symptoms of senseless brutality were by no means uncommon—particularly on Saturday nights, and in the streets of North Kensington. And there was not much 'discrimination' in such fights: they were often among white people.[39]

[36] As of June 15, 1960.

[37] *News Chronicle*, May 18, 1959. The daughter, a young white woman married to a Negro, asked for police protection after she had given information to the police.

[38] Report of the inquest. *Manchester Guardian*, August 6, 1959.

[39] The Home Secretary said at that time that during the six months from December 1958 to 31st May 1959 most cases of serious assault reported to the

As Cochrane's attackers remained unknown, there could be no definite explanation. But whatever it might have been—whether there had been a specific 'racial motive' or a complex of aggressive motiveless motives—everyone agreed that the murder had the result of increasing 'race tension'.

Three days later, *The Times* reported:

> 'Last night the police were taking no chances and extra men were standing by. Dogs and extra patrol cars were kept ready for any further incidents . . . it would not have taken much to spark off an incident that might lead to further rioting.
>
> Yesterday afternoon groups of coloured and white youths watched each other suspiciously. On Wormwood Scrubs Common the traditional Bank Holiday fair was in full swing and here, only a short distance from the troubled area, white and coloured people appeared to be joining in the holiday together.
>
> Even so, the tension was there and on several occasions only tactful withdrawal by a coloured man prevented an incident. At the dodgems, the merry-go-rounds, the lucky dips, and the coconut shies both races mixed freely, but when a coloured family and a white couple wanted the same dodgem car, the attendant ordered the coloured people off the floor and they left quietly. . . .
>
> Asked what he felt about the murder, a youth with sideburns 2 in. long and a pencil-slim tie said: "One less of the blacks—that's the way I look at it. We've got too many of them about here." '[40]

In North Kensington, the police met a "barrier of silence". Apparently the people—coloured and white—in the 'critical' streets were afraid to talk. "Curfew At Notting Hill", said a *Kensington Post* headline. "Coloured families remain indoors. Extra Police Go In Pairs." The murder

> ". . . has brought to light alleged attacks on coloured people and their property in the Notting Hill area which have been deliberately 'played down' by the victims because, it is said, they did not wish to attract publicity.
>
> It has resulted in what is virtually a self-imposed curfew by the many West Indian families in North Kensington—a precaution which has also been followed by much of the white population in this uneasy half of the Royal Borough."[41]

---

police sub-divisions covering North Kensington involved white persons only. Sixteen—out of a total of 156 such cases—involved white and coloured persons. (*Parliamentary Debates*, H.o.C., 4th June 1959, col. 370.) On the night on which Cochrane was killed, there had been another "minor riot" not far away among a crowd of white youths outside a public house at closing time. One of them was later tried on the charge of assaulting two policemen who had tried to break up the fight. The Detective-Sergeant, giving evidence in the Magistrate's Court, said: "This fighting happens night after night in this area." (*Manchester Guardian*, May 18, 1959.)

[40] *The Times*, May 19, 1959.
[41] *Kensington Post*, May 22, 1959.

Once again, the spotlight was on Notting Hill, and on the threats to social order and British reputation which this name now symbolised. There were numerous reports—some highly dramatised—and many editorials. "Smash White Gangs, Police Told" (*Daily Herald*); "Prince Philip For Notting Hill" (*Evening Standard*); "Keep Calm, Says M.P." (*Kensington Post*). "Knives in Notting Hill", wrote the *New Statesman*; "Rotting Hill", commented *The Observer*; "Awakened to Danger", stated *The Times*. The *News of the World* offered a reward of £2,500 for finding "the Notting Hill Killers".[42] The White Defence League referred to Cochrane as "this manufactured martyr".[43]

On Whit Monday, representatives of African and West Indian organisations in Britain held an emergency meeting in London. They sent an open letter to the Prime Minister, saying: "Coloured citizens of the United Kingdom and possibly throughout the Commonwealth have lost confidence in the ability of the law-enforcing agencies to protect them."[44]

They asked Mr. Macmillan to condemn the North Kensington murder publicly; and they also appealed to trade unions and churches to speak out.[45] A few days later, they formed with a number of delegates of English associations a joint committee for the "immediate protection of our persons and property", and also a larger 'Inter-Racial Friendship Co-ordinating Council'.[46]

It was this new Council which sponsored an impressive memorial meeting for Kelso Cochrane, at which some forty organisations and the three major political parties were represented. A few days later, about 800 people marched in the funeral procession behind Cochrane's coffin from the church in Ladbroke Grove to Kensal Green Cemetery. There were many notables in the congregation—the Prime Minister of the West Indies Federation, the High Commissioner for Ghana, the Mayor of Kensington. The Bishop of Kensington read the lesson. And there were many ordinary people in the procession, and many more watching. One of the photographs published in the

[42] These were headlines, titles of reports or editorials on May 19, 22, 23, 31 and on June 5 and 7, 1959, respectively. The innumerable references to Notting Hill were geographically incorrect. Cochrane had not been killed in Notting Hill, but in another district of North Kensington, in Kensal New Town, near Paddington Station.

[43] Reported in the *Daily Telegraph*, May 25, 1959.

[44] *The Times*, May 19, 1959.

[45] Mr. Macmillan made no public statement, but he convened a special meeting of Ministers. And it was reported that the Cabinet subsequently discussed the situation, and also that new 'co-ordinating machinery' on the 'colour problem' had been set up in Whitehall.   [46] *Manchester Guardian*, May 22, 1959.

newspapers showed a group of white and coloured spectators—some weeping, the others solemn. Among them was an elderly white woman in a head scarf, her left arm clasped around the shoulder of a small black boy, her right arm around a white boy of the same size and age. There was, as the caption of the photograph said, "The Sorrow of Notting Hill."[47]

The Renewed Debate

After the murder, the public discussion—in Parliament, in the Press, on radio and television—was even more intense, though also more short-lived, than it had been during the previous autumn. And while many of the earlier arguments were repeated, in sharper terms, and similar aspects were referred to, the emphasis had shifted—from talk about a 'colour problem' as such to concern with general social problems which make coloured people so visible and so vulnerable. Thus this time there was hardly any mention of proposals to control immigration or to deport criminals. Instead, attention was focussed on the causes and symptoms of tension—the housing shortage; crowding and blight; casual employment; the shortage of police; manifestations of social disorder and violence, in general; the promoters of aggressive prejudice, in particular.

Several aspects, especially, were stressed far more than previously. First, it was said repeatedly that on the whole coloured people did not trust the police. This had been mentioned earlier from time to time—for example, during the disturbances in the forties in Liverpool and elsewhere; in Nottingham before the riots in 1958; and again, more prominently, in an article by a foreign observer, published in the *New Statesman* a week before the murder.[48] But now it was stated openly and sharply by representatives of the "aggrieved minorities". Various allegations were made: the newcomers were afraid of the police; they knew of instances of police brutality against coloured people; the police tended to be harsher with coloured than with white people and were, for instance, more likely to stop a coloured driver than a white one. All this was said at a period when there was, in any case, a good deal of uneasiness about some aspects of police procedure.[49] And just then, two detective officers were tried

[47] *Evening News*, June 6, 1959.

[48] An article by Herbert Hill, Labour Secretary of the American Association for the Advancement of Coloured People. *New Statesman*, May 9, 1959.

[49] This was later brought out, and also accentuated, by a particular case: the apparently rather peculiar circumstances in the arrest of a German born Canadian, Guenter Podola, who had killed a policeman in July 1959, and who was tried and executed. In December 1959, a Royal Commission on Police was set up. Among

in Birmingham on the charge of assaulting a Jamaican in the C.I.D. room at the local police station. They were found guilty, fined and asked to resign. Shortly afterwards, a "Nigerian juryman caused a sensation at the Old Bailey when he asked to be released from a case because an experience of police methods was affecting his judgment."[50]

Second, while there were criticisms of the police, there were also complaints that there were far too few policemen, especially in the back streets of North Kensington. When a deputation from the newly formed Inter-Racial Friendship Co-ordinating Council went to the Home Office (on May 27th 1959), they asked for a greater number of police constables "to patrol the troubled areas thoroughly". "And if that cannot be done with the existing resources, permission be given us to protect ourselves. Our suggestion is the appointment of coloured and white special constables."[51]

"The black man finds it difficult to walk the streets without fear. Men go along trembling around several blocks without seeing a policeman", said one member of the Council at the Cochrane memorial meeting. There was also some talk of setting up 'Workers Defence Squads' for Notting Hill—rather hasty talk, which came from the 'Socialist Labour League', a left-wing splinter group. The idea was opposed by the migrant groups and soon petered out.

Third—and most important—in the discussion after the murder more attention was given than before to organisations which stir up colour prejudice and hatred. And indeed, they had done a good deal since the autumn events to advertise their activities. Mosley's Union Movement, the National Labour Party and the White

---

its terms of reference was the following: to consider "the relationship of the police with the public and the means of ensuring that complaints by the public against the police are effectively dealt with".

[50] In the Birmingham case, the assault occurred on April 22nd; the charge was heard by the stipendiary magistrate early in June; the trial took place at Birmingham Quarter Sessions in mid-July 1959. (*The Times*, June 1, 5, 9, 1959. *Manchester Guardian*, July 17, 18, 20, 21, 1959.) The Nigerian juryman's story was reported in the *Daily Herald*, July 23, 1959. He said that the personal experience to which he was referring had occurred in Manchester in 1950. He and a coloured barrister had gone to a public house. "It was my first visit to a British pub. I was shocked when the publican said: 'We don't serve black people here.' My barrister friend called the police. When they arrived they refused to listen to our complaint and we were hustled out. My friend and I were dragged 500 yards past the Royal Infirmary and Manchester University, watched by scores of students. It was the most humiliating and disgraceful thing that has happened to me. We were charged with behaviour likely to cause a breach of the peace. The case was dismissed. . . . My faith in the British system of justice remains unshaken. But I have still to be convinced about the honesty of police methods."

[51] *West Indian Gazette*, June 1959.

Defence League, in particular, had become increasingly vociferous in the zones of tension; and they are continuing to be so. On the side lines are the League of Empire Loyalists and the Ku-Klux-Klan. The 'Empire Loyalists' got into the news by their heckling activities at Conservative Party meetings. The "Aryan Knights", the Klan of Great Britain, seem to operate mainly by sending nasty letters to individuals and organisations. Though they demand "England Awake, Keep Britain Pure and White; Put the Traitors to the Stake", they conceal their British address. "King Kleagle Klavern No. 1, Province of Londinium, Imperial Realm of Albion" can be reached only care of a box number in Waco, Texas.[52]

As the 'Keep Britain White' agitation became louder, the recognition of its dangers became more intense and widespread, too. Previous proposals to outlaw discrimination were renewed, especially as it became well known that the racists use every opportunity to translate their theory into practice.[53] And there was, moreover, growing support for the view that special legislation was needed (or might soon be needed) to counteract—and to penalise—group defamation and incitement to racial animosity.[54] Various suggestions were made in this context. There were some who thought that the scope of the Public Order Act of 1936, passed at the time of fascist agitation in the East End of London, should be widened. The Act makes it an offence to use threatening, abusive or insulting words, or to display such behaviour, in any public place (or at any public meeting) with intent to provoke, or conducive to, a breach of the peace. The Act does not, however, apply to printed matter of a similar kind—for example, to the propaganda leaflets which the White Defence League have pushed through letter boxes in North Kensington and elsewhere. Alternatively or additionally, it was also suggested that both verbal and written insults directed against racial and religious groups, and the deliberate incitement of such insults, should be declared illegal.

The discussion of these particular issues did not stop when the intense public reaction to the Whit Sunday murder had apparently evaporated by mid-summer 1959. For although 'colour' was then no

[52] For an example of a Klan letter, see p. 180.

[53] For instance, one of the prominent members of the National Labour Party is the licensee of a public house, where he has operated a colour bar for some time.

[54] Thus *The Times* said (in the editorial 'Awakened to Danger', June 5, 1959): "In general, the attempt to curb discriminatory practices by legislation is undesirable. The ordinary laws of the land should suffice to deal with ordinary occurrences. But the Government cannot afford altogether to abandon the possibility of using this weapon, particularly against any new racialist activities which may develop." (Subsequently, 'new racialist activities' did develop.)

longer so prominently in the news, the 'Keep Britain White' groups saw to it that these questions could not be forgotten. They have continued to advertise and to expand their activities—not least through Sir Oswald Mosley's campaign in North Kensington during the General Election in October 1959. And they have thus also given new point to previous proposals to curb their propaganda. Early in 1960, this question was topical again, and not only for the coloured minority groups. There was then a rash of swastikas and antisemitic slogans, painted on the walls of synagogues (including that in North Kensington opposite Mosley's district office), on Jewish gravestones and private houses in various parts of Britain; there were also abusive telephone calls and letters to individuals. Sir Leslie Plummer and six other Labour M.P.s brought in a Private Members' Bill "To make it an offence to insult publicly or conspire to insult publicly any person or persons because of their race or religion."[55]

In talking of the disturbances in Nottingham and Notting Hill, two months after the events, the Earl of Lucan said in the House of Lords:

> "At that time the country received a severe mental and moral shock, and, as with all shocks of that kind, when we get a glimpse of unpleasant feelings just below the surface, we try to forget it. Feelings of guilt and shame are the best possible agencies for ensuring forgetfulness."[56]

Since then, the advocates of prejudice in Britain have given constant reminders.

2. 'KEEP BRITAIN WHITE' GROUPS

The Role of Racist Groups

The extreme right-wing and anti-coloured organisations have been in the news almost continuously since August 1958. Attention was drawn to their activities as soon as the 'riot' headlines appeared. But opinions on their actual role in the disturbances were divided.

[55] This Bill had its first reading in the Commons on 2nd February, 1960. It stipulates that "any person who insults publicly by speech or by writing or by illustration or advisedly incites another person publicly to insult any person or persons because of their race or religion shall be guilty of an offence". Also: "Any person who prints, publishes, distributes or circulates any written matter or illustration insulting to any person or persons because of their race or religion shall be guilty of an offence." (By June 15, 1960, the Bill had not yet had its second reading, and thus its fate was still unknown.)

[56] *Parliamentary Debates*, H.O.L., 19th November 1958, col. 684.

According to one view, then fairly widely accepted, the racist propagandists "merely jumped on the bandwagon". Thus one writer who described the 'incidents' at Notting Hill said:

> "There had been anti-coloured slogans such as 'Keep Britain White'; there had been anti-coloured pamphlets and meetings in the area. But none of this semi-political agitation had had any real support and it does not seem to have had much influence on the events that followed."[57]

Many observers and organisations thought differently. Was it mere chance that the first disorders, more infectious than the usual incidents, broke out simultaneously during the same night of August 23rd to 24th both in Nottingham and Notting Dale, before London had heard what had happened in the Midlands? And was there not far too much coincidence in that the semi-fascist and fascist groups had been busy for some time especially in the very districts in which tension became acute? Although Mosley's Union Movement, for example, had not forgotten the East End, since the late forties they had 'turned west' and had singled out North Kensington for their operations. For several years before August 1958, their speakers had put up their platform every Saturday afternoon, when the shopping crowds were thickest, at Notting Hill Gate tube station. They had held meetings at other street corners in the district and in local halls and schools as well. Their share of responsibility in the troubles, and that of kindred bodies, could not be easily dismissed.

Thus the Trades Union Congress said in their statement on the disturbances:

> "Evidence is accumulating that elements which propagated racial hatred in Britain and Europe in pre-war days are once more fanning the flames of violence."[58]

The Times commented:

> "And among other influences on the immature and excitable, the persistent agitation of 'Fascist' elements to 'Keep Britain White' is not

---

[57] James Wickenden, *Colour in Britain*, 1958, *op. cit.*, p. 40. A few paragraphs later (p. 41), the author in reporting the events of September 1st in Notting Hill said: "Monday night began with a number of incidents in the Notting Hill area, one of which was the first and only effective fascist meeting. Some teddy-boys were directly addressed and stirred up by the speakers and they moved off in an excited state." (This was the night when violence spread more widely and considerable crowds gathered.) The meeting referred to was certainly not the first one (as the author himself said on his previous page); and whether it was the "only effective" one is a matter of considerable doubt.

[58] *Report of Proceedings at the 90th Annual Trades Union Congress*, Bournemouth, September 1958, *op. cit.*, p. 458.

to be ignored. The outbreaks will have served a useful purpose if they oblige the public to understand that the Storm Troop mentality exists in England, too. It is confined to a tiny submerged hooligan element. It must be kept submerged by the contempt of the civilised majority and by strict enforcement of order."[59]

In fact, however, the "Storm Troop mentality" was not submerged. After the autumn disturbances in 1958, North Kensington heard and saw even more of Mosley, his followers and competitors than before. Their efforts were increasingly concentrated in that area. One month later, in October 1958, the Union Movement circulated the first issue of a special monthly broadsheet, the *North Kensington Leader*. It called for "ACTION WITH MOSLEY." "NOW IS THE TIME TO ACT." "FOR THE PEOPLE AGAINST THE PARTIES." "Mosley comes forward now because this is the hour when you need him."[60] Meetings were held more frequently than before; the Union Movement opened an office and bookshop in North Kensington. There was talk that one of their members would stand as a candidate at the borough council elections in May 1959, but this idea was abandoned. Instead, early in April, after his tour of South Africa, Mosley was introduced as the Movement's prospective candidate for North Kensington. The adoption meeting in a local hall—"Great, packed, historic", wrote the *North Kensington Leader* —"ended amid scenes of extraordinary enthusiasm". Several nonpartisan newspapers published similar descriptions. In his speech on that occasion, Mosley said (as was reported) that "he would send all coloured immigrants back to their homelands".[61] "We are quite a go-home-party." "He wanted Africa divided into two parts, separating black from white. He wanted Jamaicans sent back to work in their home industries. He wanted Americans to get out of Europe."[62] The Union Movement now gave new advice to their 'old and new friends':

"Do not waste your vote. Wait for the real fight when Mosley stands at the General Election. The local elections have made no difference to anyone for years past, and will not this time. . . .
Union Movement is out first to capture the main positions with your support, and is concentrating on this job. When the big fight is

---

[59] *The Times*, September 3, 1958. In the weeks following the disturbances many local authorities refused to give the Union Movement permission to use schools or town halls for their meetings. However, in February 1959 this ban began to be relaxed. During the summer of 1959, and since then, Mosley has held several meetings in town halls, in particular in Kensington Town Hall.

[60] *North Kensington Leader*, No. 1, October 1958.

[61] *North Kensington Leader*, No. 7, May 1959.

[62] *Kensington Post*, April 10, 1959.

won we will ask your support to take over the small positions. And we have good men and women in North Kensington ready for this job when the time comes."[63]

A few weeks later, on Sunday, May 10th (one week before the Cochrane murder) the Union Movement held a large scale meeting in Trafalgar Square. There Mosley "spoke up for the people of North Kensington in the very heart of Britain." "It was leader's weather, and his was leader's talk."[64]

The National Labour Party described some of its activities in Notting Hill both before and immediately after the disturbances in the first issue of its journal *Combat*, published in the autumn of 1958. "Following the outbreak of racial violence in the Notting Hill area, three open air meetings were held in ten days at Notting Hill Gate."[65] The White Defence League's news sheet, *Black and White News*, was on sale in North Kensington at the time of "the outbreak", and later re-printed. Its headlines are full of colour.

"BLACKS INVADE BRITAIN."
"REDS COUNT ON BLACKS."
"BLACKS SEEK WHITE WOMEN."
"BLACKS MILK THE ASSISTANCE BOARD."
"AMERICA POURING NEGRO TROOPS INTO BRITAIN."[66]

Subsequently, many more leaflets were distributed—at street corners and to private houses; printed slogans were stuck up on lamp posts and painted on walls; further meetings were held. Early in April 1959, the White Defence League, which was closely associated with the National Labour Party, rented a shop in North Kensington, opened an office and displayed their literature in the window.

There was thus far more awareness of the activities of these bodies even before the Whit Sunday murder occurred than there had been nine months earlier when Nottingham and Notting Hill were in the headlines. Among those who in the weeks before Whitsun expressed their anxiety about the propaganda put out by the 'Keep Britain White' agitators were the British-Caribbean Association and the Conservative Commonwealth Council. In a statement, issued on 15th April 1959, the latter gave a strong warning.

> "In the atmosphere which still exists in the Notting Hill neighbourhood, the presence and propaganda of Sir Oswald Mosley and his followers with their 'Keep Britain White' slogan could easily spark

---

[63] *North Kensington Leader, loc. cit.*
[64] *North Kensington Leader*, No. 8, June 1959. *Action*, May 16, 1959.
[65] *Combat*, No. 1, Autumn 1958.
[66] *Black and White News*, No. 1 (1st Reprint, Nov. 1958).

off new outbreaks, especially during the summer months when it is customary for both white and coloured residents to congregate in groups in alley-ways or on street corners. It is hoped that the Police will watch the activities of this fascist element, which we regard as disruptive and dangerous, especially in that part of London."[67]

Two Kinds of Organisation

During the interval between the riots and the murder, the tactics of "this fascist element" had also become better known. There is a division of labour between the two main types of anti-coloured organisation. The Union Movement, the legatee of the pre-war British Union of Fascists, and the League of Empire Loyalists are in the first group—that of those who have some aspirations to join, or to work within, the existing body politic, although they condemn all other parties, and say that "the Labour and Tory parties are making Britain the dustbin of the world".

> "We have never suffered from any illusion that the old world could go on after the upheaval of the last big war. For that reason Oswald Mosley evolved his concept of a higher synthesis of the old fascism and the old democracy immediately after the war: a political idea and faith far advanced on both."[68]

This group thus borrows phrases and notions from current established opinion and thinks it necessary to produce from time to time a programme—a "fair policy", a "peace policy", a "constructive policy"—which contains some semblance of restraint.

The second group are the National Labour Party, the White Defence League, the Ku Klux Klan and also some other local extreme right-wing splinter cliques. All these regard themselves frankly as outsiders; they are quite inflexible; and as their ambitions to gain influence within the existing political system are even more marginal than those of the Union Movement, they rarely show any inhibitions.[69]

[67] Conservative Commonwealth Council, 'Race Relations in the United Kingdom', *op. cit.* The warnings given by some individuals (for example, by Sir Patrick Spens, the Conservative M.P. for South Kensington) and by the British-Caribbean Association were very similar. On May 14th, three days before the murder, the Association issued an appeal to the Metropolitan Police "to keep a special watch on the Notting Hill area during the coming months and to make every endeavour to protect the person and property of every citizen, irrespective of colour, and deal most vigorously with any incident which may arise." (*Manchester Guardian*, May 15, 1959.)

[68] *North Kensington Leader*, No. 1, October 1958. *Action*, January 30, 1959.

[69] A member of the National Labour Party has stood as a candidate both at a local election in 1958, and at the Parliamentary election in 1959. The Party's President has also stood as an independent Parliamentary candidate at a by-election in Norfolk. But this kind of activity seems to be regarded by this group simply as another soapbox stunt.

They do not mind at all being called Fascists. On the contrary, they agree with Colin Jordan, the National Organiser for the White Defence League, who said in a Press interview: "If a Fascist is a person who wants to keep Britain White, then I am a Fascist and proud of it."[70]

Both before and during the General Election campaign in 1959, the Union Movement used emotive innuendo and insinuation rather than unbridled racist language. Its policy was "the establishment of a Europe-African economic, cultural and military force to stand between the State capitalism of Russia and the almighty dollar-worshipping United States of America."[71] Its main newspaper, *Action*, carried headlines like these: "WHITE WOMAN BULLIED"; "HOUSE BRITONS FIRST"; "BIG COLOURED THREAT TO BRITAIN'S HEALTH"; and an especially clumsy attempt at *Action*'s idea of subtle irony—"BLACKMAIL BY OUR COLOURED BROTHERS". In a pamphlet on *The Colour Question in Britain: Causes and Solution*, published under the auspices of the Union Movement, a three-point policy was put forward:

"(a) Send the coloured immigrants home, with their passage paid by the people who brought them here;

(b) Send them home to good jobs in their own countries, which can be secured by giving them the guaranteed market in Britain for which they have always asked. Give them this market, not for the 10 years they originally suggested, but on a permanent basis;

(c) Give Britain at the same time the same rights as the British Dominions, which have long exercised the right to choose which immigrants shall be allowed through their ports. The right of entry for students coming here to learn would always be respected; they would come here for a definite period, after which time they would go back to their own countries.

Under this policy the minority of crooks among them would be expelled because of their habits. The majority of decent people among them would be sent home to good jobs among their own families."[72]

[70] This was said after Mr. Jordan had been reminded that his views had been expressed before by Hitler. *Daily Herald*, June 15, 1959. (Mr. Jordan is a school teacher in Coventry.)

[71] *Action*, March 14, 1959. *Action* ("Against Communism and Corruption") is published at varying intervals. It was a fortnightly until the end of February 1959, then a weekly (*The European Political Weekly*) until July 4, 1959. At that stage, publication was suspended ("by the printing dispute and election activities") until October 17th. Since then *Action* has appeared irregularly: first as a quarterly; early in 1960 it became a monthly.

[72] *The Colour Question in Britain, op. cit.*, pp. 9, 10. The League of Empire Loyalists, too, has a varied vocabulary. The Loyalists sound more reasonable when they write letters to *The Times* than when they warn against "a mulatto Britain of the future" in their own publication *Policy for Patriots*, or when they give reports in their journal *Candour*.

Occasionally, the National Labour Party and its relative, the White Defence League, too, find it necessary to introduce a kind thought, but on the whole they are even more overtly offensive and consistently aggressive than Mosley's group. Thus *Black and White News* says:

> "In the dictionary of the communists and racial perverts, 'racial prejudice', 'racial hatred', 'bigotry', and 'fascism' are smearwords applied to any white man who wants his children to be white also in the hope of frightening him into submission to race mixture. Racial patriotism in Britain does not imply hostility to coloured people outside Britain, and the coloured people are as entitled to fair and friendly treatment in their own countries as we are entitled to keep Britain a white man's country by excluding them."[73]

In a similar vein, the National Labour Party's paper *Combat*, the 'Voice of British Nationalism', speaks of Hitler—"it is not our desire to resurrect him, or his political creed as it was formulated for a Germany of the 1930's"—and then goes on to quote *Mein Kampf* at length and with approval. "Was Hitler really our enemy?" In fact, the paper is quite certain who the enemies are, as it explained, for example, in an article on 'The Truth about World Government': "This long-standing Judaeo-Communist-Masonic plot for the enslavement of the world is the final horror prepared for all the nations of the earth."

The National Labour Party ("National because we love our country; Labour because we love our people") was formed in May 1958—primarily, it seems, by a small group of people who left the League of Empire Loyalists to set up their own 'anti-everyone' organisation. Their leader, Mr. John Bean, is the editor of *Combat* and the Party's Director of Policy. The President is Mr. Andrew Fountaine, a landowner in Norfolk, who once stood as Conservative Parliamentary candidate for a Lancashire constituency, and later, at a by-election in 1959, as an independent Parliamentary candidate for S.W. Norfolk. The Party's 'principles' are summarised quite briefly:

> "A new union of the Dominions of British blood in place of the Coloured Commonwealth. An alliance with our racial kinsmen of Western Europe. This, in essence, is the alternative that the National Labour Party offers to both Communism and Liberal Democracy, fighting its last rearguard action."

While the Party and its paper specialise in antisemitism, they never forget the 'Blacks'. Thus they also advocate:

> "Coloured immigration must be stopped. Not only does it aggravate the housing problem and constitutes a serious threat to workers' living standards in view of increasing unemployment but, most important, it will turn our nation into a race of mongrels."[74]

---

[73] *Black and White News, loc. cit.*   [74] *Combat*, No. 2, January–March 1959.

The 'mongrel' theme is a favourite one, not least with the Party's President.

> "Race mixing means the end of our race and our culture. If it is Fascist to try to stop that, then Fascism is a bloody good thing."

And another spokesman for the Party was reported to have said:

> "We are not troubled by those who compare our policies with certain aspects of Fascism. Mosley, for instance, was right before the war. But now he is a man of the past. We have nothing to do with him because we do not regard his racial views as sufficiently extreme."[75]

The White Defence League, on the other hand, has the full approval and support of the National Labour Party. It is the League which has attracted most attention since Cochrane's murder; its activities have been widely publicised, though its national organiser is rather reticent when he is asked about the leaders and members of his organisation. But they are by no means hesitant in expressing their views. The League's news sheet consists of items of this kind:

> "The National Assistance Board pays the children's allowances to the blacks for the coffee-coloured monstrosities they father, regardless of whether they are legitimate or illegitimate. . . .
> Thus material rewards are given to enable semisavages to mate with the women of one of the leading civilised nations of the world."
> *"The Right to Discriminate"*
> "The whites know that they have every right not to mix with other races if they do not wish to mix with them. One does not argue about a fundamental right; one takes it."
> *"WARNING"*
> "Civilization is only a very fragile restraint on the blacks pouring into Britain. Only a generation or two separates them from the savagery of the primitive jungle, and it doesn't require much for them to lose control, and for the savage to come to life in them."[76]

Soon after Cochrane's murder, the White Defence League published a pamphlet which implied that the public did not understand who the real victim was. The West Indian had been killed, so it was hinted, to inflame public opinion against "White resistance organisations in Notting Hill". A week after the murder, on Sunday, May

---

[75] From interviews quoted in the *Daily Herald*, June 16, 1959.

[76] *Black and White News*, *loc. cit.* The paper also carries reports and advertisements of fraternal organisations and journals in other countries—for instance, of *The Citizen's Council*, "the monthly organ of the white Citizens' Council of America", Jackson, Mississippi; of *The White Sentinal*, "the hard-hitting organ of America's National Citizens' Protective Association", St. Louis, Missouri; and the *South African Observer* ("prints the truth each month on the white man's cause in South Africa").

24th, the League and the National Labour Party held a joint 'protest' meeting in Trafalgar Square.

> "Stop the Coloured Invasion! . . .
> The nation being mongrelised. . . ."

These were the posters. The League's national organiser ". . . attributed coloured immigration into Britain to Jewish influence, and he also said that coloured immigrants were 'riddled with infectious diseases'—including leprosy." The President of the National Labour Party was no less sweeping in his condemnations. He described the United Nations as a "horde of parasitic holiday makers." He talked of a "huge coloured army invading the western world", with the West Indian immigrants to Britain as a "Trojan horse for the hordes of Asia." He called the Ku Klux Klan a "Communist organisation".[77]

In fact, however, it is only the Klan's methods which appear to differ from those of the other extreme 'Keep Britain White' groups: their views and words are very similar. So far, the Klan have held no meetings in Trafalgar Square, or even at street corners. As they say that "Secrecy is our defence against those who desire to mongrelise our proud heritage", it is difficult to find out with whom they associate and in what activities, other than letter writing, they engage. (On the next page is a copy of a letter sent to the *West Indian Gazette* five days before the troubles began in Nottingham in 1958. The letter had no post mark: it was pushed through the door[78].)

The General Election

Just because the several anti-coloured groups do not represent a united front, they cannot be disregarded as a comparatively harmless lunatic fringe. There are sufficient variations in the tenor of their campaigns to give them the chance of 'gaining friends and of influencing people' in the areas in which they operate. And they are using their opportunities. Since Whitsun 1959 'Keep Britain White' propaganda has become even louder; its echoes could be heard in the back streets of North Kensington every day, especially during the period of preparation for the General Election of October 8, 1959.

Mosley entered the field very early; he made his first election speeches in April. And throughout the summer and autumn, the Union Movement held outdoor and indoor meetings, were busy canvassing, personally and on the telephone, distributing their publications, and later also interfering at the meetings of candidates of

[77] As reported in *The Times*, May 25, 1959.
[78] Published in *West Indian Gazette*, Vol. 1, No. 6, September 1958.

Anti-Communist

Ride with the Aryan Knights
KU KLUX KLAN OF BRITAIN

We are peaceful, lawabiding and tolerant.
Secrecy is our defence against those who desire
to mongrelize our proud heritage.

Communism Enslaves, Jewish Usurers Invented It.
England Awake, Keep Britain Pure and White.
Put the Traitors to the Stake.

Anti-Semitic

KING KLEAGLE, KLAVERN NO. 1, PROVINCE OF LONDINIUM, IMPERIAL REALM OF ALBION,
ARYAN KNIGHTS KU KLUX KLAN OF GREAT BRITAIN.
C/o Box 5062, Waco, Texas, U.S.A.

The Editor,
'West Indian Gazette
250, Brixton Road,
London.S.W.9.
August.18-58.

My Dear Mr B. Ape,

Kindly post two copies of your paper to the above addressevery month
until ordered to cease.

Possibly you are wondering why we have so-far failed to pay
attention to your audacity in setting up this filthy hack-trash
of a paper?, . Pray good Sir, We, The Aryan Knights miss nothing,
close attention has been paid to every issue of this rag, and I do
sincerely assure you, the information gleamed has proven of great
value to the Klan.

May we take this opportunity to wish your ------paper every
success whilst you are able to continue printing it.

Aryan Regards,
A,Whiteman.

the 'old' parties. One of the first Mosley meetings was held on July 21st at a carefully selected spot—the corner of Southam Street and Golborne Road where Kelso Cochrane had been murdered.

It was a macabre occasion. A fine summer evening sharpening each detail of abject blight in the narrow barracks-like street that looks like an illustration for *The Bitter Cry of Outcast London*, the protest pamphlet published over 75 years ago. The double row of three-storey houses appears rejected and cut-off; dominated by the bulk of the gasworks at the back; leading into the noise and smell of railway lines at the other end. The monotonous decay of decades is written on the walls; some of it now punctuated by Mosley slogans. Peeling plaster; rotten window frames; cracked panes; sorry curtains; only here and there an odd patch of re-faced brick. The hum of people crowded together; children running in the street; women leaning out of windows, calling to one another: "Mosley is coming." Sounds of curiosity, of gladness because the street has its own show, of approval, of animosity; all blending together into one tune of expectancy: this is the second act; there is no one here who does not think of the first.

But in fact the stage told more than the play. The second act, the meeting at the 'murder corner', was rather lame.

About 300 people had come along. In my section of the crowd, there was the usual group of Mosley lieutenants and supporters: several shrill women; quite a number of men in their twenties and thirties, lower middle class in looks and accent, intense and stern; some more of the same kind selling the Movement's papers and leaflets; a few older men; and one middle-aged West End type couple, both with impeccable accents and clothes. (It was they who were applauding most regularly and emphatically.) The children from the streets nearby rushed in and out of the group.

Several bunches of onlookers—students, workmen, housewives and some coloured people, too—were standing apart from the main crowd. They talk to one another. "You see these chaps around here all the time", says an elderly workman. "People have short memories. Mosley will collect more votes than you think."

The first preliminary speeches. And then Sir Oswald arrives and mounts the platform. Cheers. More cheers. No rabble-rousing. (Not a single reference to Jews.) The usual anti-coloured slogans and innuendos; a recital of the same "constructive" policy which is published in his leaflets. He makes good use of his stage setting. He points to the forgotten people of North Kensington, to their miserable housing conditions, to "the years of Tory-Labour neglect" and to the coloured invasion, which are, he says, responsible for all this hopelessness. The solution: "Fight to end the coloured invasion. Send the Jamaicans home." Applause. The coloured by-standers listen impassively. More of the same. More applause. The meeting breaks up.

But is it really over? Everybody expects a sequel. The crowds drift along, and then bunch up again, waiting. After all, this is the Cochrane corner. The police come: "Break it up." Some men adjourn to the pub next door; another group remains outside. People look out from street doors and windows. An open loudspeaker lorry, packed with Mosley's cadets, comes along; shouts go to and fro. Suddenly the coloured people no longer walk singly. One group (the men in conductors' uniforms) stands rather tensely, half inside a street door. Theirs seems to be the sole 'coloured' house in a row of white ones. Only one Negro is still on his own; standing a few steps away on the railway bridge, in a melancholy posture of 'wait and see', even more sharply outlined than that of all the others.[79]

This kind of evening was the prelude to Mosley's campaign. Later on, the tempo was faster and tempers were sharper. North Kensington would have been in any case a strongly contested constituency. Although the sitting Labour Member, Mr. George Rogers, had won the last election in 1955 with a comfortable majority, in a straight fight against a Conservative, four years later his chances appeared to be far less favourable. Quite apart from the general change in the country's political climate, there were several specific reasons for regarding North Kensington then as a marginal Labour constituency. All the rumbling before, during and after the autumn events in 1958; Mr. Rogers' own, apparently rather ambivalent, stand at the critical time; the transitory, highly mobile and thus unpredictable electorate in the area; the possibility of a three-corner contest with a Conservative and a Liberal candidate—all these factors added to the uncertainty.

In the event, there were four candidates: Mr. Rogers for the Labour Party; one of the very rare Conservative working class Parliamentary candidates, Mr. Bob Bulbrook, for his party; a young man, Mr. Michael Hydleman, for the Liberals; Sir Oswald Mosley for the Union Movement. For some time there was also a fifth, Mr. Dhanaraj Nandawar, an Indian restaurant owner, who had been injured in the disturbances, and who decided to stand as an Independent in direct opposition to Mosley, so as ". . . to give the people of North Kensington the chance to vote for racial integration". But

---

[79] An extract from our notebooks.

Mr. Nandawar withdrew his nomination a few days before the election "in the interest of unity and the fight against racialism".[80]

Though the characteristics of the constituency, and in particular Mosley's intervention, made the 'colour question' one of the major campaign issues, not all the answers were quite direct. "We still cherish liberty for all, regardless of colour, race or creed." And: "I am fully with the decent citizens who wish to cleanse North Kensington of the undesirable elements and unsavoury conditions", said the Labour candidate in his election address. Mr. Rogers was in a rather difficult position: his previous statements at the time of the riots had been criticised right and left, by the convinced partisans of intolerance and tolerance alike. Once again, it seemed that he tried to do both too much and too little by keeping a balance between the official doctrine of Transport House and the grievances of the Portobello Road—with the risk of not expressing either. The Conservative candidate, Mr. Bulbrook, well known, popular and respected throughout the area, stuck as far as possible to general issues in terms of the straight Conservative party line, and he assured his potential voters that he would ". . . strive to serve and help everyone, young or old, in North Kensington irrespective of race, colour, creed or political belief". It was mainly the Liberal candidate who made it his business to take the offensive against the Mosley propaganda. He used every opportunity to speak against it and said in his election address:

> "The British citizens from Jamaica, Ghana and other countries, who live in North Kensington, are not the reason [for overcrowding] because the population now is lower than it has ever been since 1946. These people have not taken your homes, because the homes are not there to take. Everybody in North Kensington, everybody in the badly housed areas, whatever their colour, is equally badly housed. . . . Those who want to exploit this situation will use it to spread hatred and bad feeling. Do not be deceived into hating your neighbours when they are suffering the same misfortunes as you."

And as Mr. Hydleman is Jewish, and had an Indian election agent, the Mosleyites found it easy to retaliate in their own fashion. The Liberal candidate received antisemitic letters; Mosley leaflets and slogans were pinned on the door of his committee room. "It is hard for a doctrinaire Liberal to compete against such tactics", said *The Times*.[81]

The contest in North Kensington began to be widely known as the "ugly" election. Mosley's own election address did not make pleasant reading.

[80] *Kensington Post*, October 2, 1959.
[81] *The Times*, September 25, 1959.

"MOSLEY WITH THE PEOPLE, FOR THE PEOPLE LET HIM DO THE JOB FOR YOU"

"He has stood true to his beliefs in fair and foul weather. It surely does not matter whether you agree with him or not on long past issues. What matters is the proof that he will not let you down if you agree with him on present issues. His whole life record has proved him to be a man of principle who can be trusted to keep his word to the people."

"Dear Friend,

I came to North Kensington as your candidate at the invitation of local residents, because a grave injustice is being done. British people are being forced to accept another way of life which is alien to us. . . . All the old parties have combined to bring in more and more coloured immigrants, although their neglect of your housing problem had already caused bad overcrowding. . . .

Your vote at this election can stop at once the ruin of Britain by the immigration of more and more coloured people.

. . . a vote for any of the other parties will mean FIVE coloured men will be here after ten years for every ONE here today unless you stop it now."

The White Defence League made their contribution—writing their slogans on many walls and sticking up their posters.

"Don't vote for any supporters of coloured immigration. Send the Blacks Back."

"Stand Fast. Don't Mix. Keep Britain White."

There were Mosley meetings every night, and daily raucous calls from his loudspeaker lorry. There was the constant repetition of the same phrases: "The white man here knows that there's always a black man at his elbow prepared to work for less."

'The Mosley cavalcade moves off for a street meeting. The loud-speakers are burping and blaring. A man says: "They've got two amplifiers in there, I saw them. Marvellous equipment." Leading the way is the little van with the twin trumpets. There is also a bigger van —ugly, bulbous-nosed, looking vaguely like something out of a film about desert warfare. A crowd gathers, a lieutenant leaps to a micro-phone and reels off an impressive biography of the leader, and then Sir Oswald arrives, taut and spruce, chauffeured in a tiny grey four-seater. . . .

The leader speaks. His voice bounces down the brick alleyways like a cricket ball, echoing and re-echoing. We hear two Mosleys, one hard on the heels of the other. We hear stories about coloured people who have been assaulting, raping, keeping brothels. We are told the Union Movement is helping white residents find decent places to live.

Copies of a letter are handed out. It is from a man thanking Mosley for getting him out of a dingy basement: "God bless you. Keep up the wonderful work".'[82]

---

[82] *The Guardian*, October 5, 1959.

Still the slogans, the leaflets, the platform speeches were more restrained than the direct face-to-face encounters with opponents. Epithets were thrown at them—'Nigger lovers'; 'Jews'. There were skirmishes, especially towards the end of the election campaign.

But while North Kensington was tense, it was less turbulent than two other constituencies—Hampstead and St. Pancras North —where the White Defence League and the National Labour Party were active. Neither group was in any way inhibited by Mosley's election slogan: "the way to solve the colour problem is by votes not violence". They decided to 'keep Hampstead White' because the Labour Party in this predominantly Conservative constituency had adopted a coloured West Indian candidate, Dr. David Pitt, a local doctor. They campaigned in St. Pancras North because they themselves had a candidate in the contest—Mr. William Webster, landlord of a local public house, who was standing on an anti-colour platform.

Mr. Webster's election address read:

"Dear Elector,
The way you cast your vote on October 8 could decide the fate of the British people and the British nation. As in all other constituencies at this crucial election, my Socialist and Tory opponents will be ignoring one of the principal issues at stake.
This issue is whether this country is going to allow the flood of coloured and alien people, such as Cypriots, to continue.
The Tory and Socialist Parties have stated that the principal issues at stake are housing, unemployment and the plight of the old age pensioners. These are indeed important issues. But how can you solve the housing shortage when every day a new boatload of immigrants arrive to compete with you for the limited accommodation available? How can you remove the threat of mass unemployment when immigrants are continually adding to the pool of unskilled labour, with unscrupulous employers already taking on coloured labour at cut-rate wages? How can we ensure that the mounting number of elderly people receive the adequate pension they deserve when these foreign immigrants are milking the Welfare State and receiving priority treatment from the National Assistance Board?
Counter claims are put forward by the Tory and Socialist Parties as to who is best fitted to lead the Britain of the future, but as sure as night follows day continued coloured immigration will mean that the Britain of the future will be eliminated as a racial entity. The leader then can only be Communism!
In spite of the obvious logicality of these views, my Socialist, Tory and Communist opponents have UNITED to abuse me and make it quite clear that they stand for the continued alien invasion of our homeland.
Whatever your past party allegiances, I ask you to give me your vote and smash this Tory-Socialist-Communist conspiracy!"

"Above all—and this will solve half the housing problem—I will demand that NOT A BLACK OR CYPRIOT IS HOUSED UNTIL EVERY BRITON HAS PROPER ACCOMMODATION."

The 'Personal Notes on Bill Webster' added:

'Your candidate, a retired building contractor, has made a lifelong study of Sociology and its relationship to human behaviour and has made an intense survey and study too of Social conditions in St. Pancras.

A common saying of Mr. Webster's is: "I happen to be proud of the fact that my grandfather was a white man, and I want to see my grandchildren the same".'

Mr. Webster demonstrated his pride in a way which is rather unusual for a Parliamentary candidate. He and Mr. John Bean, the Director of Policy of the National Labour Party, were the leaders of a crowd of thirty people who forced their way into St. Pancras Town Hall during a meeting held by the Movement for Colonial Freedom shortly before election day. Fighting broke out in the hall. Outside, a crowd of about a hundred were shouting 'Keep Britain White'. Subsequently nine men were charged. Webster, Bean and five others were accused of "using insulting words and insulting behaviour whereby a breach of the peace might be occasioned". Bean was also charged with, but later found not guilty of, assaulting one of the stewards at the meeting and causing him bodily harm. Another man was facing the same charge and was later found guilty. The ninth man was charged with using insulting words, but not insulting behaviour. All the defendants pleaded not guilty.

In the Magistrate's Court, the story was told for the prosecution.

"Mr. Lane said that M.P.s addressed the meeting in the hall. Bean led the party which forced its way in. Hughes shouted to various coloured people. He refused to go away, but said to the police: 'I don't like Jews, black men, or Greeks.' William Webster shouted: 'Down with the niggers.'

William Webster, Sullivan, Frederick Webster, and van Ammel were driving round in a car which bore slogans such as 'Keep Britain White' and 'Down with the Blacks'. Barfoot was shouting similar slogans.

Police-Constable J. Chapman said that as some people were being put into a police van Barfoot took several paces towards it, stood at attention, raised his right arm in the fashion of a Nazi salute, and said 'Heil Hitler'. When arrested he said: 'Why me? Why pick me out?'

Hughes was cleared of using insulting behaviour and fined 40s. for using insulting words. Peter Webster was fined £3. Barfoot was fined 40s. for using insulting words and 20s. for using insulting behaviour.

William Webster, Sullivan, Frederick Webster, and van Ammel were each fined £10. Each gave notice of appeal."[83]

---

[83] *The Guardian*, October 16, 1959.

Mr. William Webster's appeal was dismissed; the other defendants abandoned their appeal. Two of them (one of whom was John Bean) were remanded on bail and later sentenced to one month's imprisonment each.[84]

Two days after the disturbance in St. Pancras Town Hall, there was a similar incident at Hampstead Town Hall during an election meeting at which the Labour candidate, Dr. David Pitt, was speaking. (This time, however, it was a smaller group—of about a dozen men—who went in to shout the 'Keep Britain White' chorus.) Two M.P.s, the joint chairmen of the British-Caribbean Association, wrote to *The Times* in protest. Mr. Colin Jordan, the National Organiser of the White Defence League, replied—saying that " 'better race relations' . . . is a euphemism for racial treason".[85]

Dr. Pitt was subjected to a barrage of insulting telephone calls—for example: "Nigger, why don't you go back where you came from?" Stickers appeared on his posters and also on those of Conservative and Labour candidates in St. Pancras North. There were two main versions: "For a Nigger Britain" or "Your Jewish Candidate". The loudspeaker vans of the National Labour Party and their friends screamed even more harshly than those of the Mosleyites (though they were not so well equipped).

The noise was loud enough to be heard far away; that kind of terminology was not customary at British elections. Mosley, Webster and their supporters succeeded in bringing racialism into the limelight at least in three constituencies. But on this occasion they were not able to do much more. Indeed, Mr. Webster had been right in one respect: elsewhere, most of the candidates of the established parties did in fact ignore the 'colour question'. (On the other hand, his prediction that "the next government, whether Labour or Tory, will make it illegal . . . to speak openly against coloured and foreign immigration", in his kind of style, has not been fulfilled.)

Britain's attitude to the multi-racial society at home was not a general issue in the election; there were only two other London constituencies where marginal, though still highly controversial, references to the coloured migrants were made.[86] Nor was there any

[84] *The Times*, November 11 and 13, 1959. John Bean was convicted on the charge of using insulting behaviour; the other man was found guilty of assault, occasioning bodily harm.

[85] *The Times*, October 6 and 21, 1959.

[86] One of these constituencies was Brixton, where the Conservative candidate talked of the 'colour problem'. "A flood of immigrants from the Caribbean has poured into this country and for the first time in our history we have to face the problem of large numbers of coloured people in our midst." He was also reported to have said "that it would be necessary to discourage by every possible means

evidence that the migrants themselves swung the election results anywhere in any significant way. They are far too much dispersed; they are a comparatively small proportion of the population even in those districts in which they are fairly concentrated, and because of their mobility, they are an even smaller proportion of the registered electorate. Moreover, they did not appear to vote as a block, leaning predominantly towards one party.

In view of the usual, and almost inevitably, low poll for any candidate of a small political minority, and in particular for one of a newly emerging political minority, it was certain in advance that neither Mosley nor Webster had any chance of getting into the House of Commons, or anywhere near it. And they were both defeated, and lost their deposits. But so did the Liberal candidate in North Kensington, and the Communist candidate in St. Pancras North. In fact, a comparison of the election results of the new racialist candidates with those of long established minor parties—and this is the only realistic comparison that can be made—shows that the anti-coloured vote was by no means negligible.

In North Kensington, the Labour candidate, Mr. Rogers, was re-elected. Although his majority was reduced, this was not a local phenomenon; it was in keeping with the general political swing in the country, and with the fact that at this election Labour had to compete not only with a Conservative, but also with a Liberal candidate, quite apart from Mosley's intervention.[87] The results were:

	Votes	
	No.	%
Labour . . .	14,925	43
Conservative . .	14,048	40
Liberal . . .	3,118	9
Union Movement . .	2,821	8
Total Poll: . .	34,912	100
Total Electorate .	51,492	

more West Indians from coming to Britain". He was rebuked by the Brixton Labour Party and the Lambeth Borough Council, which passed a motion deploring his action in bringing racial problems into his campaign. The former Labour Member for Brixton, Mr. Marcus Lipton, who had been criticised during the campaign by the Conservative candidate for having welcomed West Indians to Brixton in 1948, was re-elected. (*South London Press*, October 2 and 23, 1959.)

[87] At the previous General Election in 1955, Mr. Rogers had a majority of

Thus Mosley—politically a lone wolf, assisted openly merely by a small group of inexperienced social outsiders and an *ad hoc* local campaign—polled only just under 300 fewer votes than the Liberal candidate, who was supported by a long established, prominent party organisation, heard through the national media of communication; who expressed a traditional, highly respected doctrine in an up-to-date, forceful manner; and who did so, moreover, in an election in which Liberals, in general, had greater success than they had had for some time previously. Considered in its context, the anti-colour vote in North Kensington was clearly not insignificant; the fringe of overt racialism in this critical area can no longer be thought to be so small that it can be safely ignored.

Mr. Webster did not do quite so well in St. Pancras North. Even so, he collected 1,685 votes—4 per cent of the total—455 more votes than the other minor party candidate in that constituency, a Communist. Mosley and Webster had better results (proportionately and numerically) than most Communist candidates throughout the country: there were altogether eighteen of the latter; only four (in traditional left-wing constituencies like Stepney and Glasgow Gorbals) obtained more votes than Webster, but fewer votes than Mosley; and only two got more votes than Mosley, both in constituencies which had been represented by Communist M.P.s in the post-war Parliament.[88] Despite the fact that the Communists had years of work, a party organisation and a national newspaper behind them, and had nominated candidates who were personally well known locally, and popular also among their political opponents, most of them were still far less successful than Mr. Webster and his group, who had only just appeared on the political scene.

It could hardly have been mere novelty which prompted several thousand people to cast their votes for the Union Movement and the National Labour Party. Any independent, arguing for a particular

---

almost 3,000 votes, and obtained 54 per cent of the votes cast. (The turn-out in North Kensington at that election—70 per cent—was only two percentage points higher than it was four years later.) At the 1959 election, Mr. Rogers obtained 53 per cent of the combined Labour and Conservative votes. Thus the comparative strength of the two major parties in North Kensington had remained fairly stable.

[88] By far the highest Communist vote in any one of the eighteen constituencies in which Communists stood was 4,580—14.5 per cent of the poll—in Rhondda East; and in only one other constituency (Fife West) did the Communist candidate—like Mosley in North Kensington—obtain just over 8 per cent of the votes. Several Communist candidates (in working class constituencies) collected far fewer votes than Webster—just over 400, 500 and 900 votes; one to two per cent of the total poll.

cause or slogan, surrounded by some fanatics or cranks, can always collect a few hundred votes. But he cannot get much more. Mosley and Webster did get considerably more, at their first attempt, supported mainly by the noise and smears they were flinging around in the back streets, by fist-waving, verbally and physically—by their translation of the pent-up frustration and aggression in the places which used to be called 'the rookeries of London'. They could have been well satisfied with their results.

However, Mosley did not think that his was good enough. *Action* complained:

> "*MOSLEY'S ELECTION RESULT IS A MYSTERY . . .*
>
> A very careful canvass revealed promises to vote for him amounting to 32½ to 37 per cent of those canvassed, except in the rich Tory area whose strength was easily measurable on the register. The promises alone appeared quite sufficient to secure his return."

Three weeks later, Sir Oswald Mosley presented a petition to the High Court, as "the first legal step towards obtaining a judicial enquiry" into the conduct and validity of the North Kensington election. He named the returning officer (the Mayor of Kensington) and the successful Labour candidate as the respondents. His petition was subsequently dismissed.[89]

The Language of Unreason

Since the General Election, the anti-coloured groups have continued their activities; and they have also drawn closer to one another. The differences in their terminology have become slighter. Thus while *Action* was comparatively polite until and during the election campaign, and tended to speak of "coloured" immigrants, aliens and Jamaicans (the Union Movement does not seem to have heard of any other West Indians), it now usually refers to the "Blacks". "Mosley . . . stood for sending the coloured people home from North Kensington. Not in the spirit of 'race hatred'," said *Action* on October 17, 1959. Since then the Movement and its paper have changed their tone. "Go home you young ladies who love the Negroes", screech the female *Action* vendors and pickets at any woman (old or young) who is entering or leaving a public meeting at which coloured people are represented.

---

[89] *Action*, October 17 and 31, 1959. The petition was heard at the High Court of Justice on April 4–6, 1960. On the second day of the hearing, Sir Oswald Mosley wished to withdraw his petition, but because of the difficulties of the withdrawal procedure in such cases, the issue was fully contested.

In May 1959, *Action* pointed out that " 'Keep Britain White' is not an expression which Mosley has ever used." By October its own banner headlines were no less loaded[90]:

"STILL MORE COLOURED COUNTRIES HANGING ROUND OUR NECKS".

"MORE SPENT ON BLACKS THAN ON BRITISH HOMES".

"IS BRITAIN TO BE A BLACK CESSPOOL?"

The antisemitic theme is increasingly stressed (though *Action* was never in any doubt about "the original honesty of National Socialism"; its "achievements"; and the "international recognition that the Third Reich was originally founded on realism and integrity").[91] The social protest theme is becoming sharper. "Their World—And Ours", a regular column in *Action*, airs many grievances.

> "This column sets out to review two worlds as far apart as our earth and the most remote planets in outer space.
> 'Their' world of old political parties led by tired old-style leaders, bereft of ideas, incapable of grappling with the problems of the modern age.
> The world of opportunism, of materialism, of the social rat-race.
> The world of the Establishment.
> And 'our' world, of a new Movement, young in spirit and virile in action, sprung from the people and dedicated to fighting for them against oppression and injustice. . . .
> The people will turn to a Movement which opposes all further coloured immigration. . . .

---

[90] *Action*, May 2, October 17 and 24, 1959. Early in 1959, the Union Movement was anxious to point to their disagreements with the other 'Keep Britain White' groups. Thus on April 11th, *Action* criticised the President of the National Labour Party, who had managed to poll only a few hundred votes as an independent Parliamentary candidate in a by-election in Norfolk. The paper said that the candidate's failure proved that a "purely national policy" was out-of-date. "In these days a policy does not get far which just divides the world into Britons and foreigners." On May 2nd, *Action* wrote that the Ku Klux Klan had "no relation" to the Union Movement. "Oswald Mosley . . . published instructions in 1956 in which he said that no member of Union Movement could be a member of the Ku Klux Klan."

[91] *Action*, May 9, 1959. Before the election (on April 24th) *Action* asked: "Do Jews Wish To Provoke Another Fight?"—although "(1) Mosley has stated the old quarrel is over, and (2) there are not many Jews in North Kensington anyway?" A little later, the paper began to contain more frequent references to "Jewish Pressure" and "concealed Jewish control". By February 1960, though still claiming that "Union Movement is not and never has been an anti-Semitic organisation", it said: "The present wave of anti-Semitism in most countries is due to the insensate way in which many Jews sought revenge after the war. They believe in vengeance."

They will be with us in campaigns ranging from the cause of the small shopkeeper, fighting against the chain stores and the takeover bid, to that of the man behind the bar, determined that the English pub shall not be turned into an emporium for ladies' underwear."[92]

The National Labour Party is even more concerned with the fate of public houses and 'small shopkeepers'. ("The backbone of the nation is the small shopkeeper and small trader. . . . As my record shows, I am the only candidate who can genuinely say that he supports the small man", said the National Labour candidate, a publican, in his election address to the voters of St. Pancras North.) And the world of the National Labour Party and the White Defence League is even more remote from the 'old political parties' than that of the Union Movement. Even in their printed words, they make no concessions whatsoever to the conventions of published matter. Their agitation is consistently directed against all minority groups, large and small, irrespective of race, creed and nationality—against "Blacks", "Hebrews", and against those "aliens", the British citizens from Cyprus and Malta. And as the National Labour Party and the White Defence League had already collaborated in this work, they decided early in 1960 to join forces. They are now united in one organisation, the 'British National Party', which "fights to free Britain from Jewish dominance and the coloured influx", and which admits members who are "of purely Northern European racial ancestry". Otherwise, these "Nationalist battalions" or "militant columns" (as the supporters of the new party call themselves) carry on as before. They continue to disturb those political meetings to which they are opposed; to publish *Combat*, now the "Voice of Race and Nation", and also some smaller papers, such as *The Nationalist*, the "Voice of Northern European Racial Nationalism"; and to maintain their contacts with their friends overseas. Their headquarters are quite close to Mosley's North Kensington office—in Notting Dale, the centre of the disturbances in 1958.

But while the Union Movement, the British National Party and the other extreme racist cliques have a good deal of common ground geographically and ideologically, they still maintain a division of labour. There are thus still variants in the language of unreason which the 'Keep Britain White' groups speak; there are differences also in the characteristics of their supporters, and in the range and temper of their activities. Some try at times to be more respectable than others; some court publicity, others prefer secrecy. In essence their meanings are the same.

[92] *Action*, No. 58, February 1960.

3. 'KEEP BRITAIN TOLERANT' GROUPS

The anti-coloured organisations are deviants. In terms of official public opinion, they are themselves minority groups; they get no encouragement from the major organs of public opinion, from the established political parties, or from trade unions. 'Keep Britain White' is regarded as a sinister subversive slogan. 'Keep Britain Tolerant', on the other hand, sums up the official attitude which is in support of harmony, and of the attempts which are being made to promote it. Indeed, while there had been indifference or even apathy towards the problems of coloured people before the events of 1958, there had also been for some time a good deal of activity conducive to their integration in British society, or explicitly devoted to integration.[93] Since the autumn of 1958 such activities have increased, though more in theory than in practice.

Social Activities

There are several views on the means by which integration should be achieved. The most widely held one is that advocating natural absorption: coloured people should behave, and be treated, like everyone else and take part, without ado, in the social life of their communities. To some extent this has, in fact, happened. There are West Indians who are on easy, friendly terms with their white neighbours. There are also those who have joined long established organisations —churches, political parties and trade unions, student organisations, sports, jazz and social clubs. Scattered throughout London, from Woolwich to Acton, and from Hampstead to Wandsworth, there are branches of the International Friendship League, and also bodies such as the Overseas Social Centre, the All Nations Social Club and the Linguists Club. These clubs—which have a varied programme of dances, socials, lectures and tuition—are by their very nature cosmopolitan and inter-racial, for they are open to English people as well as to all interested newcomers from overseas.

Social organisations of this kind existed before, and irrespective of,

[93] 'Integration' (sometimes merely called 'good will') is a rather vague term. Though commonly used in the United States, it was in that particular American sense hardly known in this country before the events of 1958. Recently, the word 'harmony' has taken its place here. The generally accepted meanings of these terms are roughly the same: they imply 'making coloured people feel at home'; promoting social 'colour blindness'; refusal to permit differences in the treatment of black and white; improvement in race relations through various measures, including the establishment of inter-racial clubs. The term 'integration' is here used as an umbrella to cover these various meanings.

the recent West Indian migration. But there are others which have been formed, particularly since the disturbances of 1958, for the special purpose of assisting the integration of coloured people. On the whole, these do not appear to have been successful. Both the birth and death rates of such harmony clubs and similar activities are rather high—particularly in North Kensington where several groups were started with enthusiasm, and a good deal of publicity, but soon petered out.[94]

There are, however, some notable exceptions. Here and there, a particular individual—a minister of religion, a local councillor, a mayor, a writer—or a particular religious or political group—the Quakers, the Methodists, young Socialists—have established organisations, not just for the purpose of spreading harmony, but in pursuit of an 'integrated' and fairly concrete philosophy of integration. Such organisations, though usually rather modest and small, have a better chance of survival than the well-meaning *ad hoc* efforts launched as a reaction to a particular manifestation of tension —after the Notting Dale events or the Cochrane murder. Several examples of the more persistent inter-racial social activities can be found in South London. One of the best known is 'Racial Brotherhood' in Brixton, formed by a member of the Society of Friends. And the meetings and socials in Lambeth Town Hall, which were started several years ago by the Mayor in order to bring coloured and white people together, have also continued.

There is a third group of clubs—those which are intended mainly or only for coloured people. On the whole, these organisations are based on the assumption that the newcomers are often too shy to join clubs because organised social activities are not a feature of West Indian society, and that they need, therefore, a period of initiation by themselves. Thus several churches hold special services and meetings for West Indians, and so do some local associations.[95]

These various organisations—irrespective of differences in their functions, composition and lifetime—are alike in being in touch, or in attempting to get into touch, directly with the migrants themselves. But there are also other bodies which are more generally concerned with the promotion of the ideology of tolerance, both in theory and practice. Several of these organisations are engaged in

[94] Among these was a mixed youth club, the Harmony Club, which had a good start, but which survived for only six weeks. Nor were attempts by the local community centre to invite coloured people very successful.

[95] For example, the Paddington Overseas Students and Workers Committee, which is associated with the London Council of Social Service, runs an afternoon club for West Indian mothers.

advisory and welfare activities only; or they are chiefly interested in educating public opinion; some hold social functions as well.

Education and Welfare

At the local level there is the Colonial Advisory Panel of the St. Pancras Borough Council, which was re-established in October 1958, after the Panel had been dormant for some time. In the Borough of Willesden, the Mayor formed early in 1959 an International Friendship Committee "to undertake the work of helping the newcomers". Assistance is given in various ways, one of which, in particular, is a very practical one: disputes between coloured landlords and white tenants are investigated by members of the Committee, and wherever possible settled.[96]

In Kensington, the Borough Council appointed a West Indian social worker after the disturbances in the autumn of 1958; and at that time, too, the Mayor set up a 'Racial Integration Co-ordinating Committee', which consists of representatives of local organisations and churches, and of local 'public persons', white and coloured. The Committee has the general, rather vague purpose of promoting harmony in the borough.

However, there might well be a need to co-ordinate the inter-racial co-ordinators in Kensington, for there are several groups which regard it as their function to do just that. They tend to have a brief active existence. They came into being at a moment of crisis—first, after the disturbances and then, even more energetically, after the murder of a West Indian in May 1959; little is heard of them in the usual daily run. Only a few show signs of being more stable. Among these is the Universities and Left Review Club, some members of which undertook a rather ambitious 'Notting Hill project': they

[96] In general, this Committee has been rather active. It has established a club (which was intended to be an inter-racial youth club, but which is mainly attended by West Indians in the twenty to thirty years age group); it issues information, for example, on housing; it also collects information, and has sponsored a social survey of the area jointly with the local Citizen's Advice Bureau; the Committee considers complaints about symptoms of intolerance and discrimination (directed against coloured people, Jews or other minority groups); and it issues statements on such matters. One of the Committee's main functions has been the investigation and conciliation of housing disputes. In Willesden, where there are many small shabby houses, of the kind West Indians can manage to buy, the usual situation of 'mixed' occupancy is that of a coloured landlord with white tenants (generally those who were 'sitting' tenants when the house was bought). Apparently, the opposite situation—of a white landlord with coloured tenants—exists only rarely in the borough. No dispute in a case of the latter kind has so far been brought to the attention of the Committee.

N.—14

sponsored a local youth club ('inter-racial' in theory, but hardly in practice); they assisted tenants with their problems of rents and housing conditions; and thus they were also concerned with the establishment of a Residents' Association in one of the most sordid zones of transition.[97]

There is also a federal body, the 'Committee for Inter-Racial Unity in West London'. It was launched by a conference, held in July 1959, which was attended by about 100 delegates—from local branches of the Labour Party, the Co-operative movement and trade unions; from trades councils; and from various organisations of coloured people. The main theme of the resolutions passed by the conference (which its successor, the Committee, was asked to pursue) was to:

> "carry out activities against racialism in all its forms and in support of greater inter-racial unity in West London;
> co-ordinate a drive of watchful pressure and propaganda to improve welfare services and housing policies in areas of changing population, and to ensure that local authorities use to the full the powers that they already possess."

A leaflet 'Unity' was issued by the Committee, and another similar conference was held a few months later.

The potential significance of such a broadly based group cannot be easily assessed: it might help to minimise the danger of acute tension; it could also become influential in the hour of a new critical event. Meanwhile, however, the various organisations, large and small, hold an occasional meeting and announce their many good intentions. And there are also a few people (such as members of the London County Council for North Kensington) who are indeed regarded as counsellors; they have become well known because of their close personal concern with the problems of the area.

Nevertheless, the multiplicity of conferences, committees, associations and advice—all in the name of inter-racial harmony, unity and co-ordination—causes some embarrassment. Certainly, there are far more organisations and resolutions in North Kensington than

[97] This association, the Powis and Colville Residents' Association, has already been mentioned, as well as another 'mixed' Tenants' Association in Paddington. See Chapter III, footnote 11, p. 56. A general report on the 'Notting Hill Project' was given in *New Left Review*, No. 1, January–February 1960, pp. 71–2. Another organisation of a different kind, the Institute of Group Studies—formed in 1958 by Dr. Richard Hauser and his wife, Hepzibah Menuhin—is also concerned with the various social problems of white and coloured people in North Kensington. The Institute has sponsored inter-racial meetings and discussion groups.

concrete efforts. Not long ago, *The Kensington News* asked in a bold headline:

> *"Will Too Many Do-Gooders Pave the*
> *Path to Notting HELL?"*[98]

Perhaps Kensington has been particularly unfortunate, not only because the borough has been so much in the news, but also—and more important—because with its division into North and South, it is still in essence a microcosm of the 'Two Nations', even in the age of the welfare state. But of course the borough need not rely on its local organisations only; it is also within the orbit of several others whose 'parish' is the whole of London, or even nation-wide.

Among the latter groups is the Advisory Committee on the Welfare of West Indians in London, established in 1956 by the London Council of Social Service "to assemble the information needed to answer enquiries and to co-ordinate the work of the various bodies dealing with West Indian immigrants in London". The Metropolitan Coloured Peoples Housing Association was formed in May 1957 by a number of people prominent in the social services "to alleviate the housing difficulties of coloured migrants and their families, whether coloured or white, who live in London". It is the object of the Association to buy fairly large houses in less crowded areas which can be converted into flats and let to coloured tenants at reasonable rents. In that way, the Association hopes "to assist in the real integration of newcomers from overseas into the whole of London". So far, however, progress has been very slow: one house with five flats has been opened in Hackney as a pilot scheme.

In a different sphere, and far more successful, is the Race Relations Committee of the Society of Friends, which has existed for some years. Its main function is an educational one, but the Committee also advises Quakers, in general, to participate in inter-racial clubs. A group of Quakers have, moreover, given practical assistance to the people in one of the most miserable districts of North Kensington, Kensal New Town. They have helped the tenants to scrub and paint their houses, so as to give them at least a semblance of a new look.

Apart from the Society of Friends, there are many other groups whose philosophy and interests—in general aspects of discrimination

---

[98] This was the headline for the report of an interview with Councillor Mrs. Olive Wilson, L.C.C. 'Mrs. Wilson recalled the various bodies which had been formed, re-formed (and unformed!) since last year's racial disturbances. "The more there are the more they bedevil the situation", she said. "It's time somebody realised that the ordinary decent coloured working folk don't want to go to meetings and sit on committees; they want to lead ordinary lives and *forget* they are coloured".' (*The Kensington News*, 30th October, 1959.)

here and abroad or in the social problems of the Commonwealth—
have led them inevitably to a special concern with race relations in
Britain. Among these groups are the Institute of Race Relations;[99]
the Council of Christians and Jews; the National Council for Civil
Liberties; the Haldane Society; the Movement for Colonial Freedom;
the Campaign against Racial Discrimination in Sport; and the Stars'
Campaign for Inter-Racial Friendship.[100]

Finally, at the national level, a new organisation with specific purposes, the British-Caribbean Association, was formed during the
disturbances of 1958, on the basis of preparations which had previously been made. Its objects are:

> "(i) To develop and increase friendship and understanding between
>   the people of the West Indies (including British Guiana and
>   British Honduras) and the people of the United Kingdom.
> (ii) To stimulate and encourage all forms of mutual aid between the
>   West Indies and Great Britain."

The Association is well-connected. Among its patrons are the
Governor-General of the West Indies, the Secretary of State for the
Colonies, the Prime Minister of the Federation of the West Indies,
and the West Indies Commissioner in London. The Association's
joint chairmen are Mr. Charles Royle, a Labour M.P., and
Mr. Nigel Fisher, a Conservative M.P.; it has over 600 members;
among them are about sixty other M.P.s, eleven Peers, and also a
number of West Indian spokesmen in London. Thus an influential
'inter-racial' pressure group has been established. It has been active
in making friends and in censuring enemies: the Association has
repeatedly drawn attention to the 'Keep Britain White' agitators; it

---

[99] The Institute of Race Relations is in a separate category. While the other
organisations mentioned all pronounce, and indeed campaign for, the active disapproval of intolerance, "the Institute is precluded by the Memorandum and
Articles of its incorporation from expressing an opinion on any aspect of the
relations between races".

[100] The Stars' Campaign was formed, soon after the 1958 events, by a number of
people prominent in entertainment. An illustrated pamphlet (*What the Stars Say*)
explained that the Campaign intended to promote "the ideals of racial tolerance
and harmony through the example of those who earn their living in the world of
art and entertainment, and in the associated realms of journalism, writing and
the productive side of show business. Its aims are: to promote understanding
between races and banish ignorance about racial characteristics; to combat instances of social prejudice by verbal and written protests; to set an example to the
general public through members' personal race relations; and to use all available
means to publicise their abhorrence of racial discrimination." While the Campaign had a rather energetic, 'newsworthy' start (in 1958 it held an 'inter-racial'
children's Christmas party in North Kensington, which was televised), since
then it has been rather quiet.

issued warnings of tension in the spring of 1959 before the Cochrane murder occurred; it became very vocal afterwards. Its members have made proposals to outlaw discrimination (so far without success); in the House of Commons they often ask insistent questions on matters of race relations.

Thus on June 4th 1959, Mr. Nigel Fisher got up to ask the Home Secretary:

> "whether, in view of the recent murder of a West Indian in the streets of Notting Hill and of attacks upon the property of coloured residents in that area, he will issue a public statement deploring such manifestations of colour prejudice and violence; if he will draft extra police into the district to ensure the preservation of law and order and the protection of the persons and property of coloured British citizens; and if he will use the resources of his department to initiate the vigorous and sustained education of public opinion about race relations by all means and through all media available."

Mr. Charles Royle wanted to know whether the Home Secretary

> ". . . will agree that there was very little evidence of racial hatred before certain organisations became active in that area? Is it not significant that these organisations are allied in thought to organisations which created racial enmity in the 1930s? Does the right hon. Gentleman propose to take any action about those organisations?"

The Home Secretary, Mr. R. A. Butler, replied: "We are watching the situation closely. . . ."[101] And he agreed to receive a deputation of M.P.s from both sides of the House, members of the British-Caribbean Association, to discuss their proposals in detail.

Certainly, since the autumn of 1958, the questions on such matters —asked inside and outside Parliament—have become more direct, more so than the answers. Deputations, conferences, meetings, letters to the Press—the process of drawing public attention to issues of race relations continues. 'Responsible opinion' has become more explicit —not least through the activities of the many organisations, local and national, for the promotion of harmony. But has it become sufficiently explicit? Are the discrepancies between the manifold contradictory attitudes to 'colour' in British society still widening? Nobody knows.

It is true, of course, that in every sphere of British public life—in industry, in politics, in the churches, in social services, in sport and entertainment; at the local and at the national level—there are now

---

[101] *Parliamentary Debates*, H.o.C., 4th June 1959, cols. 368, 370. Incidentally, not long before, it was said in 'another place' (in a similar context) that 'watching the situation closely' may be interpreted as "officialese for 'hoping for the best'." (*Parliamentary Debates*, H.o.L., 19th November 1958, col. 656.)

groups which are aware of these discrepancies. As the need for the diffusion of unambiguous tolerance becomes more obvious, efforts to bring it about by a variety of methods are also increased. That is a positive development, though as yet it has hardly been a very effective one. While all the efforts of diverse organisations have been well-meaning, most of them have been so far rather fragmentary and peripheral.

4. WEST INDIAN ORGANISATIONS

In discussions of race prejudice and discrimination in Britain, questions are often asked on the extent of group cohesion among West Indians and, in particular, on their organisational links which might reflect, and also produce, cohesion. It is thought that if coloured people in this country felt that they were regarded as a group apart, they would surely draw together, and thus promote and assert their unity through formal association.

It is doubtful, however, whether the extent of such association can, in fact, be regarded as an index of the sense of 'community' among coloured people in this country. In many circumstances, it is an inadequate index; in those of the coloured newcomers, especially, it is certainly of rather dubious value. For many reasons, it is unlikely that the migrants would, or could, develop their own organisations on a considerable scale.[102]

It is not only their heterogeneity, in terms of origin, social class and political orientation, which makes sustained common organisation on their own rather difficult. There is also the duality of West Indian attitudes: should they take part in separate or in joint 'integrated' organisations? Many do neither; some do both, and most of those who do advocate 'separatism' regard it as a means for ultimate integration. Nevertheless, the duality remains, especially in view of the ambiguity and diversity of English attitudes, and also as a result of the divergencies in the inclinations of the different coloured groups in this country. Their views on 'mixed' or separate organisations are clearly influenced by the political status of their countries of origin within the Commonwealth. People from Northern

---

[102] It should be remembered that it would be equally unrealistic to measure social cohesion among native Londoners by the extent of their participation in organised social activities, or by similar indices—or even to expect a great deal of definite cohesion. Only a minority of the people among whom the West Indians live here take an active part in organisations, though all are more familiar with the concept of formal association than the newcomers are.

Rhodesia can hardly be expected to have the same opinions on these matters as those from Ghana or from Barbados; nor does a Jamaican necessarily agree with a man from British Guiana. First and foremost, the migrants from the various territories are pre-occupied with those events which affect their particular socio-political developments either at home or in London. And as these developments are diverse, their interests are diverse, too. It is said that activities following Cochrane's murder were more spontaneous and intense among West Indians in London than among Africans; on the other hand, it is of course the Africans, not the West Indians, to whom reports on the Hola camp or the emergency in Nyasaland are of immediate concern. Indeed, it seems that news from home—or of colonial emancipation, in general—matters more to Africans and Asians in Britain than to West Indians. Partly because they are the largest coloured group in this country, the West Indians are bound to give their closest attention to problems of their adjustment here. Altogether, the many cleavages among the migrants prevent a concerted drive towards the organisation of the coloured people on their own—either in London or in other urban centres.

But even if there were such a drive, it might not have much chance of concrete success—at least not for the time being. As the coloured newcomers live and work in various parts of London, which are at a considerable distance from one another, their organisations tend to have a limited local sphere of influence. It is not easy for those who live in Notting Hill, in Kilburn or in Stepney to attend regularly meetings in Brixton or vice versa; not can migrant associations afford the rent for premises in Central London. And even more important is the fact that the West Indians, in particular, are on the whole not yet used to being 'organisation men'. Indeed, they do not need to be organised to express their sociability; they have brought with them their talent for spontaneous, informal social contacts.

The pattern of West Indian social organisations in London is thus not a clearly defined and stable one. It includes formal associations, but as their number, their interests and their membership fluctuate, it is hardly possible to give an accurate list and description of all those which exist at a particular date. Few are well established; many seem to function for a comparatively short time—they do not have resources or premises for regular activity; others are unknown beyond their immediate neighbourhood. Often such associations are no more than small, temporarily organised offshoots of the many informal social contacts which the West Indian Londoners maintain among themselves.

Informal Social Contacts

Meetings in their rooms, at street corners and in basement areas, in the markets, cafes and barber shops, it is these which make up most of the West Indians' social life, and it is a rather extensive and lively one. The West Indian barber shops, in particular, are community centres, where West Indian newspapers can be read, and where all the latest news can be heard: information about new arrivals; about possible vacancies in jobs or houses; rumours of new chances of employment or threats of unemployment; announcements of dances and meetings. It is there, too, that stories of discrimination are told and rapidly circulated. The grapevine is very efficient, if not always accurate. Inevitably, in the re-telling, rumours gain the status of facts. And an example of a particular instance of prejudice might well have been multiplied, and become indistinguishable from a whole series of such incidents, when it has been passed around for some time.

Apart from the barber shops, there are other stores which provide special services or commodities for West Indians, and which are, therefore, also meeting places. Coloured girls and women can obtain special kinds of cream and face-powder in their hairdressing salons. Again, while some London shops now stock the foods which West Indians like, black-eyed beans and goats meat, for example, and while clothes can be bought anywhere—West Indian men and women have no particular style of dress of their own—there are also West Indian grocers, tailors, laundries and music shops selling calypso records, which are popular with the migrants.[103] The newcomers congregate in all sorts of places: in their own licensed clubs (many of which are quite ordinary meeting places, not the 'dens of iniquity' of general folklore); outside employment exchanges; and of course in shopping centres, like Brixton Market, Camden Town and the Portobello Road. They walk around, often in groups, watching the many sights of London: a church wedding; a political meeting; rush hour traffic; city lights. In the summer especially, the streets in which they live are their parlours: West Indians sit together on their doorsteps; here is a knot of people of different shades of colour (among them a white woman who is just about to take her

---

[103] Manufacture and trade by and for West Indians in London are expanding. For example, one of the migrants has set up a considerable wholesale business for the import of West Indian food products—special sauces, canned foodstuff and fruit; and he has also established a factory in London for the preparation and packing of such commodities. These foodstuffs are now sold rather widely both by English and West Indian grocers in those areas of London where the migrants tend to concentrate.

dark baby in its pram to the child welfare clinic); there is a stag party at the corner—old friends and new acquaintances.

The range of these many informal contacts is often amazingly wide: a West Indian in Paddington can give straight away addresses and news of people in Camberwell and Poplar. And as a result, the West Indians' knowledge of the total London maze tends to be better than that of many native Londoners.

Formal Associations

The formal social links among West Indians in London appear to be more tenuous, and certainly less widespread, than the informal ones. There are four main types of organisation, though the distinctions between them are not hard and fast: student groups; church groups; 'harmony' clubs which stress integration; and associations which are primarily concerned with the rights of coloured people in Britain, and also with their emancipation in other parts of the Commonwealth.

It was estimated that in mid-summer 1959 about 800 West Indian students and just over 1,000 student nurses were enrolled in the University of London, in technical colleges, in the Inns of Court and in London hospitals. (At that time, some 2,400 West Indians, including nurses, were studying in institutions of higher education in other parts of Britain.) Of course, the students join various organisations—those in their own colleges and university; those which are concerned with all overseas students in London, and also their own separate association, the West Indian Students Union. On the whole, the students remain rather apart from the other West Indian migrants: they belong to a distinct social group, and their stay here is not only more limited, but also, on the whole, more comfortable.

West Indian religious groups reflect another aspect of the social and cultural diversity among the newcomers. There are about eight gospel halls in London with West Indian congregations. Their services are evangelical, resembling or following those of the "Church of God in Christ", an American sect. The migrants who go there do so because they prefer the atmosphere to the more austere one of the Established Church.

A Congregational Minister, who has done a great deal to assist the settlement of migrants in Willesden, has described one of these services.

". . . because I still felt that many of our West Indians were not being spiritually satisfied with our services . . . I began to hold a week-night 'Evangelical Service' in the hall, particularly for West Indians.

These services I ran myself each Wednesday night and always invited one of the worshippers to lead the 'Testimony Time' and another to speak. We had some wonderful and inspiring services and I learned many choruses as well as a whole new technique in worship."

"Gradually we built up within the meeting a small orchestra, as one by one our Jamaicans either purchased an instrument of their own, or brought along friends who played an instrument. Our guitars, tambourines and trumpet could be heard all down the street, and I have often wondered what passers-by imagine to be happening inside our Tin Tabernacle! The rhythm at times would be particularly hot, and has been described by one of the young people in my church, who himself enjoys a bit of 'Rock'n Roll', as being the type that 'sends you'. Our normal pattern of worship would follow a regular line, although the time allowed for each item in the liturgy would vary according to the number of worshippers and the way in which the Spirit moved. We generally started with a hymn from *Redemption Songs*, which is the hymn book we normally used. This would be followed by a period of free prayer, in which all the worshippers would kneel and say their own prayers aloud until one by one they fell into silent meditation. The prayer time would then culminate in a petition offered by the leader, and finally the repetition of the Lord's Prayer. After this we would have another hymn and then Testimony. Between each testimony, or possibly two or three testimonies, we would have choruses led by the chorus leader and each one being quickly picked up by the various instruments comprising our orchestra."[104]

Both the harmony clubs and the associations which have the word 'coloured people' in their title have emerged mainly in response to the events of 1958. And they gained new support after the Whitsun murder in 1959. Official West Indian policy, however, is on the side of the first rather than of the second type of organisation: it is, of course, in favour of immediate integration and not of separate associations for coloured people. When the Chief Minister of Jamaica, Mr. Norman Manley, visited England in September 1958 to examine the situation, he came to the conclusion that there was a need for a full-scale programme of integration, which he called 'The Grassroots Plan'. ". . . the eventual goal had to be a network of English and West Indian committees working together in every community in this country. Local leaders would have to be trained, to serve in every area where there were sizeable colonies of coloured people, to work for a better community spirit, integration and inter-racial harmony."[105] While the attainment of "the eventual goal"

[104] C. S. Hill, *Black and White in Harmony* (London, 1958), pp. 61–63. A detailed description of a 'self-contained' West Indian congregation and their service in a Gospel Hall in Brixton is also given by Joyce Egginton in *They Seek a Living* (London 1957), pp. 117–122.

[105] *Manchester Guardian*, September 10, 1958.

is still very remote, there was certainly, after the news of Nottingham and Notting Dale, far more discussion among West Indians of the need for inter-racial organisations than there had been before, and also more interest, though not necessarily sustained, in such organisations sponsored by English people.

The most notable symptom of the new trend was the establishment of inter-racial clubs by West Indians themselves. First, the Harmonist Movement was founded by Mr. MacDonald Stanley, a blind West Indian in his early thirties, to advocate "Inter-racial Harmony amongst all peoples of the world". The Movement has rather ambitious plans: it wants to publish a journal; to obtain the support of all groups in society; to adopt its own symbol (the rainbow was suggested); and to promote various social activities. As the first issue of its duplicated news sheet, *The Harmonist*, says: ". . . there is a great surge of unharmonious thought, consciously put out to obstruct Harmonious relations, amongst the multi-racial and multi-national peoples of London. This the Harmonist movement is endeavouring to correct." The first Harmonist Club was opened in November 1958 in a church hall in Stamford Hill. Social evenings are held there every Saturday night.[106]

Another inter-racial club was founded in Clapham soon after Whitsun 1959 by a Jamaican, a post-office worker, who had served in the R.A.F. It is the object of the Clapham Club "to promote good will between peoples of all races: to foster and encourage a spirit of mutual understanding and respect . . . by study of their backgrounds

---

[106] A regular Saturday evening social at one of these clubs in London, soon after it had been opened, was described by one of our colleagues. "The church hall where we met is rather dark. Altogether, there were about thirty people there; a third were coloured. Only one West Indian girl was in the hall, another arrived late. I gathered that few of the people there belonged to the church. The main activity was dancing—including group dances. The music (gramophone and amplifier) was popular dance music. A young clergyman was busy with the amplifier. The organiser, Mrs. S., who is a member of the church, was arranging for people to dance with one another. There was no question of waiting for a man to ask a girl: the West Indians were too shy to ask the women; Mrs. S. brought them together. There were no refusals, nor any inhibitions. One white girl, engaged to a white boy, danced cheek to cheek with a West Indian. (He did that with all his partners.) Two grandmas did a very vigorous version of 'Knees up Mother Brown'. It was rather like a pub outing—and the white people were of the kind one would see in a pub on a Saturday evening (though the only drink was tea). They were working class, not well dressed: at least two family groups were there, including young children and grandparents, and also three unattached, fairly young married women. So far as I could see, no one had any family relationship with any West Indians, for instance, a West Indian son-in-law. The general atmosphere was cheerful: most people seemed to enjoy themselves once the initial shyness had evaporated."

—social, cultural, historical." The club had a good start. After it had been in existence for one month, it had equal numbers of white and coloured members—some seventy altogether.

Most organisers and some members of inter-racial clubs and committees are also active in the associations which are primarily for coloured people and for the promotion of their specific interests. Indeed, such dual participation is almost inevitable for all those who are closely concerned with race relations in London, and in this country generally. For the several 'good will' and 'harmonist' clubs are more restricted in their scope and influence than the coloured people's associations. Despite official West Indian policy, it is the organisations of the latter type, more than those of the former, which have attracted the migrants' attention, especially after the autumn events of 1958. And it is these which have been more vocal on their behalf.

The various associations for coloured people have neither a large nor a stable membership; there are divergencies amongst them; some of them have had, and others are likely to have, a rather short life time. Nevertheless, they are sufficiently alert, active and well-connected—among themselves and with other groups promoting tolerance—to exercise an influence well beyond the circle of their actual subscribers. Some organisations of this type, which existed before the 1958 disturbances, appear to have faded out or lost their individual identity—for example, the Caribbean Labour Congress and the League of Coloured Peoples.[107] But others have been either strengthened or newly formed since August 1958.

Among these are the Association for the Advancement of Coloured People, the Coloured People's Progressive Association, the United Kingdom Coloured Citizens Association, and a branch of the People's National Movement (which is the Government party of Trinidad). Although these organisations do not, of course, operate a colour bar and include white people among their officers and members, they have been founded, and are kept going by coloured men and women—mainly by West Indians.[108]

---

[107] The League became defunct after the death of its founder, Dr. Harold Moody, the outstanding coloured leader in this country before the war.

[108] The first, however, the Association for the Advancement of Coloured People, is in some respects in a category apart. It is presided over by Mrs. Amy Dashwood Garvey, the widow of Marcus Garvey who started an 'Africa for the Africans' movement in the United States in the early twenties. Mrs. Garvey runs a hostel and club in North Kensington. While she maintains her interests in African politics and art, she is of course concerned with the West Indians in her district, and she is also a member of the Racial Integration Co-ordinating Committee, set up by the Mayor of Kensington. There are several other groups which are primarily established by and for Africans. These are not mentioned here.

The Coloured People's Progressive Association was founded by a group of West Indians in North Kensington soon after the 1958 disturbances. One of its officers is a second-generation West Indian, born in this country. The Association has a list of about 500 members (though not all pay their monthly subscription of two shillings); it has a formal constitution; the executive committee holds weekly meetings; open meetings for members are arranged once a quarter. Its motto is: "United we stand—Divided, we fall." (And among its objects are these: "To protect the rights and privileges of its members as citizens; to strive for their social, economic and political advancement; to work for inter-racial understanding.") As the Association is concerned with the interests and welfare of coloured people, especially of those in North Kensington, its officers are connected with several bodies which have similar aims.

West Indian Leaders

Indeed, the same faces are seen at meetings, and the same names appear in the lists of coloured or 'integrated' organisations of various kinds—in those run by coloured people and in those run by white people. There is thus now an identifiable group of West Indian leaders in London—workers, clergymen, intellectuals, professional politicians, welfare workers, and people at the fringes of the professions. Most of them are fairly young, in the 30–40 age group, but they have lived here already for some time.

The increasing importance of West Indian leaders is the result of the network of inter-relationships which has now been formed; it does not reflect the strength of the individual organisations which they represent; in fact, it is still often out of keeping with their ascertainable actual influence. To begin with, some of the organisations exist largely on paper, or in the minds of a few friends who occasionally discuss their interests and make plans for the future in the room of one of them. A few letters are written to newspapers or M.P.s. But when new associations with a broad sponsorship are set up (as, for example, the British-Caribbean Association) they want to include representatives of migrant groups, and they naturally draw in those whose names have already been mentioned at some time or other. And as Mr. X's name is then heard more frequently, he is assumed to be influential, and indeed has a chance of becoming influential; he gains status, and so his organisation, too, may grow.

External events, in turn, make the network tighter and thus accelerate the snowball growth of influence. The Whitsun murder in 1959 brought about far more determined efforts to achieve collaboration of the various organisations concerned with racial tolerance than had so far been made. The immediate effect was a drawing together, not only for protection, but also to prepare an attack on the causes of prejudice and discrimination. The Inter-Racial Friendship Co-ordinating Council (which has already been mentioned) was set up. Initially, it included representatives of some forty organisations—established, mainly white, organisations, coloured and inter-racial ones. Two months later, some twenty organisations had paid their affiliation fees. The meetings, marches and deputations sponsored by the Council, and the statements which were issued, gave the West Indian leaders, who had previously become known, the opportunity of becoming better known still. Now they had a public platform and could, in fact, act as spokesmen for the migrants.

Systematic co-ordination is, moreover, maintained by the official bodies: the Migrant Services Division of the Commission of the West Indies Federation, British Guiana and British Honduras; and the Barbadian Immigrants' Liaison Service. It has been one of the functions of the Migrant Services Division to bring the officers of West Indian organisations together, and to give them instruction in administrative methods. In the summer of 1959, the Division established a more formal link for this purpose—the 'Standing Conference of Leaders of Organisations Concerned with West Indians in Britain'. The Conference meets monthly and is open to "leaders and potential leaders drawn from organisations working for integration". The members give reports on the activities of their respective organisations, on any general problems which they have encountered, and also discuss matters such as the drafting of constitutions and minutes, elections of an executive committee, and procedure at meetings.[109] The Division not only keeps in touch with most of the organised social activities of West Indians in London,

---

[109] Among the objects of the Standing Conference are the following: "To advise the Commission in the United Kingdom for the West Indies, British Guiana, and British Honduras on problems, opportunities and tensions in the integration of the West Indian peoples; to improve and develop liaison between the West Indian peoples and the statutory and voluntary bodies and other interested groups; to share experiences in social work; to study techniques, practice and current trends in leadership; to encourage West Indians to learn to understand local customs and ways of life and to incorporate the best of what they thus learn into their pattern of living; to promote mutual understanding between the Commonwealth peoples in Britain and to use conferences, meetings, publications and other means for this purpose; to encourage and help West Indian citizens in Britain to improve their general educational and cultural standards; to foster and encourage an appreciation of West Indian Culture; generally to promote a progressive and realistic approach to all matters relating to integration."

but also knows a good deal about their informal ones. Many migrants have at some time or other come to its offices for advice. The Division's sphere of influence is thus incomparably greater than that of any one of the voluntary associations run by and for West Indians. In considering the extent of social cohesion among the migrants, it is this official agency, above all, which must be taken into account.

The West Indian Gazette

The monthly *West Indian Gazette*, published in Brixton, is also increasingly influential in drawing the different groups of newcomers from the Caribbean together. Although it is still a very young journal—the first issue appeared in March 1958—it has established itself quickly, and has now a total circulation of about 15,000 copies.[110] On the whole, its approach is similar to that of the various coloured people's associations. The paper emphasises the special identity and problems of coloured people, and their need to stand together.

Thus in its first issue, the *West Indian Gazette* said that West Indians in Britain "form a community with its own special wants and problems which our own paper alone would allow us to meet". The editorial explained why the paper had been founded. In the summer of 1957, a group of West Indians, concerned with problems of unemployment, housing and colour prejudice, had gone around and spoken to some 2,000 West Indians in their homes, at dances and at socials. They had found that the migrants "wanted an organisation to represent their interests" and "welcomed efforts to unite and to further British-West Indian unity". As a result, and for this purpose, the *West Indian Gazette* was produced.

The journal contains a great deal of news about the West Indies, and about race relations in Britain. The items on Britain are often on questions or instances of prejudice and discrimination. There are reports on West Indian and other relevant associations and on the circumstances of individual West Indians in Britain. Stories of success and hardship appear side by side.

"U.K. SHOE CHAIN HIRES ST. KITTS-MONTSERRAT GIRL.

In Finsbury Park, a prominent U.K. Shoe Chain has hired its first West Indian salesgirl."

"West Indian attacked in Nottingham."

---

[110] Another monthly, *Link*, first published in November 1958, was less successful and was discontinued after a few issues. A year later (in November 1959) one of the people who had been concerned with the production of *Link* brought out a new monthly, the *Anglo-Caribbean News*.

"SOMETHING'S ILL—IN NOTTING HILL.

A coloured man was brutally beaten by racialists and today lies in a West London hospital."

"Most West Indians are fully aware of the fact that life in Britain is no bed of roses", comments the paper,[111] and it says that migration is continuing nevertheless because of population and economic pressures in the Caribbean territories. The journal provides a fairly wide range of information—articles not only on events and trends in the West Indies, but also on developments in Africa, and on general political matters in this country—for example, on the annual conferences of the major parties. The advertisement columns contain announcements of meetings, of steamship lines to the Caribbean, of West Indian shops, clubs and restaurants in London.

The *West Indian Gazette* organised the first 'Caribbean Carnival' in London in January 1959. The souvenir programme spoke of transplanting "our folk origins to British soil" and referred to the racial disturbances as "the matrix binding West Indians in the United Kingdom together as never before—determined that such happenings should not recur". In this brochure, the *Gazette* said that it stood for an "Independent, United Democratic State of West Indians in the British Commonwealth" and also:

> "For unity of West Indians and other coloured people in U.K.
> For friendship with the British people, based on equality and human
> dignity for peoples, irrespective of race, colour or origin."

A part of the proceeds of this brochure was intended "to assist the payment of fines of coloured and white youths involved in the Notting Hill events".

Social Cohesion

Both the West Indian Press and organisations in London reflect the dual attitude of the newcomers. There is the identification with coloured people, and with it the view that they have to unite to achieve independence abroad and integration in this country. There is also the identification with the 'British' and the wish to take part jointly with them in their activities.

The distinction between the two attitudes has not been a very definite one, and it is beginning to be less marked. These attitudes tend to merge—just because it is the first which appears to have

---

[111] *West Indian Gazette*, September 1959, January 1960. The editor of the journal, Miss Claudia Jones, is one of the prominent West Indian leaders in London.

become more dominant and certainly more explicit. As a result of the 1958 disturbances, and even more strongly in reaction to the Whit Sunday murder, the need to assert the solidarity of coloured people has been increasingly stressed. And the horizon of 'community' is expanding. Thus the "Anglo-Caribbean Unity Diary", one of the features of the *West Indian Gazette*, has been re-named the "Afro-Asian-Caribbean-U.K. Unity Diary".

Although there are now both coloured people's associations and harmony clubs, these developments do not, it seems, reflect a polarisation of opinion among West Indians in London. The same West Indians are active in both types of organisation and are bound to approach the problems of race relations in Britain from both angles.[112] On the one hand, they have recently come more into contact with people from established British parties and institutions than before—in organisations such as the British-Caribbean Association and the Inter-Racial Friendship Co-ordinating Council. Public opinion has been more outspoken on behalf of tolerance than before. Yet on the other hand, there have been many more words of assurance than concrete efforts. The causes which contribute to prejudice have hardly yet been touched. Indeed, some of them are becoming more prominent. And as integration with white British society is no longer expected as a matter of course, integration of the coloured people themselves appears to be the essential first step.

There are thus signs of growing social cohesion—in so far as it can be expected to develop among West Indians in London in a period in which they have experienced critical events, but not an overwhelming crisis.

[112] For example, the founder of the Harmonist Movement also leads the United Kingdom Coloured Citizens Association.

VI

Uncertainty

THERE was a voluble, motherly London woman, apparently an office cleaner, on the bus to Paddington. She talked about the weather, about her work and—after the coloured conductor had come round and some coloured passengers had got on—she started on the colour question. She complained that the coloured people were treated badly—"it was a shame all that fighting last year"; "they are called names"; "they have a hard time". And then she delivered her final line: "I know they ain't human, but we needn't be cruel to them."[1]

Her unusually vivid summary of a not unusual version of British ambivalence towards colour indicates why we are still so far from any optimistic conclusion on the prospect of racial equality in Britain. She did her best to explain why the arithmetic of prejudice in this country is a highly complex matter—so complex that it tends to be oversimplified and added up wrongly in the process.

Fact and Fiction

The keynote in the situation of the coloured minority in Britain is not inflexible prejudice, harsh segregation and discrimination; it is muddle, confusion and insecurity. And it is both a cause and a symptom of this muddle—of the confusion of the white and the consequent confusion of the coloured—that so little is known about the newcomers. They have been written and talked about at great length; they have been in the headlines; they have been featured on radio and television programmes. But there are very few facts about them and a great many myths.

We do not know exactly how many coloured people have come to this country in recent years; how many have left again; and how many were born here; we do not know the ages, previous and present occupations of the migrants; we have no records of their careers

---

[1] This is not an apocryphal story. It was told by a colleague in the University of London to whom these remarks were made.

and of their household composition. We do not know how they are distributed in different parts of Britain, or in what kind of conditions they live.[2]

The empty background, bereft of facts, is filled in by a great deal of fiction—ranging from the penny dreadfuls and fascist news sheets to the clothbound variety. Even the still limited concrete information which we have been able to collect—from the London Sample of West Indians and from other sources—shows that many of the notions which are floating around are misconceptions. It is widely believed that most of the migrants live in coloured quarters; but this is not so; at least not in London—as yet. Even many of the well-meaning 'hosts' are inclined to assume that the majority of West Indians have previously been unskilled labourers; that they have been used to living in pigsties; and that "these uneducated peoples" are dishonest, and generally in a primitive state of morals and manners. None of these assumptions is correct. Nor are all coloured newcomers single men who look around for white women. In the last few years, there has been a steadily increasing inflow of West Indian women and children who join their menfolk here, and a growing number of migrants have settled households. The simple fact that coloured migrants can be just as varied in their interests and aspirations as white Europeans tends to be ignored because so little is known both about their background and their present status in this country.

The current scarcity of concrete systematic information about the new minority group has obvious adverse effects. It is not an academic, insignificant matter. For it is superimposed upon the old widespread ignorance about the foreigner, in general, and the dark foreigner, in particular. There is very little to counteract malicious rumours,

---

[2] In such a situation, the snippets of hearsay information that are produced from time to time—for example, from interviews with a few officials in a few towns—tend to be useless. Some information is not necessarily better than none. It can be worse if it is not solid, and misleading because no one knows whether it is representative or not. Moreover, the mere repetition of such fragmentary titbits gives them the status of ascertained facts. Thus it is now generally believed that property values fall in districts into which coloured people move—simply because this has been said quite often—although there is no reliable evidence for such an assertion. And again, odd extracts of unemployment figures for coloured people are quoted, despite the fact that these have no meaning at all without complementary information on the dates of arrival of the unemployed migrants, the length of unemployment, and the total number of coloured workers. Similarly, all sorts of inferences are drawn from some haphazard crime or morbidity figures for coloured people, although such figures cannot be interpreted so long as no crime or morbidity rates can be constructed because the total coloured population of given areas and its composition are unknown.

stereotype notions or the very naïve misunderstandings which can offend the newcomers just as much as—if not more than—a 'nigger-hunting' cry. So long as the screen of information behind the coloured man is blank, he stands out strikingly as the dark mysterious stranger.

More important still, our ignorance about the coloured newcomers perpetuates our ignorance about ourselves. If we had a diagnosis of the 'colour problem', we would also have one of the 'white problem' which is its core. In what ways and to what extent are coloured people harassed by prejudice and discrimination? If they were not so harassed, there would be no colour problem. But perhaps we prefer to leave the questions unanswered?

If ours were a thoroughly prejudiced or a thoroughly unprejudiced society, we should not be apprehensive of the answers, and we should also be able to obtain them far more easily than we do here and now. But our society belongs to neither category. Prejudice in Britain is rarely openly self-righteous; in general it is of an uneasy and ambiguous variety. (There is no one in the seats of authority who would speak like the State Senator of Alabama, a true representative of the Southern power élite, who told me with glowing pride of a new Jim Crow statute that he had drafted.) We do not tabulate the coloured in order to keep them segregated, nor are we sufficiently free from prejudice to include a colour classification in our social statistics, without fear that this might be interpreted as discrimination; or that it might reveal, and lead to, discrimination. If 'colour' were not a loaded term in Britain, we could show colour categories in our census columns, without *arrière pensée*, just as we show age, sex and occupational categories.

It is, moreover, because British attitudes and behaviour towards coloured people are so rarely unequivocal—positively and negatively —that they cannot be easily classified. And when the attempt is made, it very often reflects the all-pervasive ambivalence. Instead of providing an account of British prejudice, it tends to be an apologia for it.

The Arithmetic of Prejudice

Thus it is frequently said that what appears to be colour prejudice is nothing but British xenophobia, either on its own or in combination with other factors—special distrust of the highly visible foreigner, class snobbery and the general habit of social aloofness. But what does this kind of sum add up to? Does it not suggest that if any one of the items is deducted, the total prejudice will be reduced accordingly? In fact, however, any one of these items cannot be deducted without the others; they are interlinked; and they are cumulative. And does it really make any difference if prejudice is called by a different name? Would it be any better if it were 'merely' xenophobia or class snobbery?

Of course, explanations of this kind can serve different purposes. They can be a part of a general critical assessment of social relationships; or they can be—and they often are—a casuistic exercise. They can so easily lead to the conclusion that there is no special problem: xenophobia, alienation and other similar characteristics are simply taken for granted.

Indeed, such evasive diagnoses of British prejudice are hampered by their failure to see the wood for the trees. They are remote from reality—certainly from the reality of life in Britain as experienced by the coloured people themselves. And the same remoteness is noticeable in some of the more elaborate, apparently more sophisticated analyses of 'Black and White' in Britain. The 'conceptual framework' is hardly compatible with the concrete configurations of altitudes and behaviour.

In the British situation, especially, classifications of prejudice—as being irrational or rational—tend to be highly misleading because they are deceptively precise. They give the impression that the different notional categories of prejudice—those which are called by different terms—are in fact clearly distinguished from one another, and that they can be separately enumerated. But this is just what cannot be done without qualifications—certainly not in this country. There is always far more in the package than any one label can indicate. Moreover, the contents of the package are liable to change. Prejudice, whatever it is called, and whatever the motivations attributed to it, is not subject to a simple quantitative, mechanistic method of analysis.

It is true that there are different kinds of prejudice—those which are more or less inflexible. It is true also that at any moment of time an approximate assessment of the distribution of such distinguishable attitudes in a given population can be made. But this is only a single part of the picture, and not by itself significant. For no attitude is self-contained; and no individual is self-contained. A particular attitude which appears to be predominant (or is verbally predominant) in an individual at any one moment is a part of many others which are not necessarily mutually consistent. It may be emphasised at one stage and submerged at another. It may be swayed simultaneously by 'rational' and by 'irrational' influences, by personal and by social factors which, in turn, interact. And how it can or will be swayed is not implicit in any one attitude census.

It is thus hardly appropriate to call the various types and degrees of prejudice by different names, and to make hard and fast divisions between them. They all belong to the same family. What is called 'antipathy' today, as distinct from 'prejudice', might well be no more than a euphemism for the harsher attitude tomorrow.

Moreover, the mere counting of prejudiced heads tells us very little about the state and prospect of multi-racialism in Britain. It has not much meaning to say that 'only' a small proportion of the British population is definitely prejudiced. The size of the prejudiced minority matters far less than its location in the society and its relation to the general spectrum of attitudes, present and potential. In a generally ambivalent society, a small prejudiced minority is potentially much more significant than a considerably larger prejudiced group would be in a society in which the leading tendencies work decidedly towards social and racial equality.

Benevolent Prejudice

British society is not of the latter type. Therefore, if we look at the components in the calculation of prejudice in this country more closely, we find scant reason for complacency.

There are strong built-in tendencies permissive of prejudice. British society consists of people who are strangers to one another: social segregation is the accepted norm. And as almost everyone has superiors, almost everyone has to have inferiors: those who are regarded as the representatives of a dependent race are an obvious choice.

However, the social hierarchy has not been an entirely inflexible one. It has been perpetuated just because individual trespassing has been allowed, or even encouraged. Social rigidity has been made tolerable by individual social mobility. And this has also had the effect that a split attitude towards members of an 'out-group' is taken for granted. A particular Irishman from Bermondsey, a Jew from Stepney or a Negro from Jamaica is accepted as a personal acquaintance, while at the same time the distance from their respective groups, and the biases against them, are maintained. There are comparatively few English people in any social class who would regard it as proper —or who could even bring themselves—to make anti-catholic, antisemitic or anti-colour remarks to someone whom they know personally. But even some highly educated Englishmen do not mind making such remarks about anonymous Catholics, Jews or Negroes, in general.[3] They are apparently incapable of translating their particularised tolerance into a general principle; of transferring it from a face-to-face relationship to a general, more abstract system of ideas. And this happens, it seems, because they are so secure in their own role that although they are considerate to those whom they happen to know personally, they see no need to consider their own dignity. They do not make a prejudiced remark to a particular Jew or Negro because (as they would say) they do not wish to 'hurt' the other man's feelings; it does not occur to them that if they did make such a remark, however politely, they would in fact debase themselves.

Such tendencies explain the striking consistency in the inconsistency of British attitudes and behaviour towards any 'out-group', and especially towards a coloured 'out-group'.[4] The same mixture exists now which has existed for so long—a curious blend of parochialism and imperialism; of inhospitality and hospitality; of animosity and friendliness. And it is found in all social strata, though there are some variations in the ingredients.

This kind of confusion has been for long—and still is—the prevalent state of mind. Unequivocal hostility or sympathy towards the dark foreigner (or any foreigner) is comparatively rare. The majority have an attitude which can be called 'benevolent prejudice'—a combination of passive prejudice and passive tolerance. One or the other of these elements becomes predominant in different situations; and in relation to coloured people, in particular, latent prejudice against strangers can easily become acute.

The vagaries in the manifestations of British prejudice are explained by the fact that by and large the latent negative attitude is intertwined with a potentially positive one. As a result the attitude of prejudice is not necessarily translated into the practice of discrimination: in fact, there is far more evidence of prejudice (expressed verbally and in casual behaviour) than of formal discrimination in our society.[5] There is widespread discrimination against

[3] However, in some circles, it appears to have become more improper to make an anti-colour remark than an antisemitic one. After the events in Nottingham and Notting Dale, in particular, colour prejudice had become a social stigma. Antisemitism, on the other hand, has been a part of the general ideology and terminology in all social strata for so long—without causing political embarrassment—that it is much more taken for granted.

[4] This consistency is reflected in several unpublished national attitude and opinion surveys, carried out at different periods from 1948 to 1958. They show substantially the same results, despite some differences in their methods and in the phrasing of questions.

[5] A different assessment was made by Michael Banton in his book *White and Coloured*, London, 1959. He wrote (p. 210) in summarising the results of an attitude survey: "The results of this survey demonstrate that—however the term be

coloured people in housing and in several fields of employment; there are colour bars in some public places. But in all spheres of public life, with the exception of housing, discrimination tends to be rather erratic and shamefaced.

Thus passive tolerance has some effect in curbing—or at least in camouflaging—prejudiced behaviour. Discrimination is not institutionalised in British society. But on the other hand, the prohibition of discrimination is not institutionalised either. Tolerance is not sufficiently active to prevent the persistence of restrictive practices in some fields, or the acts of discrimination by apparently unprejudiced persons. (It does not occur to the landlady to think that her neighbours have no right or reason to object against her taking a coloured tenant.) Time after time people act in the belief that they have to conform to the prejudice of others—without taking the trouble to find out whether this assumed prejudice really exists, and if so, to argue against it.[6] It is not widespread latent prejudice as such which makes the coloured minority group in Britain so vulnerable. It is because tolerance is so timid that prejudice is so infectious.

It is for that reason, too, that the distinctions in the motivations of prejudice tend to get blurred. There is no real brake against the snowballing of apprehension of the coloured stranger, produced by ignorance, and of antagonism, caused by economic, social or emotional disequilibrium. A bundle of quasi-rational resentment—derived from real or imaginary frictions with the coloured newcomers and from actual or potential competition with them—can so easily become entangled with irrational, stubborn hostility. Fixed stereotypes and more realistic, flexible notions exist side by side.

It seems, moreover, that economic deprivation as such is not necessarily the prime factor in generating prejudice. Undoubtedly, it activates latent animosity against the coloured 'intruder'. An economic recession or an acute housing shortage will make matters worse for the coloured people in this country. But other factors, too, can have the same result. There is no close correlation between the curves of material deprivation and of prejudice respectively: it

---

defined—colour prejudice is not widespread in Great Britain. But the evidence of discrimination is undeniable." Our own review of the situation and the analysis of other attitude surveys have led to the opposite conclusion.

[6] It is for that reason, too, that the practice of discrimination is accepted rather quickly whenever there is any external influence in that direction. Thus during the latter part of the Second World War, various public establishments which had not previously barred coloured people started to do so under the influence, or assumed influence, of American troops. Even nowadays, hotels which have American clients occasionally refuse to accept coloured guests.

cannot be assumed that prejudice will wither away with increasing prosperity.

Social Segregation

On the contrary, economic prosperity might well have the effect of sharpening the contradictory elements in British attitudes towards colour—of making intolerance more active and of making tolerance more passive still. To some extent, it seems to have had this effect already.

As prosperity spreads, social segregation—one of the main tendencies which is permissive of prejudice—is emphasised more strongly than before, in an antagonistic and in a placid manner. The ranks in the social hierarchy become more detached from one another. There is a blurring of social distinctions, and yet more awareness of them. Those who no longer take their social status for granted, but find that they are nevertheless still hemmed in, do not necessarily react by increasing their efforts to climb the social ladder. Their mode of protest (like that of the 'teddy boys') is a restless withdrawal—a sharper definition of the barriers between the 'in-group' and the 'out-group'. And their resentment of their elders and 'betters' finds an outlet in hostility against anyone who is regarded as a direct competitor or as an inferior. The coloured man is the most convenient target.[7]

But while in some sections of the society there is a new sense of insecurity, which accelerates the motor of aggression, in many others prosperity has brought about a new sense of self-satisfaction, which provides an added motive for complacency. Thus quite apart from the new hostile interpretations of social segregation, there is also—and far more widely—a smug retreat into egocentric comfort. A few additional layers of insensitiveness to any extra-personal aspects of human relationships are put on. Surrounded by the clutter of domestic gadgets, there seems to be no need to look into the store of principles of social conduct, and to recognise that it is rather bare.

For the prospect of the coloured minority in Britain, it is this kind of value vacuum—the sluggishness of good will—which is far more significant and depressing than overt malice as such. This is so not only because ambiguity is more painful than unadulterated antagonism (though it is this very fact which the self-assured Englishman

[7] This group is, therefore, likely to be susceptible to racist propaganda; and such propaganda is especially directed towards it. For example, a recent Mosley leaflet said: "Are you a youngster in a dead-end job, under the old system? . . . If so—Mosley is your man."

is apparently quite often unable to understand). More important still is the interaction between complacency and aggression. Prejudice is bound to grow—even if it is as yet tucked away in odd corners of the mind and proclaimed openly only in odd corners of the society—so long as tolerance remains inert and does not impose restraints.

Occasionally, of course, complacency gets a jolt: it becomes clear that prejudice is degrading for everyone—still more for those who express it and who allow it to be expressed than for those against whom it is directed.

Pride and Prejudice

There was such a jolt in the autumn of 1958. The news of the disturbances in Nottingham and Notting Dale came as a great shock to Britain's self-respect. And there was then a chance that tolerance would become more assertive. That is why the public debate on 'Black and White' which followed was of considerable importance. It has set the tone for some time to come. What tangible results has it had?

No doubt, it had the effect of producing at least a draft of an official opinion on matters of race relations in this country. While this opinion existed before, it began to be formalised only after the disorders. There was bi-partisan agreement in condemning prejudice and discrimination—a genuine agreement and a genuine disapproval, though expressed in varied terms, in keeping with differences in habits of thought and political vocabulary.[8]

And yet this emerging official opinion was not then—and is not now—a coherent and a unanimous one. It mirrored, perhaps inevitably, the contradictions of private attitudes in all groups of society towards a coloured minority in this country. It did so, it seems, largely because there were many public persons who—like many private persons—had not yet understood that the question of the relations between white and coloured people concerned them directly, right here at home. Like many ordinary men, the public spokesmen, too, in some quarters, were slow in acknowledging that there was a problem, and in recognising that it was their problem and their responsibility. There were those who reacted to the disturbances by saying, explicitly or implicitly: 'It is the fault of the coloured. If they were not here, there would be no trouble.' Thus it

[8] This was evident not only in the Parliamentary debates, but also on many other occasions—for example, when representatives of the Conservative, Labour and Liberal parties spoke at the Cochrane memorial meeting in May 1959.

was the question of immigration control which was the primary issue of debate. In fact, there were M.P.s, Peers and public commentators whose talk was not so very different from that of the landlady who says: "I cannot be blamed for not taking coloured tenants. It's my neighbours who object." Among them were some who argued that they were always ready to proclaim tolerance, so long as it was exercised somewhere else—on the assumption that Britain herself would not become a "community where black and white have to co-exist." There were many who did not realise that the clichés of 'passing the buck' on the colour question were spoken and practised day in and day out in all sections of society. It hurt their national and individual pride to admit that colour prejudice "penetrates right through the social system."[9] They were not prepared for the process of self-analysis, and found it painful to start it.

There were also those who did not need to start the process; their attitudes on the colour problem had already been settled, as an integral part of their general political philosophy. And it was mainly within this latter section—by no means a homogeneous one—that the controversies took place. There were three distinct points of view: the 'moral', the 'politically expedient' and the 'practical' one; and these three distinct opinions were, in fact, so categorised by their respective representatives. The divisions between them were expressed clearly in the discussions on proposals to control immigration from the Commonwealth. One group (including the official Labour Party spokesmen) maintained that the idea of limiting the number of Commonwealth immigrants had to be rejected on moral grounds. Another group said that this was not a moral issue, but that statutory control of 'colonial' immigrants was politically unwise and embarrassing, at least at that stage. A third group (apparently a small minority) disagreed with both contentions; they proposed immigration control for strictly 'practical' reasons.[10]

In looking back on these discussions, and on subsequent developments, two aspects stand out. The first is a positive one. Although there were marked divergencies of points of view—and even more in the readiness to guide opinions—the band of disagreement on the concrete decisions of the moment was rather narrow. Despite the ambiguities, there was evidence of a common ideological denominator. But this does not necessarily mean that the divergencies

[9] *Parliamentary Debates*, H.o.L., 19th November 1958, col. 699. In general, the main House of Lords debate on this subject was franker, more self-critical and more informative than the Commons debates at that time.

[10] See, for example, *Parliamentary Debates*, H.o.L., 19th November 1958, cols. 668–671, 704; H.o.C., 5th December 1958, col. 1553.

were insignificant—within the framework of British society and politics—and that the band of disagreement will continue to be a narrow one.

For there was a second aspect which reduced the actual and potential importance of the first. A unique opportunity to define a code of official standards on race relations in this country was missed. Parliament was not sitting when the disturbances occurred; and the Government issued a statement that not only urged "utmost discretion", but that was also written in terms of utmost discretion. Although it was pointed out that "these incidents have an immediate and a long-term importance", in referring to the latter ("the wider aspects of policy") merely one question was mentioned—that of the control of immigration from Commonwealth and colonial countries. The statement did not contain a single phrase on the official attitude towards intolerance. Perhaps it was thought that it was unnecessary to do so—the official insistence on tolerance was axiomatic—and that it might also be unwise to emphasise the point at that moment. It was said:

> ". . . it is important that the significance of these incidents should not be exaggerated at home or oversea."[11]

Was it wise to be so cautious? Having read the statement, *The Times* commented:

> ". . . the leaders of opinion in Britain have not been uniformly wise in their approach to racial issues. True, leaders in the Churches, Parliament, and Press have been on the whole unequivocal in pointing out the evils of racial prejudice. Thereby they have done much to form a climate of opinion in which it is hard to maintain the outward manifestation of a colour bar. But in other ways leaders and successive Governments have been cowardly. . . .
>
> The time has come to admit that there is a colour problem in our midst. It would be wrong to exaggerate it. It would be disastrous to appear to give way in the face of violence. But to ignore the existence of the problem altogether is to invite disaster."[12]

When Parliament reassembled, Government speakers repeatedly stressed the official doctrine of tolerance. But the interval was not unimportant; and Parliamentary pronouncements are, moreover, no substitute for topical public statements to the Press, on radio and television. These popular media of communication have been hardly used by official spokesmen to express their policy on the colour problem. And there was another omission: while Ministers in both

[11] The full text of this statement is quoted on pp. 152–53.
[12] *The Times*, September 4, 1958.

Houses on several occasions gave useful information on immigration statistics and on other matters concerning coloured people—information which refuted the current myths of the coloured 'danger'—no publication of any kind on these subjects was issued, either by H.M.S.O. or by Transport House.[13]

So despite all the talk and newsprint the public discussions on the mutual adjustment of white and coloured people in Britain petered out in vagueness—for want of information, and because of the official reluctance to make 'colour' a prominent, and possibly a controversial subject.

Of course, there was some plain speaking. Nevertheless, to a considerable extent, official opinion continued to reflect the general confusion, instead of giving a clear lead. And as this confusion is bound to become obvious and painful again—in some form or other, from below or from above—in a sense the debate was merely postponed.

Insecurity

There is a danger, however, that self-awareness may be delayed for too long. The disturbances of 1958 have not produced any decisive change in British attitudes or behaviour—public and private—towards colour. On the contrary, complacency was soon restored, and has so far not been seriously inconvenienced by any of the subsequent symptoms of trouble—neither by the increase in racist agitation, nor by sporadic violence which in one case, that of the murder of a West Indian in May 1959, once again dramatised the 'colour problem'. In retrospect, it is usually said that the importance of the Nottingham and Notting Dale 'incidents' (as they have been re-named) was greatly inflated. They are thought of mainly from a 'public relations' point of view—in so far as they were damaging to Britain's prestige abroad. Their actual sequence was quickly forgotten, and so was their intrinsic significance for the integrity of British society.

But there are two groups who remember the autumn of 1958 very well—the coloured people themselves and the 'Keep Britain White' agitators. Both know that the negative influences within the back street world have been reinforced, however unintentionally, by the lack of positive influences from the official world. The 'explosive matter' has not evaporated: indeed, while the display of friction in

---

[13] In the Parliamentary debates on this subject, the Government was asked repeatedly to issue a White Paper, giving such information and including also a statement of policy.

Nottingham and, in particular, in and around Notting Dale has perhaps released some tensions, it has also built up new tensions— without generating adequate antidotes. Disorder has persisted just because in the official circles of tolerance the memory of its acute manifestations has been almost suppressed. In the hinterland of blight, matters are very different: there, among those who are actually or potentially against the 'blacks', this memory is kept alive. Thus on the anniversary of Kelso Cochrane's murder, on May 17, 1960, Sir Oswald Mosley held another evening meeting at the actual murder corner (the junction of Golborne Road and Southam Street). The loudspeaker blared the by now usual anti-coloured exhortations. Apparently this was the most convenient spot for the Union Movement just on that evening.[14] No one outside North Kensington knew or cared.

The coloured people can hardly fail to care. They realise that although the racist campaign is waged in the back alleys of society, it is not for that reason any less significant to them than a few well-meaning harmony clubs or inter-racial co-ordinating committees in the High Street. For it is through these back alleys that the coloured migrants have to pass; they cannot avoid the abusive scrawls and slogans. And yet in the assessment of race relations in this country, their side of the picture is often rather strangely—or perhaps not so strangely—neglected.

It is difficult for anyone who has never been slapped in the face— or who has never had to be afraid of being slapped in the face— because of the colour of his skin or the shape of his nose to comprehend the terror of irrational hostility. It is not that it occurs, but that it might occur at any moment—it is its very unpredictability—which is so terrible. And the individual so attacked is utterly defenceless: there is nothing that he could do but to submit to the indignity of answering back in the language of brutality.

To the coloured man, it does not matter much whether it is one person who calls after him 'Where is your tail' or fifteen; the effect is essentially the same. But it does matter to him how the bystanders behave when he is insulted. Do they just listen passively, or even with a faint sneer on their faces? Do they simply walk off? Or do one or two come forward to protest? For the coloured man, it is far easier to shrug away fifteen insults if he hears simultaneously on each or most of these occasions one voice of protest, than to forget a single defamation to which he was subjected amid a crowd of sluggish onlookers.

[14] Mosley had held a meeting on that corner previously, in July 1959. (See pp. 181–82.)

Unfortunately, in Britain he is more likely to find himself in the latter situation than in the former. The general atmosphere, for better and for worse reasons, is one of tolerance of intolerance— unless the symptoms of prejudice become so violent that they are a serious threat to the maintenance of social order and national reputation. And by and large, those who rebuke defamation are not at home in the places where the insults are called out. Thus their opposition to prejudice, expressed in Westminster and Fleet Street, is not as audible to the coloured man as the 'Nigger go home' cries heard behind the Harrow Road.

Nevertheless, the random signals of aggressive prejudice would not make the coloured man feel so insecure if there were not also at the same time a profusion of benevolent prejudice which is so much taken for granted in English society that hardly anyone—apart from himself—finds it objectionable at all. He could forget the haphazard crude affronts but for the more subtle symptoms of rejection which he is liable to meet almost everywhere. And while the occasional insults are condoned in some quarters, a routine of ambiguous remarks and of some forms of polite or apologetic discrimination against the coloured is widely condoned. Landladies and employers who close their doors to dark skinned people are not censored, though once in a while there is a public protest when it becomes known that a hotel or dance hall operates a colour bar. But even those who speak against discrimination often use arguments which the coloured newcomers must find rather chilling. Do they like to be told that they are useful to the British economy because they take menial unskilled jobs which no one else wants, or because they augment the pool of unemployed labour?

When the coloured people add up the arithmetic of prejudice in Britain, they thus get a sum which is quite different from that—and apparently also more realistic than that—calculated by remote observers. In the context of the general experiences of the coloured minority in this country, the disturbances in Nottingham and Notting Dale were of great significance. For did they not show what the coloured people did not know before? One of the dreaded street corner scenes—a few aggressive hooligans watched by many impassive spectators—could be played out on a much larger scale; there was, in fact, the kind of situation in which prejudice can snowball. And having once seen this situation so clearly, and having found, moreover, that despite the warnings the inertia of tolerance is still maintained in Britain, the coloured people—or anyone who watches social trends closely—can hardly dismiss the racist agitation as unimportant either, simply because it is conducted by small marginal cliques in some marginal places 'across the tracks'. The number of these back street boys of politics is almost irrelevant as a measure of their potential influence. Their location, on the other hand, is highly relevant. They have chosen a territory for their operations where they have a chance of success.

Chain Reaction

All the factors which contributed to the disturbances in Notting Dale still exist; and some have become more disturbing since. There has been neither physical nor ideological slum clearance: the housing shortage is as acute as before; fascist propaganda is more active; South and North Kensington have remained apart from one another as 'two nations'; evidence of senseless brutality is still seen each week. Almost every issue of the local newspapers contains reports on fights between whites and between white and coloured.[15] There could be another explosion any day—particularly on a hot Saturday evening when claustrophobia in the back streets is most oppressive.

But this is not the main risk. Far more important still is the fact that while the status of the coloured minority is an uneasy one, especially in that part of London, there are signs of further deterioration. Although the problems of the migrants are still manageable, they are cumulative. If discrimination in housing and in some fields of employment continues, the coloured people will be increasingly hemmed in. And if that happens, segregation will be accentuated; mutual strangeness and suspicion between white and coloured will become harsher; additional causes of friction will develop.

At this stage, the situation of coloured people is better in the field of employment than in that of housing. However, although in general their position in British industry has improved, it is still a vulnerable one. In a period of full employment, the great majority who work in semi-skilled and unskilled occupations are not regarded as competitors; they are in jobs for which there are no local queues. But any new recession, even a minor one, can revive previous tensions and disputes.

[15] Symptoms of unrest and aggression continue to be noticeable especially in the area of the 1958 disturbances—in the Shepherd's Bush, Notting Dale and Notting Hill belt—far more in that area than in any other London district where the migrants are clustered. Since the autumn of 1958—and again since the murder of a West Indian in May 1959—there have been frequent reports from the 'disturbed' area of 'white' gang fights; of scuffles with the police; of trouble between coloured people; and of violent attacks on coloured people which are similar to the flagrant incidents which occurred before and during the 1958 turmoil. The circumstances of one or two of these cases have been not unlike those of Kelso Cochrane's murder.

And there are new difficulties ahead, or rather the multiplying effects of the existing ones.

Soon many of the newcomers will be old-timers; and as matters stand now, not only their own ambitions for advancement, but also those of their children are likely to remain frustrated. Few migrants have higher skilled and supervisory jobs, or white-collar posts. A considerable proportion have experienced a very steep occupational downgrading in this country—so steep, in fact, that it cannot be explained solely by the difference between Caribbean and English standards of qualifications and performance. Discrimination against the foreigner—and especially against the dark foreigner—has undoubtedly played a part in limiting the occupational mobility of West Indians.

The consequences of such restrictions will be felt severely by the second generation of migrants—those who are born or brought up in this country. While the first generation expected some hardships, the second generation is liable to be much more disappointed. They will face the prospect of blind-alley jobs so long as colour quotas curtail the opportunities of all coloured people, irrespective of age and origin. In such circumstances, most coloured adolescents will be unable to get financial support from their families during a long period of preparation for skilled occupations and professions; nor could they subsist unaided on the low wages of trainees or apprentices.

There are too many barriers still; the actual and potential status range of coloured people is still far too narrow. We could hardly expect multi-racial harmony at home if the new minority group were largely confined to the lowest ranks of the occupational ladder; if it became a separate section of the working class—Britain's black proletariat.

People who live in blind-alleys are prone to drift into blind-alley jobs. Indeed, the tendencies towards segregation in employment are reinforced by the even more serious tendencies towards segregation in housing. There are no coloured quarters in London as yet. But if the current trend continues, there will be such quarters before long. Central London's residential pattern; piecemeal reconstruction; the deficiency of housing for low income groups, in general, and restrictive practices against dark skinned people, in particular—all these factors will contribute to a growing concentration of the coloured minority in a few patches on the London map. And these are not healthy patches—physically or socially. Once such ghetto-like clusters are formed, the coloured are liable to become fixed in a condition of social inferiority and insecurity.

In one respect, of course, the new minority group is already 'integrated': in essence, the difficulties of white and coloured in Britain are indivisible. But, paradoxically, just for that reason the coloured people run the greatest risk of being set apart. They show us more about ourselves than we wish to know.

There is a chain reaction of resentment. It is because the existence of a coloured minority exposes the discrepancies in British society that antagonism is aroused. The 'colour problem' makes it plain that the usual complacent assumptions of general welfare, social unity and a common up-to-date ideology of reason and tolerance are far too glib. It has shown up many other problems, the immediacy of which public opinion has tended to ignore. Black blotches and tears in the social fabric have become much more visible: the long neglected slums behind the High Street, near respectable homes and new luxury flats; rapacious landlordism; widespread ignorance; lack of civic education; niggardly parochialism; xenophobia; social disorganisation; delinquency and sparks of violence; the empty boredom of adolescents; the 'militant columns' of fascist agitation. And as it is the presence of coloured people which draws attention to matters which are not conducive to the placid acceptance of the *status quo*, or to the withdrawal into separate, protected niches, it is they who are accused, consciously or subconsciously, of upsetting social comfort. There is a danger, no longer merely a potential one: here as elsewhere, the dark minority group may be made the scapegoat; it is they who tend to be blamed for the very inequalities and inadequacies in the condition of Britain which their experiences reveal.

Law and Opinion

Not all these problems can be solved overnight. But they can be clarified; and if that is done, we shall reach a less pessimistic conclusion.

There are, as we have seen, three main interrelated aspects which cause misgivings for the prospect of race relations in Britain. First, there are general features in British social structure which are permissive of prejudice. Second, the predominant attitude is, therefore, 'benevolent prejudice'—a mixture of passive prejudice and passive tolerance. Third, as a result, practices of discrimination against the coloured are condoned in some fields; and these practices contribute to residential and occupational segregation.

None of these influences is unequivocal; and thus none is inflexible. Every one of the negative tendencies leaning towards prejudice—in the social structure, in attitudes and behaviour—also has an opposite, leaning in the other direction. Indeed, it is this very contradiction which has enabled us to remain complacent. It has always been possible to point to symptoms of tolerance when symptoms of intolerance were mentioned. It can still be done; but it is no longer quite so comforting to do so.

The presence of a coloured minority in Britain has exposed the negative tendencies far more clearly than before; it has provoked their display, subtly and crudely. More important still, the experience of the coloured people has shown that there is disturbance—and that it is cumulative—not because intolerance is so strong but because tolerance is so weak. And this has occurred just at a time when we shall have to become more perceptive of those weak patches in our conduct and ideology which are incompatible with the new concept of the Commonwealth and with the changing situation of the world.

There is thus an urgent need for an explicit 'philosophy of tolerance' in Britain. It could be produced without delay because it would be derived from inherent positive tendencies. For the same reason it would also find a response. In the current state of ambivalence we can still move in alternative directions. Tolerance can be mobilised. Unless that happens, intolerance will be mobilised. Which is it to be?

It is the responsibility of Parliament to give tolerance a push; and to provide a code of standards on matters of race relations. Leaders of opinion will have to give the lead—more emphatically than they have done so far. It is hardly realistic to look to 'education' as a panacea without giving the appropriate direction to educational policy.[16] Nor is it much use to rely on the initiative of private

[16] In this context, it should be noted that several M.P.s and educationists have urged the Ministry of Education repeatedly—though so far without success—to issue advice to local education authorities on the inclusion of instruction about race relations in school syllabuses. For instance, Dr. Cyril Bibby, the author of the Unesco-sponsored handbook, *Race, Prejudice and Education* (London, 1959) said in a letter to *The Times Educational Supplement* (January 15, 1960):
"Is the question of race relations at present sufficiently pressing to demand some central initiative, or is it one of those many things which can safely be left to the slow process of pedagogic infiltration? . . . the Working Group on the Diminution of Prejudice, consisting not of a few hot-heads but of a number of eminently sober citizens of some stature, has been seeking by communication and deputation to persuade the Ministry that the time is ripe for the issue of advice to schools and teachers' colleges. We do not ask for 'directives', but simply for some indication of ministerial awareness that the matter is important. It is, after all, a well established procedure for such circulars to be issued. Have there got to be blatant acts of racial discrimination in our schools before the Ministry of Education gets around to doing something in the way of issuing advice?"

individuals and voluntary associations on their own in promoting harmony. Their efforts, however well-meaning, are bound to be marginal so long as there is a general climate of confusion. The fog has to be cleared away in Westminster first.

It is there that several practical steps can be taken. Policy statements on the coloured minority in this country have tended to be rather negative, scrappy and tucked away in odd pages of *Hansard*. Usually they have been made—not always in an unambiguous manner—to defend the right of migrants from the Commonwealth to come to the United Kingdom; or simply to assert that discrimination is 'un-British'. Could we not have a far more positive and elaborate formulation of official policy, issued as a White Paper, and published also repeatedly through the popular channels of communication?

The first principle of such a policy should be the recognition of the value of migration, as distinct from the mere apologia for migration. The exodus of some 15,000 to 25,000 people from the West Indies every year eases the pressure of overpopulation and underemployment in their home territories. The money which they save here and send home makes a small, but necessary contribution to the West Indian national income.[17] At least equally important is

---

Not long afterwards, there was a Press report which might well be quoted as a footnote to Dr. Bibby's letter. It was an account of an interview by the Coventry *Sunday Mercury* (March 20, 1960) with Mr. Colin Jordan, the prominent 'Keep Britain White' propagandist, who is a schoolteacher in Coventry. Mr. Jordan was reported to have made his usual statement: "We want the Blacks and the Jews out of Britain." He was then asked ". . . whether, with his radical political views, he considered himself a fit person to teach impressionable children. 'Of course', he replied. 'My politics take up most of my spare time. But I leave them behind when I go to school. I do not try to influence the children when it comes to politics. I think I am a pretty average teacher.' Jordan teaches a number of subjects, including history, geography and 'civics' . . . 'But the standards are so elementary that I could not possibly influence the children even if I wanted to', he declared."

A pertinent comment on the 'value vacuum' and on the kind of situation in which prejudice can become contagious.

[17] These points can be illustrated especially with reference to Jamaica for which the relevant data are available. At the end of 1955, the population of Jamaica was just over one and a half millions; the current national increase is around two per cent per year. At that rate, the population would double in about 35 years. However, as mortality will probably continue to decline, the Jamaican population growth will be more rapid still unless fertility declines, too. In such circumstances, emigration offers essential breathing space for economic and social development. If one per cent of the total population emigrate each year—that is, 16,000 people per year at present—the rate of population growth would be halved. (The actual annual migration of Jamaicans to the United Kingdom has been similar to that figure in 1955 and 1956, but considerably lower since then. See

the contribution which the presence of coloured people in this country can make to our own society and ideology. They can introduce a new element of variety and vivacity. They can help us to remove some of our blinkers to the realities of the outside world, and to develop a contemporary sense of citizenship.

So far the advantages of migration—especially to ourselves—have hardly as yet been mentioned. On the contrary, in all discussions on this subject the emphasis is always on the 'accommodation', 'adaptation' and 'assimilation' of the newcomers to the 'host society'. It is they who are always asked to conform. The fact that adaptation is a two-way process has hardly as yet been taken quite seriously; and it seems to have occurred to very few people that the 'host society', in turn, could also acquire some new interests and aptitudes from the migrants. Moreover, although the question of immigration control was temporarily shelved as being 'embarrassing' during the debates following the events in Nottingham and Notting Dale, it has since then been revived from time to time. Every new issue of immigration statistics brings forward a new proposal to limit immigration; and if there were another outbreak of 'disturbances' because of the lack of positive direction, demands to restrict immigration would undoubtedly be made more forcibly and more widely than before.[18] It is essential that we look at the other side of the coin and develop a new approach to the question of immigration.

---

p. 5.) Thus although emigrants are a 'selected' group—more skilled than the average working population—their exodus is of help in easing population pressure; and it also offers compensations to the Jamaican economy. For first, it will be increasingly difficult in the near future to find employment in Jamaica for the growing adult population; second, the remittances which are sent back by the migrants who have settled in this country contribute to the Jamaican national income. Both in 1958 and in 1959, the migrants in this country sent back almost three million pounds by postal and money orders—sums which were around 1.6 per cent of the Jamaican national income.

[18] It is likely, moreover, that such demands will be made in any case if there is a steady annual flow of immigration from the Commonwealth or—as is probable —an upward swing in the curve of immigration. Thus in reporting on the views of government departments, *The Economist* said at a time when any restrictionist policy was regarded as embarrassing (on November 29, 1958): ". . . it is no secret that some departments, looking ahead at the way the situation may develop, are considering how reciprocity may be introduced in the treatment of migrants from Commonwealth countries—especially after the colonies, and notably the West Indies, become independent. They think that the liberal line—uncontrolled immigration—can be held for a few more years, but not indefinitely. Far from thinking that the British people will get used to colour, as they are reconciled to Poles, Irish or Middle Europeans, this school of opinion in Whitehall and beyond feels that when the tide of colour rises to a certain, as yet unspecified, point, the mass of British voters will demand that some check be imposed."

It should be our policy not just to endure, but to welcome, the settlement of coloured Commonwealth citizens in Britain.

However, policy statements on their own are not enough. Equality in the status of the coloured population in this country must be affirmed in law. It should be the principal purpose of such law to remove the ambiguities in the interpretation of tolerance which still exist; and to catch up with reality. Discrimination continues to be practised although it is not officially approved. It is up to the law to take cognisance of both facts.

It is true that there are difficulties in the drafting and enforcement of such legislation. But these difficulties are not insuperable. Moreover, an anti-discrimination Act would have primarily a preventive purpose; and this is one which it could undoubtedly achieve. In the current situation, it is less important to punish the present offenders than to warn the potential offenders. It has to be made quite plain that discrimination is illegal.[19]

[19] The arguments for legal measures against discrimination have been put most succinctly in a United Nations Memorandum on *The Main Types and Causes of Discrimination* (Memorandum submitted by the Secretary-General); United Nations—Commission on Human Rights, Sub-Commission on Prevention of Discrimination and Protection of Minorities, New York, 1949. The summary of the points made there is as follows:

"Although it may not be possible completely to eradicate discrimination by law, many forms of discriminatory conduct may be suppressed or greatly lessened by legal measures.

Although law affords a powerful instrument for changing social conditions, those conditions themselves set certain limits to the scope of practicable legislation and adequate enforcement. Attempts to overstep these limits may defeat themselves and even kick back upon their authors. But there is ample scope, even with these limits, for promoting social advance through legislation.

The most important ways in which the law acts as a factor in preventing discrimination are:

(*a*) It fosters the conviction that discrimination is wrong by fixing standards which are respected by the great majority of people.

(*b*) People who have little respect for the law are nevertheless afraid of the consequences of unlawful conduct; they therefore obey the law in order to avoid its penalties.

(*c*) In both cases and whatever the motive, the resulting daily behaviour tends to create social customs which are in harmony with the law; these customs constitute a powerful collective force.

(*d*) The law can also help repair the harm produced by unlawful conduct, in so far as it can provide indemnities and reparation for the person wronged.

Social conditions in many parts of the world have developed to a point where it is possible to enact new legislation prohibiting many discriminatory practices. The very fact that the United Nations has adopted the Universal Declaration of Human Rights, and established the Sub-Commission on

This rule can be codified, in particular with reference to colour bars in public establishments—hotels, public houses and dance halls; and also with respect to restrictive clauses in real estate transactions and leases. It could be argued that the operation of colour bars in public establishments is comparatively infrequent; and that restrictive covenants are only one part of a much wider practice of discrimination in the housing market. Nevertheless, once the principle that discrimination is illegal is established in some fields, it is likely to become influential also in others, where restrictive practices are more elusive from the point of view of the law.

In industry, a great deal could be done to begin with if the trade unions conducted a determined campaign to translate their top level policy of tolerance into practice at all levels. Some unions have recognised that already; they have rebuked branches which have asked for colour quotas or which have condoned colour bars. Other unions could follow their example. It is clearly not sufficient to pass a few resolutions at the annual Trades Union Congress. A far more detailed and prolonged discussion of principles of conduct in race relations is required, and a more vigilant observation of the rules. And if that is done widely during a period of prosperity, there is less chance for resentment of coloured workers *per se* to become acute again during a recession.

Short of direction of labour, it is more difficult to change the colour quota practices of employers. Their actions are rarely in the limelight. But presumably the employers would not be immune to censure of prejudice and discrimination, expressed in public policy and legislation. The unions could, moreover, exert an influence on the employers; and so could employment exchanges, probably more than they have done so far.

It is most difficult to influence the landladies; and yet the discrimination practised in private lettings is one of the most serious kinds, if not the most serious and the most widespread kind. It cannot be controlled by legislation without the risk of interfering with common law rights. But perhaps gradually landladies, too,

---

Prevention of Discrimination and Protection of Minorities, indicates that the eradication of discrimination is considered to be possible."

These paragraphs (138–141, p. 43) have often been quoted, but as they are highly relevant especially to the British situation where social conditions are favourable for the promotion of "social advance through legislation", it is appropriate to draw attention to them again. In general, moreover, this memorandum is indispensable for anyone who is concerned with the study of race relations and with policy on such matters. Extracts from it might well be included in a school text book on this subject.

would be affected by the mobilisation of tolerance. Many of them close doors to coloured people because they believe that public opinion expects them to do so. (Or they rationalise their actions in that way.) They could hardly continue for ever to close their doors if they were told often enough that public opinion expects them to do the opposite.

There is one way, in particular, by which this can be emphasised. Indeed, there is one aspect of private lettings that can be immediately controlled by public policy—the insertion in newspapers of 'anti-colour' advertisements of flats or rooms.[20] Surely, we need not tolerate the advertisement of intolerance. If we really regard discrimination as improper, we must see to it that this offensive matter is excluded from our newspaper columns, just as other improper matters are excluded. Of course, discrimination in lettings would not stop simply because it is no longer publicised. But it would become quite clear that discrimination is not sanctioned if newspapers refused to accept such advertisements; moreover, an open insult not only to coloured people and other minority groups, but also to our national dignity, would be removed.

The catalogue of measures—large and small—that can be taken to make tolerance more assertive in this country is a long one. In discussing such proposals, state and municipal procedures against restrictive practices in the Northern United States are often mentioned. It is, however, clearly impossible to transfer the lessons of American experience directly to Britain. In terms of its history and size, the American 'colour problem' is quite unlike that of the United Kingdom; prejudice and discrimination are far more deeply entrenched and on a far larger scale in New York and Chicago than they are in London and Birmingham; and there are also relevant significant differences between the American legal and administrative machinery and ours. It is the object of American efforts in this field to turn the tide of intolerance. It is our job to make the tide of tolerance flow more strongly.

Nevertheless, American experience does provide some useful indications. It shows that governmental restraints of restrictive practices are effective—even in a situation, unlike ours, in which discrimination has for long been institutionalised, and in which, besides, public authority is far less coherent, less readily accepted and less easily diffused than it is in this country. No one who has visited the Northern cities of the United States repeatedly during the last twenty

[20] In this context, I am referring not only to those advertisements which have an explicit 'anti-colour' tag, but also to those which are more euphemistically worded, and which say, for example, 'Europeans only'.

years could doubt this result.[21] And the changes in these metropolitan areas also confirm how important it is—for the morale of both white and coloured—to board up the shop windows of prejudice. Newspaper columns are no longer filled with the kind of advertisements which we still allow—those with anti-colour, antisemitic or any other 'anti' tags. The countryside is no more cluttered up with notices of 'restricted' areas, or less euphemistic signposts of segregation. Hotels no longer display posters: 'No Negroes, Jews or Dogs'. It can now be said in New York State that "discrimination has become a dirty word".[22] It is, therefore, also becoming a dirty practice.

This is not to say that the American Negro in the North has attained a status of equality. Far from it. But in those states and cities which take active measures against restrictive practices (and there are only a few of them) there seems to have been a definite improvement in the personal relations between white and coloured. And this aspect of American experience, in particular, is one that we should note. The knowledge that discrimination is being attacked has given the American Negro a greater sense of certainty. When he meets a white man, he need not be tense and watch out for signs of animosity. Usually he knows at once whether the other man is for him or against him.

Rarely can a dark skinned citizen say the same in this country. Neither the negative nor the positive attitudes towards colour are as definite here as they are in the United States; instead, ambiguity prevails. It is that which bedevils every single aspect of the coloured people's life in England; it is an erosive factor in all their relationships—disturbing for coloured and white alike.

In the present climate of ambivalence, the coloured people can hardly ever relax—not even in harmony clubs and inter-racial associations. There is always a doubt whether any good will gesture, personal or social, is not perhaps merely another version of benevolent prejudice—a compensation for the guilt feelings of intolerance. And indeed, while the evasive policy of 'utmost discretion' in race relations is maintained, there is a tendency to cover up for prejudice by being occasionally overprotective towards coloured people—with

[21] One of the main arguments often put forward against the legal prohibition of discrimination—the fear that such prohibition might intensify rather than diminish prejudice and discrimination—has not been proved valid in the Northern United States. Across the Atlantic, in the North, governmental restraints of discriminatory practices have not had a boomerang effect; and there is every reason to assume that they would not have such an effect in this country either.

[22] This was said in 1958 by Mr. Charles Abrams, the then chairman of the New York State Commission against Discrimination, in reviewing the work of the Commission.

the result that animosity against them is intensified. In the back streets behind the zones of transition, the alleged kid glove treatment of the migrants is bitterly resented. Moreover, in the present situation, public authorities cannot compile statistics about coloured people for fear that this will be regarded as a symptom of discrimination, and that it will lead to segregation. Thus the migrants remain the unknowns; wild rumours about the dark danger spread. In this country, the wall between natives and newcomers is so thick just because it is built largely out of question marks.[23]

There can be no genuine integration of the new minority group in this country until the question marks are removed. For everybody's sake, we have to provide some yardsticks—other than 'pious resolutions'—by which our conduct can be assessed. It is for that reason above all that an unequivocal code of tolerance is required—a positive public policy, expressed in specific legislation; and followed up also in the guidance of educational curricula. Without such a code, it is hardly possible to fill the value vacuum in matters of civic behaviour. But if we had such a code, all other efforts to improve mutual understanding—made by schools, by the media of communication, by voluntary associations and by private individuals—would have the terms of reference which they need to become effective.

If the law said that discrimination is illegal, we could collect facts about coloured people, as we do about any other social group, without apprehension that our intentions may be misinterpreted, and that adverse consequences may follow. We should then obtain the information which is necessary to assess systematically the difficulties of mutual adjustment, and to take practical measures for their solution. And if we were honest with ourselves and acknowledged the risks of prejudice, we should also be more consistent and honest with the newcomers. They would no longer be given alternately cold showers and hot douches. Neither the white nor the coloured British people would then remain continually on guard in their dealings with one another. Both would know where they stand. It would become possible to distinguish clearly between valid criticisms and expressions

[23] For all these reasons, there appears to be in many situations a noticeable difference between the personal contacts of coloured and 'liberal' white people in the Northern United States and in the United Kingdom—a larger difference than could be explained by the greater reserve in British social life, in general. It seems easier for 'liberal' whites and Negroes to be spontaneous and at ease with one another in the Northern States than it is in this country. As this is a personal experience, I would not like to generalise from it, and can mention it only tentatively. It does, however, tally with the accounts of other observers—coloured and white—who are able to make such comparisons.

of prejudice; between general social hardships in the settlement of migrants and acts of discrimination. If Parliament shows the majority how to peel off some of the layers of insensitiveness, the minority would not need to be oversensitive. A firm official policy for racial equality in Britain could break into the vicious circle of tension between white and coloured at all levels and in all spheres.

Postscript

About fifty years from now, future historians—in Asia, in Africa and perhaps in England—writing about Europe in the nineteen fifties and sixties will presumably devote a chapter to the coloured minority group in this country. They will say that although this group was small, it was an important, indeed an essential one. For its arrival and growth gave British society an opportunity of recognising its own blind spots, and also of looking beyond its own nose to a widening horizon of human integrity. They will point out that the relations between white and coloured people in this country were a test of Britain's ability to fulfil the demands for progressive rationality in social organisation, so urgently imposed in the latter part of the twentieth century. And the future historians will add that Britain had every chance of passing this test, because at that period her domestic problems were rather slight by comparison with those of many other areas of the world.

All this can be anticipated. But it is still uncertain how the chapter will end.

APPENDIX A

THE 'LONDON SAMPLE' OF WEST INDIANS

Comparison With Other Data

THE sources for the 'London Sample', and the data derived from it, have been discussed in Chapter II. A detailed comparison of the Sample with the external statistics which are available was made in order to test the validity of the Sample. We are satisfied, after making this comparison, that the Sample is representative of those West Indians in London who arrived in this country after 1951. In particular, the Sample data appear to be adequate so far as male migrants are concerned; with reference to their year of arrival in the U.K., their territory of origin, their last occupation in the West Indies and their age. There were minor discrepancies between the Sample data and the external statistics; and these are discussed below.

However, as the external statistics are rather scarce, and in some respects imprecise, it was not possible to test the Sample on all the aspects on which it provides information. One general deficiency of the external statistics is, moreover, a serious one: they do not distinguish between migrants who come to London and those who arrive in the United Kingdom as a whole. Any discrepancy between the Sample and the external data might, therefore, be explained by selective migration to London; agreement, by the same line of reasoning, is not conclusive proof that the Sample represents all migrants in London. It can be assumed, however, that agreement between the two sets of statistics is not just the result of compensating errors, but indicates that the Sample reflects the characteristics of West Indians in London.

1. *Year of Arrival in the United Kingdom*
   Sources of external data:
   Arrivals up to April 1951:
   General Register Office, Census of England and Wales, 1951, *General Tables*, H.M.S.O., 1956, Table 37.

   Arrivals after April 1951:
   Figures, based on ships' manifests, obtained from the Migrant Services Division of the Commission in the United

Kingdom for the West Indies, British Guiana and British Honduras.

The figures of arrivals before 1955 are only rough estimates. Since the London Sample consists of adults only, the external data have been adjusted accordingly.

WEST INDIAN ADULT MIGRANTS BY YEAR OF ARRIVAL

Year of Arrival in U.K.	London Sample %	External Data %
By April 1951	3	12
April–December 1951 . .	1	1
1952	2	2
1953	2	2
Sub-Total	*8*	*17*
1954	13	8
1955	23	21
1956	32	22
1597	17	19
January to November 1958 .	7	13
Sub-Total	*92*	*83*
TOTAL		
Per cent . . .	*100*	*100*
Number . . .	1,070	114,502

The Sample contains, therefore, comparatively too few cases of West Indians arriving before 1951, and during 1958; and too many who arrived in 1956. The early (pre-1951) migrants were probably largely settled in jobs by the time the Migrant Services Division began to function, and they would have had no reason to apply there. Not all the 1958 migrants, on the other hand, would apply to the Division in the year they arrived. Some will have applied in 1959; others will apply in 1960 or later still. Since we only examined the records of applicants up to the end of November 1958, the Sample under-represents arrivals in that year.

2. *Proportion of Female Migrants by Year of Arrival, 1954 to 1958*
Sources of external data:

(*a*) *For migrants from Jamaica*

Data for 1954–55:

> G. W. Roberts and D. O. Mills, 'Study of External Migration affecting Jamaica; 1953–55', Supplement to *Social and Economic Studies*, Vol. 7, No. 2, June 1958.

Data for 1956–58:

> *Report on Jamaica, 1956*, H.M.S.O., 1957. *1957 Economic Survey, Jamaica*; and *1958 Economic Survey, Jamaica*, Government of Jamaica.

(*b*) *For migrants from all territories in the West Indies*

Figures obtained from the Migrant Services Division.

THE PROPORTION OF WOMEN AMONG ARRIVALS IN THE U.K.
FROM JAMAICA

Year of Arrival in U.K.			London Sample %	External Data %
1954	.	.	24	38
1955	.	.	27	39
1956	.	.	35	45
1957	.	.	41	49
1958	.	.	49	50
TOTAL	.	.	33	41

THE PROPORTION OF WOMEN AMONG ARRIVALS IN THE U.K.
FROM ALL WEST INDIAN TERRITORIES

Year of Arrival in U.K.			London Sample %	External Data %
1956	.	.	29	40
1957	.	.	31	45
1958	.	.	40	50
TOTAL	.	.	31	45

The external data in both tables have been adjusted to exclude children. The report by Roberts and Mills distinguishes between those migrating to the U.K. to seek permanent employment and those coming on a study course. The latter include a relatively large number of women, in particular student nurses. It is not clear from the other sources whether or not students have been included in the number of migrants. The effect on the figures is, however, marginal.

The Sample consistently under-represents women among the migrants, but reflects the trend towards a gradually increasing proportion of female migrants. As the data for men and women are analysed separately in the text, the undue preponderance of the former does not distort the results.

3. *Age*

Source of external data:

Roberts and Mills, *op. cit.* (Migrants leaving Jamaica between 1953 and 1955.)

AGE OF MIGRANTS FROM JAMAICA AT TIME OF ARRIVAL IN THE U.K.
FROM 1953–55

	Men		Women	
Age Group	*London Sample* %	*External Data* %	*London Sample* %	*External Data* %
15–24 . .	34	24	29	28
25–34 . .	35	42	28	40
35–44 . .	22	23	20	22
45–54 . .	8	9	20	8
55 or over .	1	2	3	3
TOTAL				
Per cent .	*100*	*100*	*100*	*100*
Number .	199	19,874	67	12,188

The Sample contains more men aged 15–24 and fewer aged 25–34 than are shown in the external data. Women are similarly under-represented in the 25–34 age group and over-represented in the 45–54 age group.

4. *Territory of Origin*

Sources of external data:

Data for 1957–58: Migrant Services Division.
Data for 1954–56 (Jamaica only): *Report on Jamaica 1956*;
and estimates of the Migrant Services Division.

(*a*) 1957 AND 1958 ARRIVALS IN THE U.K. FROM ALL WEST
INDIAN TERRITORIES

Territory of Origin	London Sample %	External Data %
Jamaica	53	61
Trinidad and Tobago	11	6
British Guiana	8	2
Barbados	5	9
Other territories*	23	23
TOTAL		
Per cent	*100*	*100*
Number	252	37,029

* Antigua (3%), Dominica (4%), Grenada (4%), Montserrat (2%), St. Kitts-Nevis (5%), St. Lucia (3%), St. Vincent (2%).

(*b*) PROPORTION OF MIGRANTS WHO CAME FROM JAMAICA, BY
YEAR OF ARRIVAL IN THE U.K.

Year of Arrival in the U.K.	London Sample %	External Data %
1954	75	80
1955	67	76
1956	50	65
1957	53	61
1958	52	61
TOTAL	58	69

The Sample contains relatively too many migrants from British Guiana and too few from Jamaica, but adequately reflects both the large proportion of Jamaicans among West Indian migrants and the gradual decline in this proportion in recent years.

The discrepancies may be accounted for, in the case of Jamaican

N.—17

migrants, partly by the under-recording of women, who (as explained in Chapter II) were less likely to apply to the Migrant Services Division, and a larger proportion of whom came from Jamaica; partly by a tendency towards selective migration to London. (For example, migrants from British Guiana may prefer to stay in London to a greater extent than other West Indians.) Since the external data refer to the United Kingdom as a whole, they give no accurate guide to the proportions of migrants from the various territories who have gone to London.

5. *Last Occupations in the West Indies*

Sources of external data:

Data for 1953–55: Roberts and Mills, *op. cit.*

Data for 1954: W. F. Maunder, 'The New Jamaican Emigration', *Social and Economic Studies*, Vol. 4, No. 1, March 1955.

Both studies are limited to migrants from Jamaica. Maunder surveyed only selected batches of migrants.

MALE MIGRANTS FROM JAMAICA BY LAST OCCUPATION IN JAMAICA

Last Occupation in Jamaica	London Sample 1953–55 Arrivals	External Data Roberts 1953–55 Migrants	External Data Maunder 1954 Migrants
	%	%	%
Non-manual workers .	13	9	9
Manual workers:			
Skilled . . .	52	61	51
Semi-skilled and personal services .	4	2	13
Unskilled . .	8	8	5
Sub-Total: Manual Workers . .	*64*	*71*	*69*
Farmers, farm labourers	23	21	22
TOTAL CLASSIFIED			
Per cent . .	100	100	100
Number . .	187	16,788	420

Discrepancies may arise from the classification of skilled, semi-skilled and unskilled manual workers. Thus Roberts did not distinguish a semi-skilled group, while Maunder allocated 11 per cent to this category. Roberts and Maunder, however, give approximately the same proportions for the three sub-totals: non-manual, manual and agricultural. It seems reasonable, therefore, to compare the London Sample and the external data with respect to these sub-totals. There is fairly close agreement between these two sets of data, though the Sample contains slightly more non-manual workers and fewer manual workers than the external statistics. This might be explained by a tendency of 'white-collar' migrants to concentrate in London.

Summary

All the data considered lead to the conclusion that the London Sample adequately represents West Indians in London who arrived between 1951 and 1958. This is true at any rate with respect to year of arrival, age, occupation in the West Indies and territory of origin. No comparisons can be made with regard to occupations in London or geographical distribution.

There are some minor discrepancies. The Sample contains proportionately fewer Jamaicans, fewer women and rather more white-collar workers than are known to have arrived in the United Kingdom. But this may be accounted for by selective migration to London. The discrepancies are in all cases too small to invalidate the main results of the analysis derived from the London Sample.

EXPRESSIONS OF PREJUDICE:
AN ANALYSIS OF PUBLIC OPINION POLLS

Questions and Answers

SOME indications of overt colour prejudice, and of the particular aspects towards which prejudice is directed, can be obtained from public opinion surveys carried out by the Gallup Poll.[1] One survey, early in September 1958, was largely devoted to questions concerning coloured people, while two other polls in 1958 each contained one further question of a similar kind. Each survey covered a sample of 1,000 to 1,500 people in all parts of Britain. The list of questions asked and the answers are set out below:

(I) GALLUP POLL 20TH–25TH JUNE, 1958

This survey was carried out soon after it had become known that the management of a dance hall in Wolverhampton had refused to admit coloured people.

Question	Answer	
Do you approve or disapprove of owners of a dance hall in Wolverhampton refusing to admit coloured people to the dances there?	Approve	22
	Disapprove	62
	Don't know	16
	Total	100

(II) GALLUP POLL 3RD–4TH SEPTEMBER, 1958[2]

The survey followed the news of the disturbances in Nottingham and Notting Dale. It was completed before the disturbances in London had petered out.

---

[1] We are grateful to Dr. Durant of the Gallup Poll who made the data used in this appendix available to us for a detailed re-tabulation and analysis. (See also pp. 122–127.)

[2] The questions which were asked in that poll are not listed here in their original sequence but—after the general questions 1 and 2—according to the degree of anti-colour bias which they evoked, ranking from least to most bias.

Question No.	Question	Answer	
1 (a)	Have you read or heard of recent disturbances between white and coloured people in Nottingham and London?	Yes	92
		No	8
		Total	100
1 (b)	If Yes: Who do you think were chiefly to blame—white or coloured people?	White people	27
		Coloured people	9
		Both	35
		Don't know	21
		Total	92
2 (a)	Do you personally know, or have you known, any coloured people?	Yes	49
		No	51
		Total	100
2 (b)	If Yes: Would you say they are better, worse or no different from white people?	Better	3
		Worse	6
		Same	37
		Don't know	3
		Total	49
3	Would you object if there were coloured children in the same class as your children at school?	Would object	7
		Would not object	81
		Don't know	12
		Total	100
4	If coloured people came to live next door would you move your home?	Yes, definitely	9
		Might do	21
		No	70
		Total	100
5	Do you think that coloured people from the Commonwealth should be allowed to compete for jobs in Great Britain on equal terms with people born here?	Yes	48
		No	37
		Don't know	15
		Total	100
6	Do you think that coloured people from the Commonwealth should be admitted to council housing lists on the same conditions as people born in Britain?	Yes	34
		No	54
		Don't know	12
		Total	100

Question No.	Question	Answer	
7	Do you think there should be laws to restrict immigration to Britain from the Commonwealth by:	White people	10
		Coloured people	16
		Both	39
		Neither	21
		Don't know	14
		Total	100
8	Would you move if coloured people came to live in great numbers in your district?	Yes, definitely	26
		Might do	35
		No	39
		Total	100
9	Do you approve or disapprove of marriages between white and coloured people?	Approve	13
		Disapprove	71
		Don't know	16
		Total	100

(III) GALLUP POLL 14TH—19TH NOVEMBER, 1958

The following question was asked as part of a poll on questions of 'political prejudice'.

Question	Would Vote for	No	Yes	Don't Know	Total
If the party of your choice	An Atheist	51	45	4	100
nominated a generally	Coloured Person	36	61	3	100
well qualified person as	A Jew	27	71	2	100
Parliamentary candidate	A Woman	21	76	3	100
and he/she happened to be	Roman Catholic	16	82	2	100
(either) a Roman Catholic,					
a Jew, a Coloured Person,					
a Woman or an Atheist,					
would you vote for					
him/her?					

Of course, it is not possible to estimate from such surveys the actual proportion of people who are or are not prejudiced. Especially in this country, colour prejudice is not a specific ideological segment that can easily be defined in quantitative terms; and that can be precisely identified on the basis of a few random questions, without repeated, far more detailed, interviewing and observation of the

same group of people. Verbal expressions on, and behaviour towards, coloured people are not necessarily mutually consistent.
Moreover, the scope of the questions was limited. And their phrasing, and the context in which such questions are asked, can also
influence the replies to some extent.[3]

Nevertheless, the results of opinion polls of this kind have a
meaning, if only a limited one. They do indicate, first, the overt
'verbal reflexes' of prejudice—how much of it is shown in immediate
replies to any questions on the subject; second, the areas and institutions—such as schools, housing, employment and marriage—in
which resistance to integration appears to be greatest; third, the
'hard core' of intolerance and tolerance alike, for it is most improbable that a thoroughly prejudiced person or a genuinely unprejudiced one would consistently give a whole series of replies
stating the opposite of his usual views.

Anti-Colour Bias in Relation to General Intolerance

The answers to the question on 'political prejudice' (in the November 1958 poll) are of special interest because they indicate to what
extent anti-colour bias is associated with general intolerance towards
any 'out-group'—including women. In the table on p. 250, two groups
of respondents were distinguished—those who said that they would
vote for a well qualified coloured candidate, nominated by the party
of their choice; and those who said that they would not do so. The
attitudes of these two groups to other 'minority' candidates—
atheists, Jews, Roman Catholics and women—can thus be compared.

Those opposed to coloured candidates were also opposed to other
'out-group' candidates far more often than was the case with respondents to whom the candidate's colour was apparently irrelevant.
The difference in attitudes towards atheist candidates was comparatively small, though still marked; but while only some 10 per
cent of the respondents expressing no colour bias were opposed to
Jewish, Catholic or women candidates respectively, the corresponding proportions among the 'colour biased' ranged from a quarter
to over half. In fact, no more than one in ten of the 'anti-colour'
respondents were biased only against coloured candidates. To judge

[3] It should be remembered that the main poll, of September 3rd and 4th, 1958,
was carried out before the ideological impact of the 'riots' had been generally
felt—that is, before public condemnation of colour prejudice had become
outspoken and widespread. Thus it is unlikely that the people questioned at that
time would have felt obliged to give unprejudiced answers in order to conform
to official opinion, and that they would be embarrassed to admit prejudice.

from these results, overtly expressed colour bias is often associated with general prejudice against other 'minority groups'.[4]

	Respondents		ALL Answering Question
	Who would NOT Vote for a Coloured Candidate	Who WOULD Vote for a Coloured Candidate	
Per cent in each group who WOULD NOT vote for:			
	%	%	%
An Atheist . . .	71	41	51
A Jew . . .	53	11	27
A Woman . . .	40	10	21
A Roman Catholic .	27	9	16
Number of Respondents	360	608	968
Per cent . . .	37	63	100

Areas of Prejudice

In general, the opinion surveys confirm once again that both consistently tolerant and consistently intolerant people are rather rare.

[4] As has been pointed out before, the attitudes which people express in an opinion poll are not necessarily consistent with their behaviour. It is well known that the personal characteristics of candidates affect the outcome of elections very little, if at all, in this country. Thus the opposition expressed in the Gallup Poll to women or Jewish candidates, for example, seems not to be reflected in actual voting, where such candidates stand. The same may perhaps apply also to coloured candidates, if one can judge by the election results in the one constituency where a coloured candidate stood at the General Election in October 1959. The constituency was Hampstead (a rather unusual one in many respects); the candidate, Dr. David Pitt, was nominated by the Labour Party (which had had a white candidate in the last Parliamentary election in 1955). If Labour supporters in Hampstead shared the opinions on coloured candidates expressed in the Gallup Poll by Labour supporters generally, and if they had translated those opinions into action, some 38 per cent of them would have abstained or voted against Dr. Pitt. In fact, the total poll in Hampstead changed hardly at all from 1955 to 1959; and the 'swing' against Labour was even slightly smaller there than in the rest of London. (The 'swing' against Labour was 3·5 percentage points in Hampstead, as compared with 3·8 in all London County constituencies.)

However, although these results are reassuring and confirm that political prejudice is not necessarily translated into political behaviour, they do not imply that such prejudice is harmless. It is still there as a latent attitude which could become active on other occasions, and which may also be expressed in other spheres of behaviour.

Thus the replies vary considerably according to the kind of topic or issue that is being mentioned—as shown in the table below, in which the questions of the September 1958 poll are listed in order of the degree of colour bias they evoked. There were some questions which were not simply dichotomous, but which also invited rather indefinite replies—for example, "might move" if coloured people came to live next door. Such replies are shown in column iv, as being 'possibly biased'.

SEPTEMBER 1958 POLL:

Questions Listed in the Order of the Respective Proportions of Biased Answers

(i)	(ii)	(iii)	(iv)	(v)
	Questions		*Per cent Biased Answers*	
No.	*Subject*	*Biased*	*Possibly Biased*	*Total cols. iii and iv*
		%	%	%
9	Mixed Marriages	71	—	71
8	Coloured People in District	26	35	61
7	Restrict Immigration	16	39	55
6	Council Housing Lists	54	—	54
5	Employment Opportunities	37	—	37
4	Coloured People Next Door	9	21	30
1 (*b*)	Blame for Riots	10	—	10
3	Mixing at School	7	—	7

The idea of mixed marriages evoked the strongest disapproval; at the other end of the scale, hardly anyone objected to the mixing of coloured and white children at school. But between these two extremes, there was considerable variation in the amount of bias shown on particular issues. A clear distinction was made between coloured people as individuals and as a group. Thus 30 per cent of the respondents said that they would, or might, move "if coloured people came to live next door"; but 61 per cent would consider moving "if coloured people came to live in great numbers" in their district. Again there was far more readiness to accept coloured migrants as competitors on equal terms on the labour market, than as competitors for municipal housing. None of these results is surprising: they are all in keeping with observations of attitudes and behaviour towards coloured people in British society. Nor were the answers hesitant: the proportion of "Don't know" replies was lower

Sending White Children to Schools with:	United States							
	North				South			
	Yes, would object	No, would not	No Opinion	Total	Yes, would object	No, would not	No Opinion	Total
	%	%	%	%	%	%	%	%
(a) a few coloured children	7	92	1	100	72	25	3	100
(b) half the children coloured	34	63	3	100	83	12	5	100
(c) more than half the children coloured	58	35	7	100	86	8	6	100

NOTE: The region of the 'South' in this table is considerably larger than the hard core of the segregationist Deep South. Almost all the answers in favour of integration come from States outside the Deep South, from those where some partial integration has already been, or is beginning to be, introduced.

than in usual polls on general political and social questions of the day.

The contrast with attitudes in some other countries is also a marked one, particularly with reference to the question on mixed schools. In an American Gallup Poll (of March 1959) white parents were asked whether they would object to sending their children to schools where (a) there were a few coloured children, (b) where half the children were coloured, (c) where more than half the children were coloured. The answers are shown on p. 252.

In the North, and to a lesser extent also in the South, it is not only people's views on the principle of 'integrated' schools which determine their answers. Their objections against integration increase greatly when they contemplate the idea that half, or more than half, of the children in the school might be coloured.[5]

Degrees of Bias

While replies to individual questions, considered separately, point to the issues on which prejudice fastens, they do not indicate how strong the prejudice of individuals is. This latter aspect begins to be visible only when we look at the opinion profile—at the range of replies which an individual gives to a whole set of questions. The main Gallup poll on attitudes towards coloured people, carried out in September 1958, provided an opportunity to trace the opinion profiles. Thus respondents were classified according to the degree of colour bias indicated by their combined answers to a set of questions. For this purpose, a modified version of the Guttman scaling technique was adopted.[6]

[5] The proportion of white parents in the North who said that they would not send their children to a school where there were "a few coloured children" was 7 per cent. It so happens that the same proportion in Britain said that they would object if there were coloured pupils in their children's class at school. And presumably the image called up by such a question in this country is one of a small minority of coloured children. It might, therefore, be thought that if the proportion of coloured children in British schools were to grow, the opposition to mixed schools would grow correspondingly, following the American trend. But this is improbable; for the analogy is not a realistic one. School integration has not been, and is not likely to be, one of the crucial issues of race relations in this country as it has been, and still will be for some time to come, in the United States. In America, there is a struggle *against* segregation; whilst here, in principle, integration is regarded as the norm, though it has not yet been fully tested, simply because the proportion of coloured children is generally so small.

[6] See S. A. Stouffer and others, *Measurement and Prediction*, Studies in Social Psychology in World War II, Vol. 4, Princeton, 1950; or for a simple description of the technique, C. A. Moser, *Survey Methods in Social Investigation*, London, 1958, pp. 239–41.

Seven questions were suitable for this analysis of opinion profiles.[7] The results showed, first of all, that respondents could be divided into two main sections. The first section—23 per cent—gave haphazard replies: they were 'inconsistent' in the sense defined by the application of the modified Guttman scaling technique. The second section—77 per cent of the respondents—who gave fairly 'consistent' replies were, in turn, allocated to four groups, ranging from group A, the most biased category, to group D, the least biased one.

The distribution of these groups, in terms of degrees of bias, is shown on the next table, on which groups A and D have each been further sub-divided into two sub-groups, so as to identify the ultimate extremes at either end of the scale. All the seven replies given by group Ai were biased; none of the seven replies given by group Dii were biased. The remnants at either end of the scale (groups Aii and Di) were also quite plainly biased and unbiased respectively, but not in quite so unequivocal a manner as their sister groups in the A and D categories.

This distribution confirms the general impression that only very small minorities of the population are thoroughly intolerant or tolerant, in their attitudes towards 'colour'. About one in eight were

---

The principle of the scaling technique is that respondents are classified, not just according to the *number* of questions to which they give a particular kind of answer (e.g., one showing colour bias), but according to *which* of the questions they answer in this way: the assessment is qualitative as well as quantitative. 'Consistency' of answers is the basis of the Guttman technique. If, for example, three questions are asked on attitudes to (a) mixed marriages, (b) movement of coloured people into the district, and (c) competition of coloured people for jobs, the three questions are then ordered according to the proportion of biased answers which each evokes. If, say, 71 per cent of respondents dislike mixed marriages, 61 per cent object to coloured people moving into the district, and 37 per cent are opposed to unrestricted competition of coloured people for jobs, the sequence will be as given—(a), (b), (c). An individual respondent is then classified as 'consistent' in his answers, if—irrespective of the number of questions on which his replies show bias—a biased answer at one point of the scale is accompanied by biased answers to all questions 'higher up' in the order. Thus a respondent who would object to coloured people moving into the district (b), is classified as 'consistent' if he also dislikes mixed marriages (a)—regardless of whether or not he is opposed to coloured people competing for jobs, because the latter question (c) is 'lower down' on the scale.

In this analysis, we have somewhat relaxed the strict criteria of consistency used by Guttman. A respondent could, for example, give one 'deviant' answer and still be classified as 'consistent'.

[7] The two factual questions, on knowledge of the disturbances and acquaintance with coloured people, were omitted. So were two opinion questions, the replies to which did not fit into the general pattern of responses: these were the questions about blame for the disturbances and about admission of coloured people to council housing lists.

at the negative end of the scale; one in five at the positive end; and only about two per cent at either end gave wholly biased or wholly un-biased replies to all the questions. The majority (53 per cent of all respondents or almost 70 per cent of all 'consistent' respondents) were in the intermediate categories: their attitudes towards coloured people were ambivalent, though this ambivalence had a coherent pattern, un-like the haphazardly contradictory views of 'inconsistent' respondents.[8]

DISTRIBUTION OF RESPONDENTS ON THE COLOUR BIAS SCALE

'Consistent' Respondents	Average Number of Biased Replies Given by Each Group		Per cent of 'Consistent' Respondents	Per cent of ALL Respondents
			%	%
Most Biased:				
Group Ai	7·0		2·2	1·7
Aii	5·3		10·4	8·1
Sub-Total A		5·6	12·6	9·8
Group B		4·0	36·8	28·5
Group C		2·4	31·2	24·1
Least Biased:				
Group Di	0·7		16·6	12·9
Dii	0·0		2·8	2·2
Sub-Total D		0·6	19·4	15·1
TOTAL		3·0	100·0	77·5

NOTE: The remaining respondents (22·5 per cent) were classified as 'inconsistent'. The total number of respondents was 1,500; that of those in groups A to D was 1,160.

[8] Of course, the nature of the scale and the consequent classification of respondents depend upon the content of the questions asked. Had the scale, for instance, been based solely on questions concerning issues which evoke overt colour bias most often, the distribution would have been 'skewed' in the direction of much greater prejudice. But in fact the scale used covers the range of topics on which in this country colour bias tends to fasten to a varying extent; and it thus gives a realistic indication of the general attitudes.

Moreover, the distribution of colour bias in the population indicated by this analysis of the 1958 Gallup poll is very similar to that shown by a nation-wide survey in 1951, the results of which are not available for publication.

A more recent survey of attitudes towards coloured people is reported in Michael Banton's *White and Coloured*, London, 1959 (Appendix II). A total of 600 respondents were interviewed in six localities, which did not include London or any other large city, except Leeds. The questions asked were rather general in character and some of them are said to have been frequently misunderstood. To judge by the analysis presented in the book, the results are inconclusive. Taken in conjunction with other external evidence, they do not seem to provide sufficient support for the author's conclusion that ". . . colour prejudice is not widespread in Britain".

	Men Aged:			Women Aged:			All	
	16–34 %	35–64 %	65 or more %	16–34 %	35–64 %	65 or more %	Men %	Women %
'Consistent' Respondents only:								
Group A	16	15	8	7	12	16	14	11
Group B	34	41	26	32	41	32	37	37
Group C	36	29	29	33	31	26	32	31
Group D	14	15	37	28	16	26	17	21
Total Groups A to D	100	100	100	100	100	100	100	100
All Respondents:								
'Consistent'	74	76	82	75	82	81	76	79
'Inconsistent'	26	24	18	25	18	19	24	21
GRAND TOTAL								
Per cent	100	100	100	100	100	100	100	100
Number	247	369	76	257	413	130	692	800

Who is Prejudiced?

This opinion survey indicated once again, moreover, that colour prejudice is spread fairly evenly throughout all social strata. Thus no significant differences, in terms of degree of colour bias expressed, were found, for example, between manual workers, non-manual workers and people with no gainful employment. Nor were there any striking variations in this respect between supporters of the Labour, Liberal and Conservative parties, though the latter had a slight tendency to show rather less tolerance, and also to give fewer haphazard answers, than Labour and Liberal supporters.

However, there were some differences between the various age and sex groups, as the table opposite shows. Apparently, the most prejudiced sections of the population are young men and old women. Among 'consistent' respondents, 16 per cent of each of these sections had the highest bias rating (group A). By contrast, old men and young women are the most tolerant sections—37 per cent of the former and 28 per cent of the latter had a low bias rating (group D). In general, however, women of all ages appeared to be slightly more tolerant than men.

There were also a few noticeable differences between the various parts of the country. Respondents in the Midlands showed relatively much bias, those in the North showed relatively little. Both in Greater London and in Scotland, expressions of marked intolerance as well as marked tolerance were comparatively frequent, while intermediate responses were less frequent than elsewhere. (See p. 258.)

Acquaintance with Coloured People

Altogether just about half (49 per cent) of the respondents interviewed by the Gallup Poll in September 1958 said that they personally knew, or had known, any coloured people. The proportion was rather higher among men (58 per cent) than among women (42 per cent), and for both men and women rather higher among the young than among the old. Regional variations were slight: only in the North was the proportion of respondents who knew coloured people significantly smaller (43 per cent) than elsewhere in the country.

Those who knew, or had known, coloured people personally expressed less bias than those who knew none: to each attitude question asked, the former group gave intolerant answers far less frequently than the latter. And indeed, in the replies to some questions, the differences between these two groups were particularly striking. Thus 37 per cent of those with coloured acquaintances blamed

	Midlands %	Scotland %	Greater London %	Wales %	Rest of South and S.E. %	North %	Total %
'Consistent' Respondents only:							
Group A	20	15	12	10	9	8	13
Group B	44	26	35	41	37	35	37
Group C	23	33	28	43	37	34	31
Group D	13	26	25	6	17	23	19
Total Groups A to D	100	100	100	100	100	100	100
All Respondents:							
'Consistent'	83	83	80	67	73	74	77
'Inconsistent'	17	17	20	33	27	26	23
GRAND TOTAL							
Per cent	100	100	100	100	100	100	100
Number	329	147	257	76	269	422	1,500

NOTE: The differences between the 'bias ratings' of the various regions have been tested to see whether they are attributable to variations in age and sex composition. It was found that this is not the case.

The regional divisions are those used by the Gallup Poll. The North contains the Registrar General's standard regions North, East and West Ridings, and North West; the Midlands contains the standard regions Midland, North Midland and East; the South and South East contain the standard regions of the same name and also the South West; Greater London is the conurbation as defined by the Registrar General.

white people for the 'disturbances', as compared with only 22 per cent of those without such acquaintances. Again, 46 per cent of the former group approved of the admission of coloured people to housing lists, and 60 per cent of their competition for jobs on equal terms with people born in Britain; while the corresponding proportions among those who knew no coloured people were 23 per cent and 37 per cent respectively. Even to respondents with coloured acquaintances, however, mixed marriages were usually objectionable: only 19 per cent definitely approved—though this was still nearly three times as many as the proportion (7 per cent) among those who did not know any coloured people.

	Respondents who said that they:		All Respondents %
	Knew Coloured People %	Did NOT Know Any Coloured People %	
'Consistent' Respondents only:			
Group A	16	9	13
Group B	26	47	37
Group C	34	28	31
Group D	24	16	19
Total Groups A to D	100	100	100
All Respondents:			
'Consistent'	75	80	77
'Inconsistent'	25	20	23
GRAND TOTAL			
Per cent	100	100	100
Number	740	751	1,491
Per cent	49	51	100

When the opinion profiles are analysed, in terms of the colour bias scale, the greater degree of tolerance of those with coloured acquaintances is again quite plainly indicated (as shown in the table above). Fewer of those who knew coloured people had strong leanings towards prejudice (group B) than those without coloured acquaintances. And while about one in four of those with coloured acquaintances were almost or wholly unbiased (group D), only about one in six of those without coloured acquaintances were in that category. On the other hand, it may seem curious at first sight that the proportion of strongly biased respondents was also greater among those who know coloured people (16 per cent) than among those who know none (9 per cent). But group A represents the 'hard core' of prejudice in the population: though over three in every five of these respondents claimed to know coloured people, their hostility was presumably too deep-seated and rigid to be shaken by personal experience. For the majority of British people—who have an uneasy, secret kind of prejudice—matters are different. The majority (as the bias scale indicates) may be influenced, if only marginally, slowly and haphazardly, by acquaintance with coloured individuals.[9]

[9] It has to be remembered that in this respect the situation in Britain is quite unlike that of a country such as the United States: in some regions, ideas of prejudice and habits of segregation are so deeply rooted that personal acquaintance with coloured people is likely to be a symptom, rather than a cause, of tolerance.

APPENDIX C

'TEDDY BOYS' AT SHEPHERD'S BUSH

*An Interview by Barry Carman, a B.B.C. Reporter**

Interviewer: How old are you?
Voice: Twenty-four.
Interviewer: What job do you do?
Voice: Machinist.
Interviewer: And what do you reckon about the coloured people coming into Britain?
Voice: They shouldn't be allowed in. They should be kept out. They shouldn't be let in in the first place.
Interviewer: I mean what sort of objections have you got?
Voice: I don't like 'em with white girls, I don't like 'em at all, they're too filthy—I know I've mixed with them, I've worked with them, I don't like them at all, they're no good.
Interviewer: And what sort of special reasons—I mean are there any special incidents you've seen or anything that . . .?
Voice: Well, they done my friend up, that's how that riot started down the road.
Interviewer: You knew . . . (inaudible).
Voice: Well, my friend they done—well he's not actually a friend of mine, but he's a friend of a friend of mine, you know what I mean—there's fifteen of 'em jumped him, cut his back open and broke his arm, that's how the riot started. So they done the niggers, they burnt his house out or his room out, whichever it is anyway.

* Transcript of the tape record of an interview conducted for the B.B.C. after the disturbances in Nottingham and Notting Dale in the autumn of 1958. The breaks in the transcript occur when the record was either inaudible or unprintable.
A number of 'teddy boys' from Shepherd's Bush (mainly from one large estate) were involved in the so-called 'Notting Hill' disturbances in the autumn of 1958. The first incidents on 14th and 26th July and on 17th August, before the rioting spread, were attacks by gangs of boys from that estate on coloured people in Shepherd's Bush. The prominent scene of the later disturbances was a road in Notting Dale near Shepherd's Bush. A number of boys from Shepherd's Bush were arrested during the disturbances, and some of them were regarded as the main culprits. (See Chapter IV, pp. 134–36, 142–43.)

Interviewer: Now was this—did this happen before the riot started or during . . .?

Voice: That's how it started—that's . . . the same night it started. Well they come down, fifteen of them, right—they done him, so naturally his friends went down and done them. That's how it started. Everybody come out then.

Interviewer: Had there been anything before this at all?

Voice: No, not much.

Interviewer: (unintelligible).

Voice: Just that a lot of ponces live round there. I mean, it's not very nice to see a coloured bloke with a white girl out in the streets, is it? I don't mind white people doing it but not black.

Interviewer: Well, why don't you like to see a white girl with a black fellow?

Voice: Well, it's not them it's the children—they're half-castes. You want to know about the kids—the half-castes. Well we don't want a lot of half-castes running around, do we. I don't mind Irish, Scotch, they all belong to the same country, don't they? You don't want a lot of foreigners in here, especially black anyway. In my opinion they ought to be shot—the whole lot of them. What do you say Peter?

Other Voice: I agree with you.

Interviewer: Just a minute, we'll try and go round the circle in a minute. Now these brawls over girls like—I mean you had them in Scotland between Poles and Scots during the war. I saw them in Sydney between Australians and Americans. Do you think that it's just a fight over a girl—do you think the colour . . .?

Voice: I don't fight over no girl but I still don't reckon a black man should go with a white girl. If they're going to marry at all let them marry their own kind—if not sling them out. You go down to Lyons's—you can't get a job in Lyons's because a black man'll go cheaper. Any place. I worked in a factory that wouldn't employ a white man, only a black man, because he'll work cheaper —I got the sack through it. In my opinion they should be thrown out the whole lot of 'em.

Interviewer: How do you find them as work-mates?

Voice: Terrible. Lazy sods. (Background noise.) If they can get a white man to do the job they will. And they'll sit back and cop the wages.

Interviewer: What about this idea that a lot of them come over here and after a while they buy cars, they buy houses?

Voice: I'll tell you how they get them (unintelligible) off the backs of white girls, and black girls now. You go up Bayswater Road you'll see black girls out on the game now.

Interviewer: Now do you reckon that the sentences on the fellows that went up to court can stop any trouble?[1]

Voice: No. Definitely not. Not in my opinion. I think it will cause more. If they don't get the sentence stopped there'll definitely be a lot more trouble.

Interviewer: Is there trouble going on around here now, do you reckon?

Voice: Well, it's coming up again, I think. If it does I shall be there, don't worry about that.

Interviewer: Did you see the actual trouble when it was on here?

Voice: Yes. I was down there the night it started.

Interviewer: Now I've done a lot of programmes and so forth with Teddy Boys or what are called Teddy Boys . . .

Voices: We're not Teddy Boys.

Interviewer: Yes, I know. And I know they often like to have a go amongst themselves. Was this that sort of thing or . . .?

Voice: No, it was not. I'll tell you it straight—this fellow—I won't say his name, or anything like that, but I know for a fact that he's got a weak heart, and he was standing there minding his own business. He was talking to three friends of his and fifteen spades come up and done—and had a go at him—one done his back, slashed his coat open with a knife and broke his arm—so naturally, I mean, if that happens, you have a go back, don't you?

Voice: Excuse me, sir. I see that performance up at Shepherd's Bush that night. I'm going to the pictures and I see these three darkies coming in a car so this man was on a scooter with his girl friend, so the darkies—the car pulled in and the darkies stopped, so the man on the scooter got off, and they started an argument saying he was on the wrong side of the road. So then one of the darkies hit the man straightway, no messing about. So myself and my mate went over and just stood by to see how the way things were going, and two darkies—outsiders—stepped in and so my mate and myself stepped in, so we just had it there and then and that's the way it happened.

Interviewer: Do you know any of them personally?

Voice: No, but that's what happened that night at Shepherd's Bush, just down the road here. We were going to have a drink and we just see this car pulling up—next we see the scooter pulling up next to it. The darkies accused the man of being on the wrong side of

---

[1] The judgment on the nine "nigger hunting" youths who were each sentenced to four years' imprisonment in September 1958. Seven of these boys lived in Shepherd's Bush. (See Chapter IV, pp. 135–36.)

the road. As the darkies got out of the car the man with his girl friend . . . (unintelligible) so the man got off the scooter, and one of the darkies hit him across the face.

Voice: We were walking down the road and a bloke comes along on a scooter. He is supposed to have dented this darkie's car. And these two darkies step out to him. Three more joins them, that's five. They get on to this bloke—he's on a scooter, he's got his scooter in gear, with his girl on the back—probably his wife—now the argument's on. One of these darkies strikes this bloke on the scooter, now he's got to leave go his clutch to fight back, so us took them on. Well to finish up there's about five darkies, but there's three of us, and they're still afraid of us.

Another Voice: Well I'll tell you something about a darkie—I'm an Irishman and a foreigner to England—but I'll tell you one thing, that the darkie is ignorant and I'll tell you something, as far as I've travelled which is a long ways I can name the causes for (unintelligible). The darkies are ignorant. You go on a bus—to a white conductor you'll ask for a tuppeny fare, they'll say thank you —you go on one with a darkie, you ask for a fivepenny fare, he'll say fares please and just walk away. They're as ignorant as I've ever met, and I'll have a go with them any day they fancy. That's all I've got to say to you.

Interviewer: Do any of you know any of them that you like?

Voices: No—never known one I like.

2nd Voice: Yes—that's right, I reckon the girls here are the start of it all. I mean if it weren't for the girls going with them they wouldn't have the influence of running the brothels and what have you. I mean they start it all don't they?

Interviewer: Why do you reckon the girls go with them?

Voice: (Laughter) I could answer that one and all. No, well I mean you could gather that for yourself, but mainly I mean they got the money. That's one of the big items towards it, isn't it?

2nd Voice: Yeah, yeah, that's another thing, I mean down the labour exchange, I mean you go in there, we were in there today, three of us, and we're standing waiting for our pay and we see one darkie go up, he drew eight—seven pounds something, we see about six whites go up, draw three pounds, another darkie go up and draw eight pounds and so forth and so on. And it's nearly all blacks down there except for the few whites. Spades, I'm sorry—spades.

Interviewer: Now do you make any difference between West Indians, West Africans, Pakistanis, Indians, Nigerians?

Voice: But they're all spades if it comes down to the same thing—

all spades. But the Jamaicans are the worst in my opinion . . . so . . .

Interviewer: Now let's have another look at this idea of why the girls go with them.

(Break)

Interviewer: I know what you mean, since we're talking of this I'll say that the coloured peoples are supposed to be more virile, let's put it that way.

Voice: Yes, that's right, yeah, well put it that way then. They're able to entertain a girl more so than a white chap is.

Interviewer: But do you reckon that's so or do you think it's just a vague idea this?

Voice: No, I reckon it's so. I know a few girls who go out on the game and I reckon it's so, they all say it's so and so on.

Interviewer: They do reckon it's so, the girls themselves?

Voice: Yes, definitely, definitely. But I mean the Labour Exchange is one of the biggest problems, isn't it?

Interviewer: Do you know any coloured people personally?

Voice: Yes, I do, and I mean the few that I do know, I mean the majority are terrible but I mean a few I do know they're very polite and good manners. There is a few, like I say, but not many.

Interviewer: But what do you reckon ought to happen then? What do you think the solution is to the problem?

Voice: Well I mean if I was in the Government I'd say stop 'em coming over, and just stop 'em coming over, I mean they can't send them back, so I mean they've just got to stop sending them over. That's the only thing to do, isn't it?

Interviewer: I mean, the reason why these characters come over you see, they know they've got the right to come over.

Voice: Yeah, yeah. But if an Englishman went over to their country and behaved the same way they do, running the biggest brothels, they'd be kicked out, straight away.

2nd Voice: Could I ask a question?

Interviewer: Who to, me or . . . ?

2nd Voice: Well, to all concerned. Right?

2nd Voice: Who is a British subject? Is a darkie a British subject, correct, an Irishman isn't, right? Now who would you sooner have in your country an Irishman or a darkie?

Voices: An Irishman definitely.

Interviewer: An Irishman definitely, why?

Voice: Me old man's Irish isn't he?

2nd Voice: Well, O.K., why would you prefer an Irishman in your country, because, not because your old man's Irish, but why would you prefer an Irishman in your country to a darkie?

Voice: Why because they're not so much scandal are they?

2nd Voice: Not so much scandal? Well I'll contradict you there, an Irishman can be the worst man out.

Voice: Well, it all depends under what circumstances.

2nd Voice: Under what circumstances? He can drink (yes), fight (yes), he can run brothels, same as the darkie (yes). He can do anything.

Voice: But they're not so bad as the darkies are they? Are you running your own country down?

2nd Voice: No I'm not running my own country down, no, no, but I've seen myself in Shepherd's Bush, in Acton, in Camden Town, in numerous parts of London, I've seen Irishmen in trouble.

Voice: So you condemn all the blacks?

2nd Voice: No, no, I'm not condemning the Irish or the black men. But I do believe this, I've met Englishmen that condemned the Irishmen. My name is Danny and they condemn me because I'm Irish. They know my name is Danny but they won't call me Danny, they call me Pat, but when they meet the darkie they'll call him by his name.

Interviewer: What difference does that make?

Voice: No, if you go out to Australia, you're English and they call you a pommie, you can't get rid of it.

2nd Voice: Oh you can.

Voice: No you can't.

Voice: Yes, by telling somebody . . .

Voice: You go to New Zealand they call you Snowie. Well what difference does it make?

Voice: Oh I haven't been there.

Voice: So what's the difference between Pat—Paddy or Danny, or whatever you happen to be called. (Talking together.)

Voice: An Irishman is called a Paddy isn't he? Or if he's a Scotsman he's called a Jock? The same as a darkie man is called a . . .

Voice: Same as a Geordie is called a Geordie.

Voice: You must agree with that point then sir?

Voice: You're running on to the Irish instead of the blacks now. I mean we was telling about the blacks not the Irish.

Voice: Well actually I tell you something. A darkie . . . you can think what you like, I'll tell you something, I have no time for a black.

Voice: Do you know any spades in person?

Voice: I do, I know . . .

Voice: And what do you reckon on them?

Voice: Well, I reckon this, as I told you before tonight, that I wouldn't walk across that street in front of any one of them.

Voice: And I tell you what, there's a bird up on the hill I'd go anywhere with. And anybody said anything to her I should like to know.

Voice: No, no not Jessie. There you are, and I f—— think—sorry for swearing—I think she's very nice. There you are.

Interviewer: She coloured, is she?

Voice: Yes she's coloured, Jamaican. I reckon she's very nice, couldn't find a better girl. I'm not running 'em up or not running 'em down. That's just one person in particular.

Interviewer: Well what—how do you feel about the sentences of these boys?

Voice: Well I reckon it was a right liberty. I reckon they—I reckon they took further steps than necessary, because I mean I know the bloke, I know a couple of the blokes in person. And I mean they're damn nice fellas, and it wasn't just that six, I mean there was hundreds of people. And why condemn just six of 'em? I mean it just wasn't right.

Interviewer: Do you reckon they were within their rights in whatever they did?

Voice: Definitely. If they were in the right the other hundreds of people were as well. I mean, so they should have condemned the hundred that was in it instead of just those few.

Interviewer: Well now, were they what you'd call Teddy Boys?

Voice: No, no. A couple of 'em were, what you might call Teddy Boys, but the others they were hard working blokes.

Interviewer: And why do you reckon that they individually were steamed up about this?

Voice: Well just because they got caught carrying something to defend themselves with. I mean it was no good just walking round with nothing in your pocket, I mean you're likely to get chipped anywhere.

Interviewer: Tell me why you reckon the girls start going with the coloured fellows?

Voice: Well I reckon, first of all, for the money. Well I mean the darkies entertain them pretty well . . . they got plenty of stuff, plenty of drink, chuck a bit of dope in the drink, and the girls want to stick with 'em. Put 'em out on the game, and take in their earnings. So all right they're able to buy a couple of more cars. So that's how they carry on, just keep getting more money all the time. Like that.

Interviewer: But how do you reckon they get this money, somebody else has just been telling me that they work for lower wages?

Voice: Who—the darkies? Oh well they might do, work for lower wages so they can't get nicked for immoral earnings. I mean, like I say, they send the girls out on the game, the girls bring in—the darkies tell 'em to bring in so much every night, so they stay out until they bring it in.

Interviewer: Now there are a couple of hundred thousand coloured people in Britain, how many of them do you reckon are ponces or run brothels?

Voice: Well ninety-five per cent.

(Break)

Voice: In this district, Shepherd's Bush, . . .

Voice: Shepherd's Bush, Paddington.

Voice: There was a story about a darkie who came to England, and he went to the London Transport—we don't know how true this story is—but that he went along to the London Transport, he had a permit to stay in England for six months. And he asked for a job as an Inspector. And it takes years to attain the position of Inspector. Another thing is that in the trade you'll find that the black man is working his way in so much that he's making way for his own . . . friends and the white man cannot get a job.

(Break)

Interviewer: . . . About a white man going with a coloured girl?

Voice: Oh I still feel the same about them. I don't think that they should mix. I think like, whites should go white and black with the black. If the whites went with the whites and the blacks went with the blacks there'd be no trouble in London. And as far as work is concerned, if any of them go to work, they always work for less than a white man. That's how this work is getting very bad.

Interviewer: Well about this idea that they've got lots of money then?

Voice: Well, see, a lot of them have lots of money because they have two or three birds on the game for them, you see. That's how they have a lot of—that's how they all get their cars.

Interviewer: Well I don't think you could really expect West Indians, particularly, to appreciate this business that they shouldn't go out with white girls. Because West Indians are descended from white men and coloured women.

Voice: Well it's not only West Indians like. I know there is white like out in West Indies. But as far as the Jamaicans is concerned they're the people that's really starting the trouble in London.

Voice: Maltese.

Voice: And the Maltese.

Interviewer: Why those two do you think?

Voice: Well the Maltese they're the same thing. They won't work at all. So if they find our girls, or particularly down Whitechapel— I've lived there and I know—they just get all these kids, you know girls only fifteen—sixteen and they put them on the. . . . They won't work either. (Unintelligible.)

Interviewer: Just a minute—O.K.?

Voice: I said put them back to Africa, get rid of the lot of them. Let them live with the monkeys, they can trade with them. That's my opinion of them.

APPENDIX D

PARLIAMENTARY REFERENCES

A list of the main recent Parliamentary references to the coloured minority group in Britain is given below. This list includes debates and policy statements on immigration from the Commonwealth; the condition of coloured people in this country; colour prejudice and discrimination; racial disturbances; group defamation; and other relevant matters. The dates on which short verbal or written answers to particular Parliamentary questions were given are not included here.

More detailed references to several of the debates listed below are given in the text.

Hansard

House of Commons

18th February, 1954	Columns 2154–2155
5th November, 1954	821–832
12th June, 1956	247–250
10th May, 1957	1425–1438
24th May, 1957	1602–1608
3rd April, 1958	1419–1431
30th April, 1958	387–388
8th July, 1958	205–207
29th October, 1958	195–206
30th October, 1958	415–422
5th December, 1958	1552–1597
4th June, 1959	368–372
5th November, 1959	1199–1201
2nd February, 1960	796–801
23rd February, 1960	331–339

House of Lords

20th November, 1956	391–400; 403–422
19th November, 1958	631–724

Index

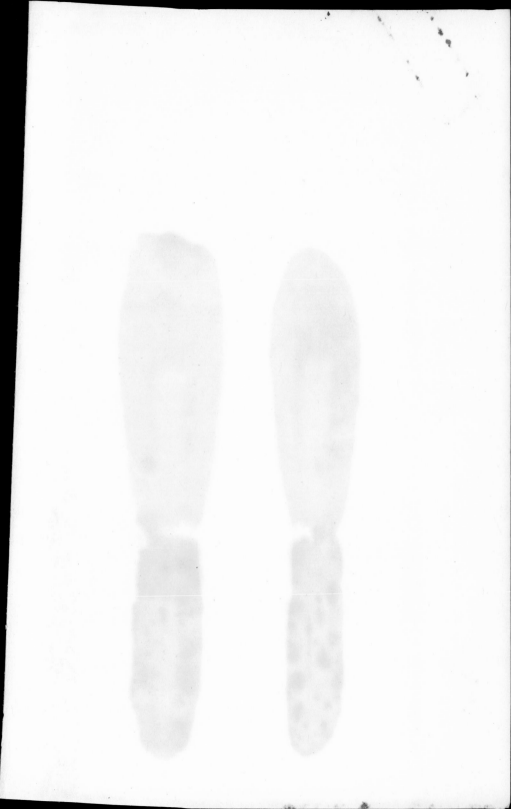

42909

GLASS, RUTH
  LONDON'S NEWCOMERS.

DA
125
W4
G7

DATE DUE	

GAYLORD

PRINTED IN U.S.A.